P9-API-759

THE FBI PYRAMID From the Inside

W. Mark Felt

THE FBI PYRAMID From the Inside

by

W. MARK FELT

G. P. PUTNAM'S SONS
NEW YORK

 Published simultaneously in Canada by Longman Canada Limited, Toronto.

Library of Congress Cataloging in Publication Data

Felt, W. Mark, Date.
The FBI pyramid from the inside.

1. United States. Federal Bureau of Investigation.
I. Title.
HV8138.F45 1979 353.007'4 78-24257
ISBN 0-399-11904-3

Printed in the United States of America

ACKNOWLEDGMENTS

This book would not have been possible without the unflagging assistance of my wife and family whose suggestions and editing were invaluable. I want also to thank Ladislas Farago for the inspiration while I struggled to give birth to this history of my life in the FBI.

Material in this book is based upon my personal recollections, considerably refreshed by reviews of voluminous FBI records which were made available to me under the provisions of the Freedom of Information Act and of the many detailed reports of the Senate and House Select Committees on Intelligence. Most of the conversations which are set out in quotes were taken directly from the transcripts of the Nixon White House tapes and from various Senate and House documents.

DEDICATION

This book is dedicated to the FBI and all its employees, past and present, whose conscientious efforts through the years have made our country a better and safer place to live.

THE FBI PYRAMID From the Inside

CHAPTER ONE

We must not turn the Bill of Rights into a suicide pact.

—MR. JUSTICE ROBERT H. JACKSON
UNITED STATES SUPREME COURT 1941–54

In the late Sixties and early Seventies, the country was at war—civil war—but only a few knew it. The Weather Underground, Cuban-taught, self-proclaimed Communist Revolutionaries, publicly declared war on the United States. Claiming credit for scores of bombings and boasting of their ties to Fidel Castro, these young anarchists actually believed they could overthrow our Federal Government by force and violence.

I took part in the successful FBI struggle against these bomb-throwers and my battle decoration came on April 10, 1978, when Attorney General Griffin Bell announced that I, along with L. Patrick Gray III and Edward S. Miller, had been indicted by a Federal Grand Jury in Washington, D.C., for violating the civil rights of members and supporters of the Weather Underground.

I retired from the FBI on June 22, 1973, after thirty-eight years of Government service—thirty-two of them as a Special Agent and a Field and Headquarters executive of the FBI. I was—and I remain—proud of my years of Federal service, particularly those which I spent chasing bank-robbers, kidnappers, bombers, hijackers, and foreign intelligence agents in every state of the Union. Now I would rest and get my blood pressure back to normal. I would devote more of myself to my loyal wife, who had put up with moving seventeen times and thousands of hours of waiting for me to come home from assignments at all hours—day or night—while she shepherded a daughter and a son all the way from nursery school through master's degrees (at Stanford University and Virginia Polytechnic Institute, respectively).

I could not have been more mistaken! Since my retirement, I have been pursued by the Executive Branch, pressured by the Legislative Branch, and prosecuted in the Judicial System—always concerning matters which I handled as Acting Associate Director of the FBI while I was doing my utmost to serve the best interests of my country. I have never been accused of doing less than what my conscience and my FBI training told me were expected of me. Neither personal malice nor selfish motivations colored my actions or judgment at any time in my career.

Of course, it is perfectly clear now that I would have been much better off to retire when J. Edgar Hoover died on May 2, 1972. At that time, I had reached maximum salary and retirement benefits; however, I decided to stay on for a while to help the new Acting Director, L. Patrick Gray, who was a neophyte not only to the FBI, but to the profession of law enforcement.

As Acting Associate Director under Gray, I was responsible for the day-to-day operations of the Bureau, while Gray spent most of his time "on the road"—visiting all but one of the fifty-nine FBI Field Offices and making endless public appearances, not to mention six weeks of sick leave for abdominal surgery in November and December of 1972.

During my last thirteen months of FBI service, I wore many hats—trying to help and protect a new Director while coping with the intricate investigative problems of Watergate, Wounded Knee, and many other crises—and trying to appease and placate subordinate officials puzzled by Gray's constant absence from his command post in Washington and unsettled by the unquestioning receptiveness he appeared to show to requests from Administration insiders.

Looking back on the events which occurred during Pat

Gray's tenure as Acting Director—as well as the headlines which some of those events continue to capture—I marvel at the successes which the Bureau achieved despite the often formidable obstacles it encountered. Politics wielded a heavy influence in the Department of Justice in 1972–73, and the same is true today. Political considerations are too often superimposed over professionalism to the disadvantage of the FBI, then as now, the epitome of law enforcement professionalism.

Thus, the FBI's role in the ITT-Dita Beard case was subject at all times to partisan instructions and pressure (see Chapter 13); and the perils presented by the confrontation at Wounded Knee, South Dakota, in 1973 were escalated when long-standing rules governing the FBI's use of firearms were annulled by a political appointee in the Justice Department (see Chapter 19). There was tremendous public and political pressure on the FBI to solve and stop the bombings of Government buildings and of business and industrial facilities, crimes which had become a "fact of life" by the early Seventies. And because of the timely and effective action taken by FBI Agents in the Sixties and Seventies, caches of explosives were tracked down, bombings were thwarted, and major inroads were made against the forces of terrorism.

The FBI must have been doing something right, for it met the challenge of terrorism which was on the rise in the United States during the early Seventies. Al Fatah, the militant wing of the Palestinian Liberation Organization, planned a series of terrorist acts in the United States—plans which evaporated when the FBI began a program of in-depth interviews of Al Fatah adherents in the United States. Violence-oriented young devotees of the Jewish Defense League were prevented from committing acts of violence. This is what was expected of the FBI.

Foremost among terrorist groups in North America during the late Sixties and early Seventies was the Weather Underground, a band of young men and women who aspired to achieve a degree of notoriety in this country akin to that reached by the Tupamaros in South America, the Japanese Red Army, the terrorist branch of the Palestinian Liberation

Organization, the Irish Republican Army, the Baader-Meinhof Gang in West Germany, the Moluccans in Holland, and the Red Brigade in Italy, which came close to toppling the Italian Government with a series of assassinations and other acts of terrorism.

The Weather Underground caused the most difficulty for the FBI. We succeeded in dispersing the members and stopping the bombings, but their lawyers are well on the way to emasculating the FBI with civil suits and the fear of civil suits. Sympathizers and supporters of the Weather Underground describe its members as "dissenters" or "anti-war activists" and liken their activities to those of our Eighteenth Century forefathers who pledged their lives, their fortunes, and their sacred honor in the cause of freedom. The comparison is grotesque. (More about the Weather Underground in Chapter 23.)

Because terrorism in the United States was largely contained and we have been relatively free from it for several years, complacency has developed. Few believe that this great country could drift into the kind of frightening chaos which gripped Italy. The FBI knew of the danger, but by one of those bewildering shifts in public opinion, partly because of the Watergate syndrome, J. Edgar Hoover and the men who worked under him became the "enemy." On the other hand, there were sympathetic words for those who were plotting to destroy the domestic tranquility of the United States—and a barrage of criticism which undermined the effectiveness and morale of the FBI and other law enforcement agencies. In the face of a clear and present danger, it seemed that many were determined to look in the other direction, ignoring the admonition of former Supreme Court Justice, Robert H. Jackson, who said, "We must not turn the Bill of Rights into a suicide pact."

Set forth in the chapters which follow is an account of how I came to the FBI, my early years as a Special Agent, and the events which propelled me to the top of the FBI Pyramid. There is a blow-by-blow account of the "palace intrigue" wherein former Assistant to the Director, William C. Sullivan, seeking "revenge" against Hoover, set in motion the unfortunate chain of events which trouble the FBI today. And finally, I describe my twelve hectic months under Acting Director, L. Patrick Gray III, and the job-related events which have plagued me since retirement.

CHAPTER TWO

Sunday will be your day of rest.

—HUGH H. CLEGG

It is sometimes said that an FBI Agent is born, not made. Perhaps this is so for some who see the Bureau as a vocation rather than a job. But whether the agent is born or made, it is a fact that the FBI puts a stamp on him—or her—almost as indelible as the mark on a veteran of the U.S. Marine Corps. In my case, the FBI was an escape from a humdrum and ill-paying job on the legal staff of the Federal Trade Commission, and a step up the economic ladder to what, in the days following the Great Depression of the Thirties, was the munificent salary of $3,200 a year. I was also attracted by the prevalent belief that FBI Agents led a life of daily excitement tracking down bank robbers or engaging in gun battles with desperados.

My background was what we now call "middle American"—a pleasant boyhood in Twin Falls, Idaho, where, until the Nation's economy started crumbling in 1929, my father was a moderately successful building contractor. My boyhood was healthy but undistinguished. I liked sports and debate; and, at my mother's insistence, I even took piano lessons. If there was any criticism of me, it was what one of my favorite teachers said, "He does not live up to his potential."

With no thought that a law degree was one of the prerequisites for employment in the FBI, I decided to become a lawyer because that profession promised an interesting and prosperous career. Like many other children of the Depression, I worked my way through college waiting on tables and stoking furnaces. For me it was the University of Idaho, and when I received my Bachelor of Arts degree in 1935 (I was president of my fraternity, Beta Theta Pi) I had one year of prelaw to my credit. In 1935 a college degree was not necessarily the ticket to a good job. However, I had heard that there were government jobs in Washington, D.C., which would give me an opportunity to go to law school at night. I appealed to Idaho Senator James P. Pope for help in getting such a position, and to my great good fortune he found an opening for me in his own office as a correspondence clerk.

The hours were long and at 4:45 in the afternoon I would dash off to George Washington University Law School to attend classes from 5:00 P.M. to 7:00 P.M. and then return to Capitol Hill to finish my work. In spite of the pressures, my life was happy, my work interesting and my law course stimulating. There was an additional cause for my happiness. A beautiful and intelligent girl, Audrey Robinson, who had attended the University of Idaho with me, was working in Washington with the Internal Revenue Service. We began dating and in June, 1938, we were married by the Reverend Sheara Montgomery, Chaplain of the House of Representatives.

Until 1940, when I received my Bachelor of Law degree, I attended classes by night and worked for Senator Pope and then for his successor, D. Worth Clark, who also arranged my schedule so that it would not interfere with my education. Then, having successfully passed the bar examination in the District of Columbia, I immediately applied for a legal position with the Federal Trade Commission and was accepted. I could hardly wait to get my first assignment, but wait I did. Finally, when I could no longer stand the inactivity, I asked my supervisor for an assignment. He gave me a complaint the FTC had received and asked me to prepare a report on it.

Skipping lunches and working at night, I completed the report in short order and was complimented for the job I had done. But the penalty for completing an assignment rapidly was to go without another one for a long time—several weeks in this case. And when it came, it was hardly one to set my heart pounding. I was to determine whether people using Red Cross brand toilet tissue did so because they thought it had some connection with the American Red Cross. My research, which required days of travel and hundreds of interviews, produced two definitive conclusions:

1. Most people *did* use toilet tissue.
2. Most people *did not* appreciate being asked about it.

That was when I started looking for other employment.

Two very good friends who worked for the FBI urged me to consider applying, and seven months after joining the FTC I decided to make the change. I did so, well aware that J. Edgar Hoover was a tough disciplinarian, that the work was demanding, and that the Bureau imposed strict conformity. But I was looking for a career of more substance than interviewing reluctant consumers. Europe was at war and I wanted to be involved in work that would be significantly helpful to my country.

In November of 1941, I applied for a position as a Special Agent with the FBI. Applicant screening processes for new Agents were very demanding and very thorough. The primary requirement was a law degree or an accounting degree with three years of experience. In addition, I filled out a detailed application form with questions covering every phase of my life. Some ten days later I was told to report to FBI headquarters in Washington for an interview. This consisted of going over my application question by question and probing my experiences. The interviewer, an official of the Administrative Division, wanted particularly to know why I was applying. Did I intend to make the FBI a career or was I simply looking for a way to avoid military service?

My answers must have been satisfactory; the next step was a legal examination. Most of the questions described a factual situation, cited the law, and asked if the facts constituted a violation. If so, what investigative steps would I pursue to establish the evidence needed for prosecution? Having taken this hurdle, I was subjected to a rigorous physical examination. Then I waited for weeks while FBI Agents checked out my educational and employment records and interviewed friends, neighbors, teachers, and associates. Finally, on January 19, 1942, two months after I had filed my application, I received a letter informing me that I had been accepted.

The letter, bearing the printed signature of J. Edgar Hoover, instructed me to report for duty at Room 5231 in the Justice Department Building at 9:00 A.M. on Monday, January 26. I arrived there feeling both nervous and elated, and lugging a suitcase with enough clothing to last me for the introductory three weeks of training at the Marine base in Quantico, Virginia. This was to be followed by another thirteen weeks of training in Washington. (I learned later that the FBI was undergoing the greatest expansion in its history, from fewer than 600 Agents to more than 4,000 by the end of World War II.) When we had been assigned seats in the classroom, Assistant Director Hugh H. Clegg, in charge of the Training and Inspection Division, walked briskly into the room. After some introductory remarks about the Bureau, he laid down the law.

"Gentlemen," he said, "this is a very serious occasion and must not be taken lightly. We expect the very best from all of you and anything less will be completely unacceptable. You are on probation for one year and if you don't measure up to FBI standards, you will be dropped from the rolls. The passing grade in all courses is eighty-five, and any failing grade will result in dismissal. On weekdays, classes will be held from 9:00 A.M. until 9:00 P.M. with one hour each for lunch and dinner. On Saturdays, classes will be held from 9:00 A.M.until 6:00 P.M. Sunday will be your day of rest with classes from 1:00 P.M. until 6:00 P.M.

"You will learn the rules as you go along, but let me stress a few of them. There must be extreme moderation in the use of alcohol. There is to be no consumption of alcoholic beverages when you are on assignment, regardless of the hour of day or night, and there must be no excessive drinking when off duty because you can never know when an emergency will call you back to the office. Violation of these rules will result in dismissal with prejudice." *

* An employee dismissed with prejudice loses not only his job but is also barred from other employment in the Federal Government.

After many more instructions and admonitions, Clegg said, "Gentlemen, if any of you has any doubts about it, now is the time to withdraw before I administer the oath of office." There was a long silence, then he told us to stand up, raise our right hands and repeat after him, very solemnly, our promise to defend the Constitution and protect the Nation from all its enemies, "foreign and domestic."

For the rest of the day, until 4:40 P.M., we filled out forms, were photographed for FBI credentials, and received further indoctrination. We were issued briefcases which contained a .38 calibre police revolver, a holster and an Agent's badge. There were also two large looseleaf books—a Manual of Rules and Regulations and a Manual of Instructions focusing on the investigative methods and reporting procedures in the more than 100 different types of cases handled by the FBI at that time. (By the time I had retired, the number of categories had increased to more than 150 as Congress added to the FBI's responsibilities.)

Promptly at 4:40 P.M., we gathered up our belongings and piled into Bureau buses which took us the thirty-eight miles to Quantico where the new and spanking clean FBI Academy was located, almost in the heart of the large Marine Corps Base. After dinner we were told how to maintain our quarters, how to make our beds and fold our blankets in strict military fashion. It was after 11:00 P.M. when I found my assigned bed and locker space and gratefully turned in.

For the next two weeks—ten hours of each weekday—we were lectured and drilled on rules and regulations, and we took copious notes of these lectures. The only break in this instruction was a daily session in the gymnasium doing calisthenics and learning the principles of judo and disarming tactics. The purpose of this training was not so much to put it into practice but rather to illustrate what can be done by skilled and dangerous adversaries unless the Agent is always on guard and knows what to expect when making arrests. As the end of the second week approached, we were deeply worried about the impending examination on the rules and regulations we had been studying night and day. It was not that they were unduly complicated but simply that there were thousands of them to be remembered. Fortunately, some last minute cramming by our instructor, covering the specific questions in the examination, carried us through with scores well above the passing grade.

I was perhaps more concerned over the next week's training on the firearms range. I had absolutely no experience with guns, and I knew that the FBI considered marksmanship as important as the academic side of training. There are very few instances in which Agents engage in gun battles, and one of the reasons for this is the reputation established by G-Men in their early days for a willingness and ability to shoot it out with desperate criminals. Agents are to use their weapons only in self-defense, but when they shoot, they shoot to kill.

FBI firearms training is calculated to weed out the unfit. The FBI teaches agents to fire the .38 calibre police revolver, the standard weapon issued to all Agents; the .30 calibre rifle, needed where shooting must be at a distance greater than the fifty-yard effective range of the pistol; the .45 calibre machine gun; the 12-gauge shotgun with its awesome firepower; and the 37 millimeter "cannon," which is occasionally used for lobbing tear gas projectiles into a room occupied by fugitives resisting arrest. Trainees also had a chance to fire the impressive .357 Magnum revolver, which is powerful enough to stop an automobile by penetrating the motor block.

As in the military, we spent hours learning how to strip and assemble these weapons, how to care for them, and how to fire them. Safety rules were also drilled into us. And before we went to the range, we had a session of "dry firing" without ammunition, to teach us what is essential in marksmanship—squeezing the trigger slowly and smoothly so as not to anticipate the weapon's recoil. Because I had no previous experience with firearms, I was actually ahead of some of the men who had to unlearn bad habits.

Other than during training, I never had to fire a weapon in my Bureau career, but the knowledge of firearms ingrained in me during the many training sessions was of tremendous value. I knew how to handle weapons safely and this was extremely important because there were many times when they were drawn and ready during raid and arrest situations. I knew how dangerous a firearm was and appreciated the rigid discipline necessary to protect others from injury.

Our three weeks at Quantico completed, we returned to Washington to learn the routine of FBI work. We studied the various laws over which the FBI had jurisdiction and the essential elements of each violation. We were taught investigative techniques used to develop evidence. Report writing differed, depending on the type of case, and we learned to know these differences. We saw at first hand the extraordinary capabilities of the FBI Laboratory and how evidence is prepared for examination. We observed the work of the Identification Division and became adept at taking fingerprints and dusting for latent prints. I even learned how to pick locks.

Much of the instruction was known as "project training," in which we worked on simulated cases, interviewed "suspects" and "witnesses," wrote reports, and testified in Moot Court. The last week of training was at the Washington Field Office (WFO), where we were supposed to work on actual cases under the guidance of experienced Agents. But for my class, which was number fifteen, it did not quite work out that way. The WFO was being reorganized, and we spent our time moving desks and other office equipment. The only cases I worked on were the cases of files which I pushed from one location to another.

During the last week of training, a reception was held for Class No. 15 at the Mayflower Hotel. It was to be our first opportunity to meet Director Hoover, and we were carefully instructed on how to handle ourselves. It was important, we were told, not to crowd around him when he arrived. We were to form a line and march by to shake his hand, but we were not to delay the proceedings by unnecessary conversation. It was extremely important that our handshake be firm, but not too much so. Hoover reacted as much against a "bone crusher" as he did against a limp one. He particularly objected to moist hands, and those subject to this failing were told to have a dry handkerchief ready to wipe their palms unobtrusively just before the crucial handshake.

J. Edgar Hoover arrived precisely at 6:30 P.M. He strode into the room briskly with Associate Director Clyde Tolson, who, as always, remained a few steps behind. My impression of the Director was sharp and distinct. He was vigorous and alert, dignified but friendly, and in complete control. He was forty-seven years of age at that time and at the peak of his physical capacities. He was stocky but not fat. Perhaps more than anything else, I noticed his immaculate appearance. He looked as if he had shaved, showered, and put on a freshly pressed suit for the occasion. Through the years, I never saw him when he looked otherwise.

The handshaking ceremony, each of us getting a quick tight smile from the Director, took less than fifteen minutes. As the last member of the class was approaching to be introduced, Tolson, who had scrutinized us as we stepped forward, approached the Director and whispered in his ear. A few seconds later, they were both on their way out of the room, Tolson still a few steps behind.

I was to see this pattern of behavior many times during my career in the FBI. Tolson was not the innovator. He was the buffer between Hoover and everyone else in the Bureau. His job was to protect Hoover and to make sure that the Director's energies were expended efficiently.

CHAPTER THREE

This man needs roughening up.

—Ross Prescott
FBI Instructor

Ross Prescott, one of my instructors at Quantico, was a Texan. If he liked you, he would recommend, "This man needs roughening up. Send him to a Texas office." I like to think that this was the reason my first assignment was to Houston, Texas.

I had known that transfer to the Field was a certainty. It was FBI policy to assign new Agents for three months to their first office, six months to the second, and three years to the third. Agents could then expect to remain in their fourth office of assignment from seven to ten years. Hoover wanted Agents to be experienced in dealing with different types of people and differing conditions in all parts of the country. He wanted every Agent to fit into any Field office at any time. Since he had never been transferred and did not have a family, he had no idea of the financial and personal hardship involved.

To cover moving costs, Agents were allowed the price of a first-class railway ticket plus six dollars a day for expenses en route. It was, however, permissible for an Agent on transfer to travel in his own car at the rate of five cents a mile, plus the six dollars for daily expenses. The Agent could only ship 500 pounds of personal effects by Railway Express.* Married

* Today, transfer policies are far more liberal. The transferee is allowed expenses for his family as well as himself. The government pays moving

Agents like me had no choice but to travel by personal car when moving from one assignment to another, in order to cover their wives' traveling expenses. But for the extra time it took to go by car, the Agent lost out on annual leave.

Audrey and I elected to drive from Washington to Houston and, in the one day allotted to us, managed to find a pleasant furnished apartment. Leaving the job of settling in to her, I plunged into my new assignment. The Houston FBI office was located in the center of the downtown area. The space had once been excellent, but when I arrived, three times the number of people were crowded into it than it had originally been designed for. The territory we had to cover was, like everything else in Texas, very large—forty-five counties, stretching from the Louisiana border to Beaumont and south almost to the Mexican border. The Special Agent in Charge (SAC), Ray Abbaticchio, was a kindly man but thoroughly intimidated by J. Edgar Hoover. As a result, he made the Houston office ground rules one notch tighter than the Bureau required.

Exceeding Bureau policy, the Houston office required that each Agent must wear his revolver at all times while working. For an Agent doing little else than interviewing friends, neighbors, and references of applicants for government jobs, carrying a three-pound revolver in a heavy leather holster in the Houston heat was more than a little burdensome. It also precluded taking off your coat to cool off. The SAC also excluded all Agents from the office during regular working hours except to dictate their correspondence. Organization of work, reviewing files, preparation for dictation, and reviewing notes all had to be done during overtime hours. Hoover would not have objected to any legitimate activity in the office, and Abbaticchio's rule created more problems than it solved. Because of the serious overcrowding, it was next to impossi-

---

costs for up to eleven thousand pounds of furniture and for an inspection trip by Agent and spouse to search for housing prior to their move. Costs of storing household goods for up to sixty days are paid, as well as a temporary quarters' allowance for thirty days. Real estate commission of up to $8,000, and settlement and closing costs for a new home of up to $4,000 can be allowed.

ble to organize work or prepare for dictation before 8:30 A.M., when the regular working day began. New Agents frequently left the office without enough investigative leads to keep them busy during the day, and when these were completed they were afraid to return to the office. Not knowing what to do, some just wandered up and down the streets.

My solution was to go to the public library where I could organize my work for the following day. I made it a practice to carry all my papers and documents in my briefcase so that I could have access to them in the library. As a result, my reports were just what Hoover wanted—terse, succinct, and relevant. This, perhaps, is what started me up the promotional ladder. One particular report, a wartime Plant Protection Program, on which I spent considerable time in the library, was detailed and innovative enough to bring me Bureau commendation.

Three months to the day of my assignment to Houston I received my second transfer letter. San Antonio was my destination, and though Audrey had to resign her job with the IRS in Houston, we were pleased. The San Antonio office covered even more territory than Houston's—sixty counties—and the Special Agent in Charge kept most of us out of the city to handle the vast territory for which he was responsible. My new SAC, Maurice W. Acers, was always cordial and considerate to me, but he was not popular in the office. Agents resented some of his management techniques, particularly the pressures he exerted to keep the San Antonio "voluntary overtime" or VOT, the highest of any office in the FBI.

Acers accomplished this by compiling a list which showed where every man stood on the VOT totem pole. The four low men were given weekend duty during the ensuing month to "assist" them in moving up the list. This meant a "voluntary" eight-hour shift every Sunday of that month. He augmented his overtime by claiming as VOT the time he spent on overnight train rides to and from his frequent engagements out of the city. It pleased me very much when Hoover subsequently disallowed credit for travel time.

My work in San Antonio was routine until I had settled in. Then Acers gave me what he touted as a "very important" assignment—the Waco road trip. Each Monday morning, I started out from San Antonio loaded with leads to be covered in the territory between Austin and Waco, most of which was on the Fort Hood military reservation, an Army tank corps battle training area. My job was to track down persons who had given the name of a tank trainee as a reference for positions in the FBI, the Justice Department, or the Office of Strategic Services (the wartime predecessor of the CIA). It was grueling work in which I spent long hours on the road or on the rough tank trails, driving to each interview. I had almost no time at home, and when I managed a few hours with Audrey I was too tired to do anything except fall into bed. It was very good news when I was transferred again, this time to Washington.

J. Edgar Hoover grandiloquently referred to Bureau headquarters in the capital as the "Seat of Government"—otherwise known as SOG. This was the nerve center of a tightly controlled and disciplined organization. SOG, which occupied 40 percent of the block-square Justice Department building on Pennsylvania Avenue, directed all field operations. The Special Agents in Charge of Field offices across the country had autonomy in directing investigations, but they were under constant supervision from headquarters through correspondence, the careful review of their reports, and a system of annual inspections. In turn, SOG was subject to close scrutiny by Hoover, who kept his finger on everything and made all the decisions. The whole operation was a pyramid, with everything funneling up through ever tightening lines of responsibility until it reached Hoover.

Headquarters operations at that time consisted of eight separate Divisions. The administrative side included the Identification Division, the Administrative Division, the Crime Records Division, the Training and Inspection Division, and Files and Communications. The investigative side was made up of the General Investigative Division, the Domestic Intelligence Division, and the Laboratory. There was considerable competition among the different offices of the Seat of Government to extract the maximum amount of work from the field. The SACs had to juggle operations in such a way as to keep all eight of those Headquarters divisions happy.

The device which permitted direct contact between SOG and the Field Agent was In-Service Training, a two-week session held at regular intervals in Washington and at the FBI Academy in Quantico. New Agents were brought to SOG after having served from five to twelve months in the field. More experienced Agents were required to take In-Service Training every two years. Because of cost factors, these intervals have been substantially extended since those early days, but I had only been in the field for six months when I received orders to report to SOG for my In-Service Training.

Some disagreed, but I thought this training was valuable for passing on the benefit of other Agents' experience and the sharing of new investigative techniques. The first week of training was usually held in the large FBI classroom in the Justice Department building. All classes were from 9:00 A.M. to 6:00 P.M. The first week in Washington consisted entirely of lectures by Bureau supervisors. Each of these supervisors was an expert in his field. For example, there was a bank robbery desk with eight or ten supervisors, each responsible for his area of the country and its problems. In addition to these lectures, there were two full days of firearms training at Quantico, hours devoted to the solving of hypothetical arrest problems.

During the first week of my In-Service Training, I received my third transfer letter assigning me to the Seat of Government as a Bureau Supervisor. Though there was no increase in pay, it was a promotion. I carried this happy thought with me when I was interviewed by Harry Kimball, Chief of the Espionage Section. This was part of In-Service Training. Kimball thumbed through my personnel file very carefully as he questioned me about my assignments in Houston and San Antonio. He seemed impressed, and congratulated me on the promotion when he saw it noted in the top serial number of my file. When I asked him if he could tell to which division I would be assigned, he said there was no clue in the file. But, because of my lack of experience, he was sure I would not be assigned to the Espionage Section.

Two weeks after my interview with Kimball, I found myself reporting to him in the Espionage Section. He made no reference to our talk and I never learned whether he had asked for me. I did discover, however, that there were positions in the section which could be handled by a novice: I was assigned to assist three other supervisors at the General Desk, where all the unimportant cases were handled, and they numbered in the thousands.

The Assistant Director in charge of the Domestic Intelligence Division was D. Milton (Mickey) Ladd, a highly capable and hard-driving official. Much of the Bureau's success in combating German espionage and sabotage was due to his effective leadership, and he was very popular with the supervisors under him. When the Director disapproved of something done or not done by the division, Ladd took the heat and never passed it down.

Though I did not at first handle any important cases at SOG, I did learn the tricks of the trade. I quickly found out, for example, that Hoover would not accept a long memorandum. I also learned to use the "abstract"—a three-by-five-inch typed slip with the title of the document, the date, to whom addressed, the name of the writer, and a one- or two-sentence description of the content of the document. Hoover, who went through a tremendous volume of reports and letters each day, frequently read only the abstract. Only if interested did he read the document itself. Unlike many Agents, I realized the importance of writing a good abstract. With careful wording, it was often possible to point Hoover in a desired direction. A good abstract had a subtle influence, but this was a technique which not many applied.

However valuable this knowledge may have been during my rise in FBI ranks, it was secondary to my work on the General Desk of the Espionage Section. America was at war, and concerned citizens passed on to us every suspicion of a possible saboteur or espionage agent. Relatively inexperienced in such matters, the FBI opened investigations on nearly every one of these reports. Wiretaps, microphones, and physical surveillance were reserved for the major cases. In minor cases, because of limited manpower, the investigations consisted of regular contacts with neighbors and employers of the suspect, and spot checks. All of this created a tremendous volume of work for the General Desk.

From the first day of my assignment, my responsibility was to review as many cases as possible—fifty or more files a day—of the thousands of cases which poured in for scrutiny by our four-man team. New to the work, we were overly cautious and we tended to resolve doubts in favor of continuing the investigations. In time, we realized that ninety-eight percent of the cases could have been closed immediately and we made substantial reductions in the case load. The work I did was routine and hardly thrilling, but I became familiar with the major cases, sharing in the excitement. I also learned a great deal about German espionage techniques, thereby preparing myself for a promotion to the Major Case Desk.

The experienced Agents handling the big cases had a very condescending attitude toward the neophytes on the General Desk. And they kept the good cases to themselves, passing the humdrum cases on to us. But in April of 1944, one of the major case supervisors missed one. Having casually reviewed a four-volume file involving a Nazi sympathizer, being investigated for possible denaturalization, he routed the case on to me.

The subject, Maximilian Gerhard Waldemar Othmer, had been born in Germany, immigrated to the United States in 1919, and was naturalized in New Jersey in April of 1935. The very next day he had joined the German-American Bund and had become the local fuehrer before the year was out. He had made no secret of his Nazi sympathies and had returned to Germany several times. On one of these trips, he had been given an espionage assignment by the *Abwehr*, Germany's spy service. Subsequently, he obtained a job at Camp Pendleton (near Norfolk, Virginia) as an electrician and part-time stevedore. In 1942, he had been relocated to Knoxville, Tennessee by the Army under its wartime powers.

The investigation of Othmer had been inconclusive and denaturalization proceedings against him had never been instituted, nor had there been any suspicion that he was a Nazi agent. But in studying Othmer's file, I came across several things which aroused my interest. To begin with, I knew that the wide mouth of Chesapeake Bay between Norfolk and Hampton, where he had lived in Virginia, was the assembly point for convoys bound for England. The German submarine command seemed to have detailed an uncanny knowledge of this activity.

I noted, too, that Othmer had received $500 from Shanghai through the Chase National Bank. The amount was insignificant, but the *Abwehr* funneled money to its agents in this manner. And buried away in the file was the information that a Trenton dentist had casually mentioned having received a letter from Othmer pleading for a prescription for Pyramidon, a commonly used pain-killer in Europe. (The doctor had told Othmer to use aspirin.) This last fact was the real tip-off for me. Pyramidon was used by *Abwehr* agents for making secret ink. The process was simple. A tablet was dissolved in water, and the solution was used to write an invisible message between the lines of a seemingly innocuous letter. The receiving agent heated the letter and the secret writing appeared. This highly effective technique is used by spy networks to this day.

Convinced that Othmer was a spy, I prepared a carefully worded memorandum recommending that the case be reopened and that Othmer be interviewed again as soon as possible. To make sure that the Agents asked the right questions, I made out a detailed summary and outlined what he should be asked. Impatiently, I waited for the results of the new investigation. And then the word came—Othmer had confessed! He told his questioners that he had been sending secret-ink messages to his German superiors in 1940 and 1941, via a letter drop in Milan, Italy. These were radioed to the German High Command, which in turn passed them on to German U-boats preying on Allied shipping. Because it took days to assemble the convoys and then for them to reach submarine hunting grounds, Nazi raiders had sufficient time to sink many Allied vessels.

Othmer was charged with violations of the Federal espionage statutes. But he denied having sent any messages after Pearl Harbor and refused to implicate other German agents. When I questioned him myself—arguing, pleading, and even threatening him with a maximum prison sentence—he refused to budge. However, during that day of interrogation, he let slip one bit of important information. He identified his mail drop as R. A. Homburg, 46 Via Gran Sassa, in Milan and a file search disclosed two other suspects using the same drop.*

There was one unusual turn to the Othmer case. One of the Agents who had interviewed Othmer when he admitted his spying was David Scruggs. While Othmer was on his way to the Federal Penitentiary in Atlanta, he wrote to Scruggs, who had been compassionate, asking him to handle some personal matters. Scruggs was glad to do this, and it was fortunate that he did. When, a few weeks later, Othmer requested permission to see Scruggs, permission was granted in the hope that the spy might be ready to talk.

"You have been kind to me," Othmer said to Scruggs, "and now I want to do something for you." This was one way of putting it, but another would have been that Othmer realized that by being cooperative he might shorten his prison sentence. "I have a steamer trunk full of books in storage at the YMCA in Knoxville. Look at the one entitled *Weiers Taschenbuch der Kriegsflotten—1940,*" he said.

When the book was examined by the FBI Laboratory, a frame of microfilm was found concealed in the binding, the negative of a photo of a typewritten page. What Othmer had given us was a code for use when writing in open text, as opposed to secret ink. A message in this code would appear to be innocuous. For example, "Mrs" meant a convoy. If the proper name started with an *A*, it would indicate a convoy of under ten ships. *B* would indicate ten to twenty ships, *C* from twenty to thirty, and so on. "Suitcase" meant a destroyer. Any date was ten days less than stated. We found the double-

* Othmer was sentenced to twenty years, the maximum sentence for espionage when the crime had been committed before we entered the war. After the German defeat, Army Intelligence teams found *Abwehr* records which showed that Othmer had volunteered his services in 1937. Though Othmer had claimed to be a minor agent, his dossier showed that he was probably one of the most valuable *Abwehr* spies in the United States, furnishing reports on damaged British warships being repaired in Norfolk, on the details of departing convoys, and on tank production. Based on what he sent, the *Abwehr* was able to piece together a picture of naval aid to Great Britain and America's growing preparedness at sea.

meaning code exactly as it had been placed there by the authorities at Nest Bremen, one of the *Abwehr* subdivisions, at which Othmer had been trained. This was a valuable find because the same code, prepared on the same typewriter, had been used by other German agents. It proved to be an important link to other Nazi espionage cases.

My role in the Othmer case came at an opportune time for me. When a vacancy on the Major Case Desk occurred, I was promoted from the General Desk, still at no increase in pay. Involvement in the case had made me something of an expert on Nest Bremen and I was assigned to coordinate all information on this operation and to familiarize myself with its personnel. This assignment was both interesting and important because, as we came to learn, Nest Bremen had primary responsibility for *Abwehr* operations directed against the United States.

Information about Nest Bremen was routed to me for study and indexing. Much of our knowledge came from MI-5, the British counterpart to the FBI, which had caught and debriefed a number of German agents trained at Nest Bremen. I used this information, along with what the FBI had gathered exclusively, to prepare brief dossiers on each staff member, and these were furnished to MI-5 so that they could complete their records. As my knowledge increased, I was able to identify other German agents just by reviewing the files which had been accumulated.

But this was not my only assignment. The Agent I had replaced on the Major Case Desk had been handling the Mexican microdot case, one of the great breakthroughs in our counter-intelligence efforts. German agents in Mexico, abusing that country's neutrality, accumulated vast amounts of information about the United States—far too much to be sent by radio. In order to send it by mail, the Germans had devised a process of photographic reduction—prints so small that they could be disguised as a period on a typewritten page. The Germans had developed such a fine grain emulsion that the surface of the microdot would look smooth even when magnified 100 times. The finest photographic emulsion in America at the time was so coarse that a 100-X magnification looked like a field of pebbles and was impossible to read.

This mode of transmitting information might have gone undetected but for the alertness of an examiner at the British censorship station in Bermuda. He had opened and examined a letter bearing a microdot, detecting nothing, but as he put it aside, he noticed a shiny spot. Examining the letter more carefully, he saw that what seemed to be a typewritten period was actually a dot glued to the paper.

The letter and the problem it posed were turned over to the FBI. It was imperative not to let the enemy know that their process had been discovered, yet we could not allow vital information to reach Germany. These factors have to be evaluated in every espionage case. As a general rule, the best procedure is to contain, and possibly to control, a foreign agent. With containment, you learn much about enemy intelligence operations and other agents can be identified. With control, the submission of false information can mislead and confuse the enemy.

After consultation with the Joint Security Council (JSC), we decided to let that particular letter go through. The information on the microdot had come from various American publications sold openly in Mexico. But by the end of the war, more than 300 microdots had been intercepted. All were reviewed by the JSC and many were cleared to go to the enemy. Such was the pace of our military production and our developing technology that it did more to discourage than to help the German High Command. Where the information was too sensitive to be passed on, the microdot was rubbed off so that it would appear to have come loose in transit.

My work in the microdot case brought me into close contact with the Joint Security Council, and this association was very helpful in the next case which I handled. Code-named "Peasant," it was a double-agent operation designed to provide misinformation to the Japanese military, and was a part of a much bigger misinformation program conducted during World War II. "Peasant" was so important, that what we transmitted to the Japanese made it possible for General

Douglas MacArthur to land almost without opposition in the Philippines toward the end of the war.

Early in 1944, Nest Bremen had trained an espionage agent for assignment in the United States, his messages to be sent by Morse code. Since each person's touch on the wireless key is unique—telegraphers call it his "fist"—Nest Bremen had made a tape recording of the agent's way of transmitting to serve as his signature. The agent, Helmut Gold, had left Germany with $5,000 in cash. In Lisbon, on his way to Washington, Gold had promptly defected to the Allied cause, revealing his whole operation to the British Embassy there. At first, the British planned to make Gold their own double-agent. But he was completely unreliable in his personal habits, and an aggressive woman-chaser as well, so they turned him over to us. Warned of Gold's propensities, however, the Bureau decided it wanted no part of him.

What to do with Gold? Because he had been trained at Nest Bremen, the question was referred to me for recommendation. I recommended that we take the case but leave Gold in England, in protective custody. We would create a fictitious Gold who would come to Washington and set up an espionage operation. Thus we would not only control what information went to the Nazis but also use the bogus Gold to ferret out the spies he was to work with. Hoover agreed. The critical point—and most of my memorandum to Hoover was addressed to this—was the ability of an FBI radio specialist to duplicate Gold's "fist" at the Morse key.

Working on this case was one of my most fascinating assignments for the FBI. On the one hand, I was involved in fooling the Nazis. But I was also learning much about the thinking and the problems of important German officials. We got corroboration, for example, of the German military's growing confusion and despair over the magnitude of America's war effort. On one occasion, the *Abwehr* asked "Gold" to procure the production figures for two-engined transport planes in the United States. Knowing the impact the true figures would have, the Joint Security Council decided to supply them. The *Abwehr* radioed back to Gold that his source obviously did not have access to the facts and he was instructed not to use it any more.

Most of the information "volunteered" to "Gold" by his "high level contacts" was designed to be of more interest to Japan than to Germany. The Joint Security Council deliberately prepared fragmentary data which it knew would be given to the Japanese by the Germans. "Gold" was only one channel. Pieces of the jigsaw puzzle were leaked to Japan from many "sources." In Tokyo, they would be put together by specialists into one erroneous picture. A message to Gold's superiors in Bremen would contain a small amount of valid information and misinformation relating to United States military operations in the Pacific. A few days later, the Signal Security Service,* which had broken the Japanese diplomatic code before the outbreak of hostilities, would intercept a message from the Japanese Embassy in Berlin to Tokyo. Its substance would be what "Gold" had transmitted to Nest Bremen.

* The Signal Security Service was later merged into the National Security Agency.

CHAPTER FOUR

A Burning Desire.

—J. EDGAR HOOVER

For those of us who worked in the Espionage Section, Seat of Government, World War II came to an end on May 7, 1945—V-E Day, when the Third Reich surrendered to the Allies. Terrible battles still raged in the Pacific, but for the FBI the ineffective Japanese espionage apparatus posed few problems. The wartime "alliance" with the Soviet Union, however, had opened up the United States to the Kremlin's spies, and the FBI was busy learning to cope with the Russian agents and their American supporters who manned the underground apparatus. But this aspect of FBI work was being handled by the Internal Security Section of the Domestic Intelligence Division. Less than a week after V-E Day, Hoover abolished the Espionage Section for reasons of efficiency and economy. This meant that each of the twelve Supervisory Agents in that section, myself included, had to be transferred to other assignments. Ordinarily, this would have been handled by the Administrative Division strictly on the basis of the manpower needs of the various field offices, and we could have been assigned almost anywhere, from Alaska to Florida.

But "Mickey" Ladd, the Assistant Director in Charge of the Domestic Intelligence Division, took good care of those who worked for him. At his prompting, Hoover agreed that each of us could choose where we wanted to be transferred. Some of the Agents in the Espionage Section chose one of the Bureau's Field Offices and others opted for remaining at the Washington headquarters. My choice, for both personal and professional reasons, was the Seattle Office. Three weeks after I began my duties there, however, I received orders to report to Washington, D.C., for In-Service Training. This was not bureaucratic bungling. The Espionage Section had been excused from this training for the duration, and that requirement had finally caught up with me.

I expected a two-week stint and a return to Seattle, but this was not to be. Elizabeth Bentley, a courier for the Soviet espionage apparatus, had defected. A woman with little imagination but a prodigious memory, Miss Bentley had given the Bureau a full account of her activities, her espionage contacts in the Federal Government, and the extent of Soviet penetration.* In the course of her debriefing by the FBI, she named a considerable number of suspects in the Washington area, and it fell to the Washington Field Office to investigate her allegations. With the sudden demand for extra manpower there, the budget-wary Bureau assigned the two classes then taking In-Service Training to the Bentley case. More than seventy Agents were "shanghaied" for the task of physical surveillance of suspects—8:00 A.M. to 10:00 P.M., seven days a week. Since most of the suspects worked in downtown Washington, the surveillance agents were constantly crossing paths and we frequently had problems keeping out of each other's way. For some, this was rewarding work, but my job was limited to the surveillance of one individual who never did anything suspicious. The surveillance was thorough, uneventful, and unproductive—and the only thing I caught was a cold, brought on by the unusually rigorous Washington winter.

Just before Christmas, I was reassigned to the Seattle Office where I spent two years working on general assignments. My

* In the summer of 1948, Elizabeth Bentley's testimony before a congressional committee created a nationwide furor. This, in turn, led to the testimony of Whittaker Chambers and to the Alger Hiss and Harry Dexter White cases.

background as a supervisor in the Espionage Section was of value once when I was assigned to the surveillance of Nicolai Reddin, a Russian naval officer stationed in Seattle in a liaison capacity. Reddin had bribed a technician at the United States Naval Shipyard in Bremerton (a ferry ride across Puget Sound from Seattle) to furnish him with information about our ships. The technician had contacted the FBI and was told to continue his contacts with the Soviet intelligence agent.

Reddin was no unsuspecting amateur like the suspect we had tailed in the Bentley case. He was a trained agent, familiar with all the tricks and alert to any surveillance activity. He made left turns where they were prohibited and we either had to follow or lose him. He slowed down when approaching an intersection, and as the light turned red, he would drive through. He rode up and down elevators in order to spot those who were following him. Our orders were not to arrest him unless he boarded a Russian freighter. This was precisely what happened. Reddin was subsequently tried on charges of espionage. But he was acquitted, in part because the government could only prove minor violations of the espionage statutes, and in part because the Russians were still considered "allies."

My next assignment was as Firearms Instructor, a position I held for two years. Then, relieved of my firearms duties, I was again promoted to the rank of supervisor (which I had lost when I left the Espionage Section), and resumed the climb up the FBI ladder. Congress had just passed the Atomic Energy Act, which transferred supervision for the production of atomic warheads from the military, which had successfully supervised the wartime Manhattan Project, to the newly created Atomic Energy Commission. In a sense the AEC was a giant government-owned defense contractor, and the FBI was given the responsibility of conducting the AEC's personnel security investigations and guarding against the theft of our atomic secrets.

The major plant for the production of plutonium was at Hanford, in the state of Washington, which fell within the jurisdiction of the Seattle office. Conducting personnel clearance investigations of AEC employees (including the many contract employees having access to atomic facilities) was a tremendous burden for the FBI, and particularly for those Field Offices near AEC installations. As the supervisor of this activity in Seattle, I found myself overseeing as many as 1,500 pending cases at a time. In time, and at my urging, routine personnel investigations were turned over to the Civil Service Commission.

There was, however, an occasional moment of drama to our work. One day we received a breathless report that eleven ounces of plutonium were missing. The eleven ounces consisted of minute machine filings, the by-product of lathing down raw plutonium into the shapes necessary for an atomic explosion. The scientists at Hanford were worried because the chemical composition of the filings would disclose to a Russian chemist the processes used in refining the plutonium.

To investigate the alleged theft, I took a squad of Agents to the Hanford Laboratory and made a thorough examination of their procedures. It was apparent almost at once that it would have been virtually impossible to steal the eleven ounces of plutonium. We therefore checked the clean-up and accountability procedures. The floors in the laboratory, we learned, were covered with brown wrapping paper. Periodically during the day, one man circled the laboratory and if he detected signs of radiation in any area, the paper was rolled up, sealed in a large cardboard box, and buried under tons of dirt. This was also done at the end of the day, whether radiation was detected or not. Eventually we were able to convince the scientists at Hanford that the missing plutonium was a result of their rigorous safety measure rather than Soviet espionage. In that spy-conscious time, I suspect that some were not entirely convinced.

But however interesting my work in the Seattle office may have been, it did not satisfy my ambition, modest enough, to become a Special Agent in Charge. It was common knowledge that J. Edgar Hoover was interested in promoting only those who had demonstrated commitment to the Bureau and a "burning desire" to rise in its hierarchy. I felt that I qualified on that score. My experience was such that I had few doubts that I could handle a SAC's job, and this was confirmed by Richard Auerbach, the Seattle SAC who had repeatedly recommended me. In May of 1951, when I was scheduled for another round of In-Service Training in Washington, Auerbach called me into his office for some friendly advice.

"You've got to call yourself to Hoover's attention," he said. "I'm a good friend of Clyde Tolson. Ask to see him and tell him it was my idea. Explain that you want to be a SAC and feel you're ready for the responsibility. Ask him to help you."

On the last day of my training, the supervisor who was lecturing us announced, "Mr. Felt, Mr. Tolson wants to see you right away."

"Hello, Mr. Felt," Tolson said and motioned for me to sit down on the long couch at his right. I had not seen him since the day of the reception to welcome new Agents more than eight years before. Now I was really looking at him for the first time. He looked drawn and tired, and smiling seemed to be an effort for him. Very thin and aging, he appeared to be much older than the Director. He was very remote, very impersonal. When I outlined my Bureau experience and expressed my desire for the responsibility of a SAC assignment, he told me, "I am glad to know that you are interested. Your record is good. I will make a note of your visit."

Whatever note he made had no effect, and almost three years later, when I was once again scheduled for In-Service Training, I decided that the only way I would achieve my goal would be to personally contact the Director. My request to see Hoover was granted and, again on the last day of my training period, I found myself walking through a large conference room at least fifty feet in length. Large portraits and other pictures covered the walls. In the center of the room was a large conference table and beyond it the executive desk Hoover used for ceremonial purposes. In a small private office beyond this room sat J. Edgar Hoover. His desk was piled high with papers and files. The Director held out his hand and said, "It's nice to see you, Mr. Felt."

In my twelve years in the Bureau, I had only been face to face with Hoover once before. My earlier impression had been a fleeting one but I saw now the power and strength of this imposing man. The squareness of his face was accentuated by a jutting jaw. His piercing eyes looked squarely into mine, sizing me up. A little on the stocky side, he was not fat as some have described him, although in later years he had some difficulty in maintaining the weight standards he imposed on others. He carried himself with a military bearing which made him appear taller than his five feet and ten inches. His voice was strong and cultivated, with a trace of Southern accent. I particularly remember his necktie, which was very bright. The small private office was plain, almost Spartan. The furniture was old and he sat down behind the desk he had used from his first day as Director (and would use until the day he died).

I did not feel intimidated or uncomfortable and he was cordial and gracious as I made my prepared presentation. "Mr. Hoover," I said, "I feel ready for more responsibility. My ambition is to be a Special Agent in Charge. I feel confident I can handle the job whenever you feel I am ready for it."

Hoover looked pleased. "Mr. Felt, I am glad to hear that. We need ambitious, hardworking young men. You can be sure I will give you consideration when promotions are being made," he answered.

Then he launched into a discussion of the problems facing the FBI. He spoke in a forceful and staccato manner of the demands of the Congress and the Atomic Energy Commission for the need of Bureau clearance investigations. I took copious notes of what he was saying, but after ten minutes or so, I began to wonder if I was being tested. It was not easy to interrupt J. Edgar Hoover, but when he paused for breath, I broke in. "Mr. Hoover, this is a particular problem of the Seattle office where we conduct thousands of these investigations. Most of them are routine and could be handled by the Civil Service Commission. The FBI has more important things to do and we should be responsible for only the top positions."

Hoover thought for a minute and then told me, "You are probably right. We'll have to take a long, hard look at this problem." He did, and perhaps my career turned on this exchange. From that point on, I injected myself into the conversation whenever possible, and Hoover was always interested in what I had to say. We talked for about thirty minutes and then he rose, holding out his hand. "Mr. Felt, I enjoyed this conversation," he said. "You can be sure you will be kept in mind for a promotion."

Six days later, back in Seattle, I received a letter from Hoover transferring me to the Seat of Government as an Inspector's aide, the next step on the promotion ladder. I was not too happy to serve on the "goon squad"—which is what my fellow Agents called the Inspection staff—but there was no other way to go if I wanted to rise in the Bureau. Inspections have always played an important part in the FBI, and Hoover referred to his Inspectors as his "eyes and ears." Each Field Office and each division at the Seat of Government were to be inspected at least once a year, and more often than that if there were problems. This meant that the Inspectors were constantly on the road, which made it difficult for those who were married.

Inspectors were required to check into every phase of Field Office operations and to review a substantial number of cases to detect errors—either "form" errors relating to procedure or "substantive" errors which might have adversely affected the outcome of a case.

Inspector in Charge Edmund Mason, my superior, was known for maintaining tight control over his aides. He had risen to power by ingratiating himself with the Director. Other Bureau officials and Agents in the field distrusted Mason and feared his power. He delighted in finding errors which he called to Hoover's attention with recommendations for disciplinary action. He exploited Hoover's determination to ferret out errors and weaknesses and his belief that the Inspector who found the most things wrong was the most efficient. So I was pleased when after only two months in the capital, I was transferred to New Orleans as the Assistant Special Agent in Charge, even though this meant another move for me and my family just as we were settling down in Washington. The possibility of a raise in pay also helped.

The FBI office in New Orleans was average in size—fifty-one Agents and twenty-six clerical employees. It was the nerve center for all FBI activities in Louisiana, with suboffices in Baton Rouge, Shreveport, Monroe, Alexandria, and Lake Charles. The SAC, Morton P. Chiles, supervised most of the major cases and had overall responsibility for the office. As Assistant SAC, I handled everything else in the criminal field and supervised the Criminal Informant Program, which was very active in sinful New Orleans.

The Bureau's method of training new Assistant SACs was to take someone like myself and let him learn from experience under the tutelage of an older and experienced SAC. But this was particularly tough for me because I had virtually no experience in the day-to-day management of an FBI Field Office. And, unlike the average Agent, I had no background in the criminal field which constituted more than 80 percent of the Bureau's work. I had spent my first five FBI years in Washington supervising espionage cases. Without grounding in bank-robbery investigation, the apprehension of criminals, and the criminal justice system, I quickly earned five censure letters, the bane of an Agent's existence, for the mistakes I made. These letters were sent out over Hoover's signature, written in doomsday language, and typically began, "I am amazed and astounded . . ." etc. Censure letters were more than a written slap on the wrist for they could hold up a prospective raise for as long as six months. Because they were often earned for insignificant errors, they were resented by Agents who felt that their transgressions should have been overlooked. But if Hoover was quick to blame, he was even quicker to praise—and letters of commendation often accompanied by a cash incentive award, outnumbered censure letters by three to one. In my case the censure letters did nothing to hurt my FBI career.

Censure letters or not, within fifteen months I was transferred to the Los Angeles office, second in size only to the New York office and another step toward promotion to SAC. The work in Los Angeles was hard, but in a few months I accumulated more on-the-job experience than I would have received in three years at a smaller field office. Of prime importance was what I learned about administration and personnel management. And not the least significant training I received was in the handling of the "baggage detail" in which I was dealing directly with Hoover.

To get away from official Washington, he and Tolson made several trips each year, the one they enjoyed most being their annual trip to Los Angeles and La Jolla each summer. Preparations were made far in advance because Hoover insisted on the same seats in the plane, the same rooms in the same hotels, the same restaurants, the same haberdasher, and the same pleasure ride—each in the same sequence. My responsibility in this operation was to handle the luggage, a precision operation. When Hoover and Tolson departed from Washington, airline officials arranged for their suitcases to be loaded last into the forward baggage compartment. Numbers on the claim stubs were telephoned ahead. It was my job to get the luggage off the plane and to deliver it to Hoover's hotel room exactly three minutes after he entered it.

I must have done it right because, almost two years to the day that I had sat in Hoover's office, I was promoted to SAC, the job I had asked for. My new assignment was Salt Lake City, and once again my family pulled up stakes. The Salt Lake City office was one of the smaller ones, but it included Las Vegas and Reno—and it was here that I became a part of the FBI push against the Mafia. It has been charged that Hoover did not move against organized crime until forced to by Attorney General Robert F. Kennedy. I know differently because, in 1956, as SAC of a field office whose territory included Nevada, I was under continual pressure from the Seat of Government to move against Mafia infiltration of the gambling casinos in Reno and Las Vegas. Without adequate laws such as the Congress enacted in the Sixties, we could do little more than gather information through the use of informants and electronic surveillance, and this is how we discovered that the underworld owners of the gambling casinos were not informing Federal and state authorities of the full extent of their profits—or "skimming."

Arduous as my work as SAC may have seemed at the time, I was glad to be in Salt Lake City and looked forward to remaining there for at least three years. But this was not to be so. In February of 1958 I received the bad news. I was being transferred to Kansas City, known within the Bureau as the Siberia of Field Offices.

CHAPTER FIVE

Shape up or ship out.

—DWIGHT BRANTLEY
FORMER SPECIAL AGENT IN CHARGE AT KANSAS CITY.

Discipline in the Bureau was extremely tight, and in very serious cases the penalty was usually a transfer to another field office. And for the most severe disciplinary cases, Hoover had a "dog house" Field Office—in Kansas City, where for many years Dwight Brantley, the roughest and toughest SAC of them all, ran a reform school for fallen Agents, as well as an excellent investigative office. When an Agent in trouble was sent to Brantley, it was either "shape up or ship out." But in actual fact, the Kansas City office was anything but a Siberia. Living conditions were outstanding and the staff there had been welded into an effective and highly cohesive unit. It was and is one of the finest FBI offices in the country.

My misconceptions about the new assignment and the thought of once more pulling up stakes made me reluctant to move, but orders were orders. Leaving my family behind until the end of the school year, I took off for Siberia, my only consolation being that the Kansas City Field Office was larger and more important than the one in Salt Lake City. The Kansas City office's territory covered half of Missouri and all of Kansas. And on arriving, I quickly realized that my fears were not warranted. Instead of the collection of misfits I had expected, I found a group of Agents who had been tried and passed with flying colors. Any real misfits had long since fallen by the wayside and instead I had an investigative crew which could handle the wide variety of major cases which had fallen to the Kansas City office during the entire history of the FBI. Something important happened every day. There were more extortions, kidnappings, bombings, gangland slayings, and dangerous fugitive apprehensions than in several other large FBI offices combined. The city was a transportation crossroads and it was also the headquarters for one of the more important Mafia "families" in the United States.

The Mafia leaders called themselves the "Clique." They lived in an enclave of fancy homes in North Kansas City occupying an entire block. Though polite when interviewed, they of course gave us no cooperation and when summoned to appear before Federal Grand Juries, they usually invoked the Fifth Amendment. Less important members, known as "soldiers," were arrogant, crude, and very much aware that any of their number who turned informer would end up in the Missouri River in concrete boots.

There were few Federal laws on the books then which covered the activities of the Mafia, but SOG pushed hard to get us to uncover evidence which could put the leaders behind bars. Though we knew the favorite meeting places of the Mafia, physical surveillance was extremely difficult and I discovered that we were operating in the dark much of the time. The answer seemed to be the use of planted microphones to eavesdrop on what went on at one of the "Clique's" meeting places, which was legal under the standards of the time. Today, the Omnibus Crime Control and Safe Streets Act of 1968 permits electronic eavesdropping, provided that court approval is obtained.

After securing Bureau approval, I therefore assigned Max Richardson, the electronics specialist, or "sound man," in the office to set up microphone coverage. The meeting place he chose was located in a very old building, and Richardson rented a small apartment right above it. For three weeks, working late at night so as to avoid discovery, he slowly cut through the timbers of the old floor and through to the space above a false ceiling. To his chagrin, however, the members of the "Clique" congregated some thirty feet from the spot where we had planned to lower a microphone. Undaunted, Richardson wired large fish hooks to an arrow. Then, hanging by his feet, he shot the arrow in the direction of the general area where the Mafia types played cards. The hooks caught, and by the use of pulleys, he was able to maneuver the microphone so that it picked up the conversation below.

But our "invasion" of the privacy of organized crime in Kansas City netted us nothing but the conversation of a continuous high-stakes poker game and the clinical descriptions of the sexual exploits of various "Clique" members. Later, when we were able to place a bug in the private office of a prominent second-echelon member, we could record only the squeakings of an old couch and the sounds of his daily fornications. In both instances, this microphone surveillance was quickly discontinued. The FBI had more important matters on its mind.

When Robert F. Kennedy became Attorney General in 1961, there was increased pressure to obtain probative evidence against leading figures in organized crime, and this meant more microphone installations. Later on, he would deny all knowledge of this activity. I have no way of knowing what he learned at other FBI Field Offices, but I do have direct knowledge of what he learned when he visited the Kansas City office. I gave him a guided tour and personally escorted him into the "plant"—the room where the microphones were being monitored. Admittedly, he was very busy shaking every hand in sight, but I find it difficult to believe that he did not hear what I explained to him.

Bobby Kennedy also knew that the FBI's efforts against the Mafia were hampered by the lack of Federal legislation giving us jurisdiction—and to his credit, he pressed for and obtained passage through Congress of Federal gambling statutes which gave us a handle to use against organized crime. Once Congress put teeth in the law, the Bureau developed so many cases that the Federal Criminal Justice System was clogged with them.

Pressure from the Seat of Government was particularly fierce in extortion cases, and the Kansas City office handled more of these than either Los Angeles or New York, the two largest offices. In coping with the crime of extortion—and because Hoover expected the Special Agent in Charge to personally direct the stakeouts set up to catch extortionists—I learned a great deal about those who commit it. Unlike kidnapping or bank robbery, extortion requires little courage. With the exception of Mafia figures, the extortionist is usually unprepared physically or emotionally for violence, though he threatens it. And in case after case, the extortionist is too frightened, as I learned after many freezing hours on stakeout duty, to come for the money he is attempting to extort.

In my years as a SAC, however, the most relentless arm twisting from the Seat of Government involved the "Top Ten" fugitive program—the FBI's "Most Wanted" list. Conceived in 1950, it was a brilliant idea and it served two purposes. On the one hand, it served to put the most dangerous criminals behind bars quickly. On the other, it gave the Bureau great and favorable publicity. The idea was to focus the spotlight of media attention on the fugitives, and both newspapers and television cooperated fully. An alerted public was requested to notify the nearest FBI office if they learned anything about the wanted man.

On the day a new name was added to the list, FBI offices all over the country received hundreds of tips from people who believed they had useful information. These leads were immediately checked, and as a result most "Top Ten" fugitives were caught soon after they achieved this dubious distinction.

My most frustrating "Top Ten" was the search for Frederick Grant Dunn, an escapee from the Lincoln County jail in Kansas, who was wanted on a variety of armed robbery charges. There were reports that Dunn was moving from city to city with impunity. When he was placed on the "Most Wanted" list, the pressure on the Kansas City office and on me mounted as the days and weeks went by with Dunn presumably still at large. Supervisors at the SOG could not understand why we could not locate the elusive Dunn. The investigation became so extensive that one Agent working full time was needed just to handle the paperwork, and demands made on me were becoming embarrassing. Like so many "problems," this one solved itself when the Sheriff at Ellsworth, Kansas, called to say that he had found what he believed to be Dunn's remains in a wheatfield. We were satisfied that the case was closed but Hoover, who reviewed all the "Most Wanted" cases, had to be shown. It was not until after the grisly task of gathering up Dunn's mortal remains, scattered over the landscape, had been completed—and after examination by the FBI Laboratory, a Smithsonian Institution anthropologist, and a prison dentist—that Hoover took Dunn off the list.

Another cross I had to bear was the strict enforcement of the FBI's weight standards. Throughout his tenure as Director, J. Edgar Hoover had always insisted on these standards but during the early years the rules were moderate and casually enforced. Weight standards for new Agents were occasionally waived if the overage was not excessive. The Administrative Division recorded an Agent's weight at each annual physical examination, and "fat" letters were sent to those who were overweight.

During the early fifties, this changed drastically, and under the stern eye of Hoover, the entire Bureau began fighting the "Battle of the Bulge." Hoover had studied life insurance weight charts which suggested for each height and frame the categories of "minimum," "desirable," and "maximum." The average was not good enough for him and he made the arbitrary decision that each Agent must fall into the "desirable" category. The new standards were just plain healthy for most Agents, and in my case it meant bringing down my weight from 181 pounds to 171, for which I am thankful.

Hoover himself had slipped to well over 200 pounds through the years. But, full of enthusiasm for his new program, he plunged into a four-month regimen of diet and exercise which brought his weight down by thirty-three pounds. He made the desirable bracket, but he couldn't hold it and at the time he died he was sixteen pounds over the standard which he demanded of others. Most Agents, however, could adjust to the new standards without difficulty. But for a variety of reasons, there was a handful who found it impossible to comply and theirs was an excruciating problem, since Hoover refused to make exceptions. Even those with letters from personal physicians stating that further weight reduction would be injurious to their health were not excepted. The penalty was "limited duty" status, which cut them off from dangerous assignments or any strenuous physical exertion, with an added forfeiture of overtime pay.

Fortunately, Agent ingenuity came to the rescue. A sympathetic examining physician could be talked into listing an Agent with a medium frame as having a heavy frame, a difference of fourteen pounds in allowable weight. Or he might add an inch to an Agent's height, which added five pounds to the allowable weight. The examinations were made by military doctors who often felt that Hoover's standards were too stringent, and the weight program, excellent as it was, became self-defeating through Hoover's lack of flexibility.

It was not long before I became aware of what some Agents were doing to solve their weight problems. Because I felt, as did most SACs, that the rules were overly rigid, I did nothing to stop these practices. But as the pressure from SOG increased, it became more difficult for a SAC to circumvent them. The Bureau instructed each SAC to obtain scales and height-measuring equipment. Agents on record with weight problems were to be weighed and measured by the SAC every thirty days until they were within the desired bracket. I learned not to notice when an Agent wore his shoes while being measured for height and to indulge in the other measures necessary to keep SOG from descending on those who sinned by a few pounds from the Hoover standards. And this was necessary. One of my Agents was spending hours in the steam room and taking no liquids for days before the weigh-in. Another, with an unusually heavy bone structure, was becoming almost skeletal in his appearance—and my conscience made me order him to gain ten pounds.

Before I left Kansas City, I played a role in bringing Clarence M. Kelley, who became FBI Director during the series of shake-ups which followed Watergate, back to his hometown as its Chief of Police. Kelley, a friend for many years, was the SAC in Memphis, Tennessee, and we frequently consulted each other by telephone on FBI business. In March of 1961, during one of our conversations, Kelley told me that he was planning to retire and would like to return to Kansas City.

"I was born and raised there and went to law school at the University of Kansas City," he told me. "I'll be fifty in a few months and I have over twenty years of service. That makes me eligible for retirement."

I knew that the Kansas City Crime Commission was looking for a new Chief of Police. I called one of the commission members and told him, "I've found just the man you are looking for. He's Clarence Kelley, the SAC in Memphis. He has twenty years of experience in the FBI and the military. He is thoroughly qualified and would make a great chief. And, most important, he's a native of Kansas City, so you would avoid the criticism of bringing in an outsider. The police force will accept him."

The commission member called the following day to tell me that his colleagues were very interested in Kelley. "Call him," he said, "and tell him to submit his application as soon as he possibly can." Kelley, of course, was delighted. "Want it?" he said. "I'd love it." And so it was that on August 28, 1961, Clarence M. Kelley became the Chief of Police of Kansas City.

I have many pleasant memories of Kansas City. But there are bad memories as well, and one of them grew from J. Edgar Hoover's determination to make the FBI as perfect as it was humanly possible to do, pressing constantly to "ferret out" all mistakes, weaknesses, or indiscretions. When he found them, the guilty could expect to be dealt with summarily and drastically. This was what made the FBI such a finely tuned instrument.

But Hoover's Draconian approach to discipline had another consequence which I am sure he never fully understood. It could be used for vendettas within the Bureau. Knowing Hoover's reaction and overreaction to allegations of wrongdoing, disgruntled employees discovered they had a safe weapon for getting even with superiors—an anonymous letter to Hoover. He paid as much attention to the unsigned letter as he did to a signed communication. Any allegation against Bureau personnel had to be fully resolved to his satisfaction, regardless of the source. On Monday, August 11, 1959, I became the victim of an anonymous letter. It came at a particularly bad time.

Three days earlier, Audrey and I and the children had left by car for a two-week vacation in Idaho, at the Clark-Miller Dude Ranch near Sun Valley. This was on a Saturday. The following Friday, my trout fishing was interrupted by a United States Forest Ranger who had driven all the way from the Ranger Station at Obsidian with a message that I was to call the FBI office at Kansas City. It had to be important because I had left instructions that I was not to be called except in an emergency. When I was able to reach Kansas City by phone, I was startled to learn that an FBI inspector, W. W. "Smokey" Wood, an old friend from my Espionage Section days, was there to accept my call. I was shocked when he told me that I was to return immediately because of an anonymous letter about me which had been sent to Hoover. Leaving Audrey and the children behind, I hitch-hiked, drove, and flew back to Kansas City. "Smokey" Wood, who had taken over my office, placed the anonymous letter before me. I read:

Kansas City, Missouri.
Dear Mr. Hoover,

As a profound admirer of the great organization which you so capably represent, I am confident that you will appreciate having certain matters brought to your attention in connection with the Kansas City branch of the FBI, especially in view of the fact that it has resulted in unfavorable comment among citizens of this city.

Each day, between 8:30 A.M. and 9:00 A.M., ten to fifteen Agents of the Kansas City office gather at Bonura's Restaurant, where they spend the following hour or more drinking coffee and gossiping about their various duties, usually in a loud tone which is clearly audible to other customers in the restaurant. For example, one individual was heard to remark that the person in charge of the Office here in Kansas City had instructed them during the month of July not to complete any pending work, in order that there would appear to be more work than is actually the case, and to justify the present staff of employees. They also expressed their personal satisfaction that Mr. Goddard had been transferred and can now have it easy. The same individuals can usually be located between 4:30 P.M. and 5:00 P.M. at the Hotel Pickwick Coffee Shop.

A break in the daily routine for refreshments is, of course, helpful, and it is not my purpose to cause any difficulties for any employee of the Office here. However, this matter has been the topic of much unfavorable comment and one individual has suggested writing a letter to the editor of the Kansas City Star."

The envelope was marked "Personal" and those in the Bureau knew that such mail was sent, unopened, directly to Mr. Hoover. Before he had half-finished the letter, my career was in jeopardy. The matter had to be resolved at once and "Smokey" Wood was on his way to Kansas City that same evening.

The author of the letter had been very clever in selecting allegations that were guaranteed to inflame J. Edgar Hoover. Coffee drinking on government time was, for example, a mortal sin in the FBI catechism. The second allegation was equally damning. If I had actually told the Agents not to close any cases in July, I would have been fired on the spot. It was not that Hoover had any objection to carrying a high case load, but he didn't want to get it by doctoring the records. That Agents were talking about their work in a loud voice was also calculated to bring down the wrath of the Director. If each of these allegations was designed to raise Hoover's blood pressure, the last paragraph was the topper. It contained a threat to put the Bureau in a bad light through a letter to the editor.

Fortunately for me, Wood had made his investigation in a highly professional manner. He had photographs of every Agent in the Kansas City office, and when he arrived in town he did not check in. Instead, he went directly to Bonura's Restaurant on his first morning in Kansas City and sat there in a corner booth until 10 o'clock. Whenever a male walked in,

Wood thumbed through his photographs to see if he could identify him as an employee of the Kansas City office. From 3:30 P.M. until 6:00 P.M., he repeated this procedure at the Pickwick Hotel. After three days, he had identified no FBI coffee drinkers and he so informed Washington.

His next step was to check case closings. Contrary to what the anonymous letter had said, the closings were higher for July than for any previous month. It was apparent then to Hoover that a Bureau official had been falsely accused, and he was equally incensed. With a barely perceptible shift of gears, the aim of the inquiry became to identify the anonymous letter writer—and it was for this that my vacation had been canceled. Since it was clear from internal evidence that the writer was familiar both with the routine of the office and with what would incense Hoover, we knew that the writer had to be one of us. It could not, however, have been an Agent who would have known that the charges could easily be disproved. Bonura's had long ago been a favorite coffee-drinking spot for Agents. It was therefore clear that the writer had to be an older clerical employee.

I was sure that I knew who that employee was, but since I could not prove it, I felt that to make an accusation would only disrupt the office. Perhaps I benefitted from the experience. Hoover, I am sure, realized that the letter was an indication that I was not afraid to discipline an employee if it was necessary. There were other ways to demonstrate my administrative competence—ways less painful—but I did not let it rattle me. It was part of the job.

I was not quite so philosophical when, in September of 1962, I received a transfer letter. I had expected a promotion for the work I had done in Kansas City. Instead, I was being returned to Washington as "Number One Man to the Assistant Director in Charge of the Training Division." Not only did I consider this a demotion, but I had very little interest in training. This was the only time in my FBI career that I thought seriously about resigning. But at forty-nine years of age, I was not eligible for retirement and would lose the attractive benefits provided for all Federal investigative employees when they left the government.

It was not, however, the demotion I thought. For some time, Hoover had been dissatisfied with the operations of the Training and Inspection Divisions. To shake up the organization, he had separated Training and Inspection and brought in officials from the field to make them more efficient. As second in command, I was a kind of Dean of the Faculty for all the training programs in Washington and Quantico. Nevertheless, it was a humdrum job, and I would have retired on August 17, 1963—my fiftieth birthday—had it not been for a very interesting development. Impressed by the quality of FBI training of local police and appalled by the continuing rise of crime, Congress authorized the expansion of the FBI Academy in Quantico.

As a result, I became deeply involved in the planning for the new Academy. It was also my responsibility to review all memoranda and other material, and I made it a point to insist that every piece of paper that was to be read by the Director be short and to the point. And because my new job was less demanding, I was able to polish and perfect my own memoranda—and this was noticed and appreciated by those above me. This was a factor in my movement up the pyramid of FBI responsibility.

CHAPTER SIX

I am designating you Chief Inspector.

—J. Edgar Hoover

In May of 1924, when Attorney General Harlan Fiske Stone asked J. Edgar Hoover to take over the Bureau of Investigation, the Justice Department's investigative arm was widely categorized as a "national disgrace." Hoover accepted the job on a series of conditions. "The Bureau must be divorced from politics and not be a catchall for political hacks," he told Stone. "Appointments must be based on merit. Promotions will be made only on proven ability. And the Bureau will be responsible only to the Attorney General."

"I wouldn't give it to you under any other conditions," Stone answered.

And over the years, that guarantee by Harlan Stone had allowed Hoover to make the FBI—the "Federal" was added in 1935 to the Bureau's official designation—the fine instrument of law enforcement that it had become by the time I enlisted in the ranks. There was only one attempt, as far as I know, to make it a "catchall" for political appointees, and that was in the early Roosevelt Administration. But Hoover remained firm and thereby improved his standing with FDR, with the Congress, and with the press. The FBI may have been listed as a subsidiary bureau on the Justice Department's table of organization, but in actuality it was an independent agency.

In 1961, when President John F. Kennedy appointed his

younger brother to be Attorney General, Hoover and the FBI faced their first serious challenge. Prior to this time, Hoover had gotten along well with most Presidents and their Attorneys General, although there had been some friction during the Truman days. But the Kennedys were something else again. JFK's advisers, friends, and supporters included those who resented Hoover's undeviating opposition to Communism and his determination to uproot subversion. Bobby Kennedy—brash, ruthless, and politically motivated—resented the FBI's independent status. He saw it not as a law-enforcement agency but as an arm of "his" administration.

For the first time in his career, Hoover and the FBI were up against a President and an Attorney General who were openly antagonistic, who wanted to dislodge him, and who saw the Bureau as a weapon for political guerrilla warfare—an adjunct of the Kennedy wing of the Democratic Party rather than as a nonpolitical investigative force. And it was made very clear that Attorney General Kennedy thought of the FBI as a kind of private police department, with Hoover its desk sergeant. Bobby would not only storm into Hoover's office unannounced, or summon the Director to his own palatial suite in the Justice Department building as if Hoover were an office boy, but he also struck directly at Hoover's authority by calling a Special Agent in Charge or an Agent on a case directly, violating the traditional chain of command—something no other Attorney General had ever done.

The result was ill-disguised friction between Hoover and Robert Kennedy, which affected all of us in the Bureau and struck at our morale. Perhaps the single most disturbing act of the Attorney General was his circulation among high government officials of a memorandum prepared by Walter Reuther, president of the United Auto Workers, and his brother Victor. Entitled "The Radical Right in America Today," it included a sharp attack on the FBI and Hoover, both lumped under a "radical right" which consisted of everything from extremist kooks to the Republican Party. To the Reuthers and to Kennedy, the "right" posed "a far greater danger" to the United States than the Communist movement.

This kind of warfare, however, was less troubling to the Bureau than Bobby Kennedy's determination that Agents be taken off important investigations to do political jobs for the Kennedy Administration. Agents were assigned to pick up unfavorable comment made about President Kennedy by members of the press, and those who had spoken their minds were summoned by Administration officials and roughly scolded—and since the Bureau had been the instrument of this snooping, press anger was aimed at all of us, and it resulted in the publication of stories leaked by the Justice Department which were derogatory to the FBI.

On one issue, Hoover and Bobby Kennedy battled head to head. The Attorney General demanded that FBI Agents be detached from the Bureau and assigned to his "Task Forces" to investigate the organized crime syndicates. Hoover argued strenuously that his Agents must remain under the direction of the Special Agents in Charge but he agreed to work closely with the Task Force attorneys. But when Hoover's objections were leaked to the press by Kennedy, they suffered a sea change. What reporters were told was that the FBI did not believe organized crime really existed, and even if it did, attempting to cope with the syndicates would reduce the FBI's impressive statistics of arrests and convictions in less important cases.

To counter the Kennedy onslaught, Hoover created a new division at Headquarters, the Special Investigative Division, and it was no coincidence that he selected Courtney A. Evans to head it. Evans had handled liaison with Kennedy when the latter was Chief Counsel to the Senate Labor Rackets Committee. Knowing that Evans had Kennedy's confidence, Hoover also made him responsible for liaison between the FBI and the Attorney General. It was a logical choice, but Evans soon found himself trying to serve two masters. The situation grew quite untenable, and at a particularly difficult period Evans remarked to me, "Last night, I told my family I was sure I was going to be fired, but I didn't know whether it would be by Hoover or Kennedy."

It was one of Evans's duties to serve as go-between for

Hoover and Kennedy on the touchy issue of telephone taps and electronic surveillance. The Attorney General had been lobbying on Capitol Hill for the unrestricted use of these devices in internal revenue cases and other unspecified "serious" crimes. Contrary to the view held by many, both then and now, Hoover believed that wiretaps and bugs should be used very sparingly. To protect himself and the Bureau from repercussions that might result from any disclosure of the extent to which electronic devices were employed, Hoover made certain that the Attorney General was kept fully informed and that his approval was carefully noted. As noted earlier, I myself had discussed with Kennedy the FBI's use of these devices when I was Special Agent in Charge at Kansas City.

The wisdom of Hoover's procedure became apparent after Bobby Kennedy left the Justice Department and was serving as a United States Senator. Times had changed, and he was leading the fight against wiretaps and bugging. When an instance of FBI bugging during his tenure at Justice became known late in 1966, Senator Kennedy launched an attack on the Bureau, deploring what he now saw as a dirty business. In response to a letter from Representative H. R. Gross requesting clarification, Hoover wrote, on December 7, 1966:

> Your impression that the FBI engaged in the usage of wiretaps and microphones only upon the authority of the Attorney General is absolutely correct. You are also correct when you state that it is your understanding that "full documentation" exists as proof of such authorizations. . . .
>
> . . . you will find attached to this letter a communication dated August 17, 1961, signed by former Attorney General Robert F. Kennedy, in which he approved policy for the usage of microphones covering both security and major criminal cases. Mr. Kennedy, during his term of office, exhibited great interest in pursuing such matters and, while in different metropolitan areas, not only listened to the results of microphone surveillances but raised ques-

> tions relative to obtaining better equipment. He was briefed frequently by an FBI official regarding such matters. FBI usage of such devices ... was obviously increased at Mr. Kennedy's insistence while he was in office.

A memorandum on Justice Department stationery, with "Approved" and the signature "Robert F. Kennedy" was attached. It discussed the future use of microphone surveillance in New York, which the telephone company would agree to, as it had always done, if it was authorized by a letter which the Attorney General had approved.

> We have not previously used leased lines with microphone surveillance [the letter signed by Bobby Kennedy continued] because of certain technical difficulties which existed in New York City. These technical difficulties have, however, now been overcome . . . this type of coverage can be materially extended in security and major crime cases. Accordingly, your approval of our utilizing this leased line arrangement is requested. . . .
>
> Approved: Robert F. Kennedy

The former Attorney General immediately charged Hoover with being "misinformed" and made public a letter from Courtney Evans which tangentially seemed to support Kennedy's contention that he may have signed his approval without reading the document in question. Hoover countered with two documents from Courtney Evans recounting meetings with the Attorney General. The first noted that Kennedy "was pleased" with the manner in which the FBI had used electronic surveillance and asked for a complete list of all such activities. The second recounted a detailed conversation with Kennedy concerning the "leased lines" situation in New York and reported that he approved the "proposed procedure" before signing the authorization. Kennedy's answer was that Hoover had at no time "discussed this important matter with me"—technically true, since all discussions had been with Courtney Evans, the FBI-Justice Department Liaison Agent.

There is no doubt that Hoover considered Attorney General Kennedy, in the words of another writer, "brash, impetuous, bad mannered, and undisciplined." He was also more than irritated that Kennedy demanded a "hot line" between the Attorney General's office and his. The first time it was used, Hoover's secretary answered. "When I pick up this phone," Kennedy said rudely, "there's only one man I want to talk to. Get this phone on the Director's desk immediately." The phone remained there until after President Kennedy's assassination, and then was returned to Miss Gandy's desk.

There was one amusing side, if you can call it that, to the Attorney General's imbroglio with Hoover. At a time when the White House had declared war with United States Steel, there were press stories that seemed to reflect on anti-trust violations by Bethlehem Steel. Robert Kennedy called Hoover late in the evening and demanded that the writers of those stories be questioned "immediately." Hoover might have waited until the morning but, perhaps with a touch of malice, he did exactly what Kennedy had demanded. Reporters were routed out of bed in the wee hours of the morning to be questioned, and they were as incensed at this as they were at the Attorney General's assumption that he could compel them to reveal news sources.

This state of affairs ended when John F. Kennedy was assassinated in Dallas. RFK's influence declined abruptly and he could no longer have his way simply by murmuring, "Do you want me to talk to my brother about this?" On September 3, 1964, he resigned.

While JFK had been alive, it was generally assumed that some politically safe method would be devised to replace Hoover with Courtney Evans. The date suggested by inside sources was to be soon after the 1964 election. But because of the concessions he had made to RFK, Evans's power in the Bureau hierarchy dissolved and he applied for retirement. Approval was prompt, and Evans went into private law practice.

Hoover quickly acted to restore the FBI's prestige and independence in the government. His replacement for Evans was James H. Gale, a tough and highly competent veteran of the battles in the Field—and someone who could stand up to the Justice Department. But the reorganization also affected me. On Friday, November 13, a few minutes after he had given Gale the Evans assignment, Hoover summoned me to his office. I still remember the exact minute that I entered Hoover's inner sanctum—3:53 P.M.—with no idea what the meeting was to be about.

"It's good to see you, Felt," the Director said as I shook his hand. "How have you been?"

"I'm fine," I said, relieved by the cordiality of the greeting.

Hoover wasted no time. "Felt," he said, "Evans has applied for retirement and I have approved it. I have just designated Gale to replace him. I told Gale that Evans had been wishy-washy in dealing with Justice. Gale knows I expect him to stand up to them."

"You picked the right man," I answered, wondering where I fitted into the picture.

Hoover continued: "I'm transferring you to the Inspection Division to replace Gale. I'm designating you Chief Inspector, and if you demonstrate that you can handle the assignment, you will be promoted to Assistant Director."

"Thank you, sir," was all I could manage.

"I want you to be firm and tough—but fair. I want you to be my eyes and ears. You will report directly to Tolson."

Again I managed a "Thank you, sir."

"I want you to handle a Seat of Government inspection under Gale's supervision before you take over. After that, you will be on your own. However, I want to talk to you personally before each inspection of the New York office." This I could understand. There had always been a subtle rivalry between the New York office, the FBI's largest, and the Seat of Government.

For the third time, I said, "Yes, sir"—feeling foolish but not knowing how else to respond. In my past conversations with Hoover, I had tried to contribute something, to show interest and aggressiveness, but this time I was too stunned. In the space of a few minutes, I had found myself standing at the door to the FBI's top echelons.

"That's all, Felt," Hoover said. "I expect you to do a good job."

"Mr. Hoover," I said, "I'll do the very best I can. You can count on it."

"I hope so," Hoover answered, and picked up one of the memoranda on his desk.

My transfer to the Inspection Division marked a great change in my relationship with Hoover. Prior to that time, as a SAC, I saw him once a year for no more than thirty minutes. During my tenure in the Training Division, I saw him only a few times. Now all that changed. He would call me on the intercom and I saw him with increasing frequency for personal conferences. During his last year, I saw him or talked with him on the intercom or telephone several times a day. This association was strictly business—and my only social contact with him was at a banquet of the Society of Former FBI Agents, where he was the guest of honor shortly before his death.

The Chief Inspector occupied a unique position in the FBI hierarchy. Operating under the direct supervision of the Director and with authority to inquire at any time and any place on any matter, the Chief Inspector was both feared and respected. Shortly after my transfer to this Inspection Division, another Assistant Director said to me, "You are in a position where you can do a lot of good or a lot of harm." I knew what he meant. During my movement up the FBI pyramid I had learned that there was a major difference between constructive and destructive criticism. I was determined to be as constructive as possible, and I think it is fair to say that during my six years as FBI Chief Inspector I lived up to that resolve. I tried to achieve a balance between the rigid demands of Hoover and what I felt were the best interests of the Bureau and its personnel.

No organization operates completely without error and the FBI was no exception. Hoover knew this and he demanded that all errors be uncovered and all responsibility fixed. When

Inspectors detected mistakes, they initiated corrective action and made recommendations for suitable discipline, almost always by letter of censure—which all good Agents strove desperately to avoid, since it brought down on their heads the Director's wrath. Field Agents complained of "nit-picking" and of censure letter "quotas" imposed upon Inspectors and their aides. The Chief Inspector bore the brunt of this criticism no matter how fairly or compassionately he tried to act.

However understandable the Agents' reactions, their complaints were, more often than not, unjustified. For one thing, Hoover just would not accept an Inspection Report which found a Field Office or SOG division to be in perfect condition. Had I submitted such a report it would have been inaccurate, and Hoover would have removed me from the Inspection Division at once. In addition, I could not accept as fact the assurance of an Inspector that he had reviewed hundreds of case files and found them to be completely error-free. Given the tightness of Rules and Regulations, there were always mistakes of varying magnitude in the investigations of complex FBI cases.

Most Inspectors unofficially corrected minor errors which might have aroused Hoover's ire and led to disciplinary action—and they saw to it that the burden of censure letters was equally shared by a number of Agents. And there were enough serious matters to report to satisfy Hoover's appetite for disciplinary action. Recommendations for this kind of action, moreover, had to be carefully evaluated and worded since Hoover or Tolson would sometimes upgrade the punishment despite the Inspector's recommendations. If there was bias on our side, it was in the direction of leniency. But at no time could I let the Director get the impression that the Inspection Division was "soft." This created something of a dilemma for me, making it vitally important that the language of a memorandum proposing disciplinary action exactly justified the recommendation—no more and no less. It was also essential to avoid words and phrases which might inflame Hoover. It was in the editing and rewriting of these memoranda that my years of experience in preparing material for Hoover's eyes stood me in good stead.

CHAPTER SEVEN

I agree with the Inspection Division.

—J. EDGAR HOOVER

The responsibilities of the Inspection Division, as described on the inter-FBI Organizational Chart, fell into three categories: "Inspections Field and SOG, Special Projects and Surveys." Of the three, inspections of Field Offices were the least pleasant. They involved the painstaking annual search at every FBI Field Office for errors, lax discipline, and infractions of the many rules that had been set down by the Director. It also meant reporting these sometimes minor irregularities to Hoover, to the chagrin of those Special Agents who had stepped over the line.

The most interesting, and by far the most sensitive, of my responsibilities came under the heading of "Surveys and Special Projects." There was no official distinction between the two, but I regarded surveys as relating to administrative matters and special projects as involving operational aspects. Surveys were special problems referred by Hoover to the Inspection Division for resolution. One of the most common resulted from the practice of Bureau officials when faced by a touchy problem, particularly one where no answer was apparent or where a dispute with another Division was involved, to write a memorandum outlining the facts, with calculated bias, and recommending that "this matter be referred to the Inspection Division for Survey." As Chief of the Inspection Division, I was responsible for reviewing reports on major investigations to determine whether they had been thoroughly and completely conducted.*

My previous inspection experience had been very limited, and as part of my education, I resolved to personally conduct several Field investigations. New York, the largest FBI Field Office, was next on the list. For as many years as I could remember, that office was the first to be inspected each calendar year. There were good reasons for this. Its size required the entire inspection staff to take part. Only at one time during the year were the Inspectors and their aides assembled together conveniently and economically—over the Christmas holidays when the annual Inspector's Conference was held. Following this, the entire squad would descend on New York.

I decided to change all that and surprise the New York office by holding its inspection in April or May. To me, it seemed hardly fair that only one office should have a guaranteed inspection date, thereby enabling it to achieve "spit and polish" conditions. I also wanted to have the experience gained in inspecting smaller offices before I tackled the largest of them all. That January (of 1965), therefore, I not only surprised the New York Office, which had expected the annual visitation, but five other Field Offices as well, whose SACs were certain that the entire Inspection squad would be busy elsewhere. In this, I was carrying out Hoover's objective that the Inspectors should see an office as it normally operated, not as it peaked for visitors. (Much later, Acting Director Gray took the surprise element out of his inspections by ordering that offices be given two weeks' notice. This may have created a more relaxed atmosphere, but it did not contribute to an on-your-toes efficiency at all times.) I also decided that with enough advance preparation on my part, the New York inspection could be cut down to three weeks from its usual four. This would not only save precious time for the Inspection Division, but also relieve the New York Office of 25 percent of the inconvenience of having Inspectors in its hair.

My planning completed, I asked for an appointment to see

* It was in this role that I reviewed the reports on various aspects of the case involving Dr. Martin Luther King, Jr.

the Director, disguising my need to confer with him to prevent the unlikely possibility that New York might be tipped off. Two days later, I was in Hoover's office. He was very cordial and asked me what the purpose of my visit was.

"Mr. Hoover," I said. "You told me that you wanted to confer with me before I began an inspection of the New York office. I am planning to take the entire staff up there on Sunday, April 4, and commence the inspection on Monday morning."

Hoover looked at me steadily. "That's fine, Felt. I was beginning to wonder when you were going to start."

"That's why I didn't want to wait any longer. I have completed inspections of two medium-sized offices and I think I am ready to take on New York."

Hoover smiled, and I suspect that he realized why I had put off the New York inspection. "I am not sure that I ever had a Chief Inspector who was really ready to take on New York. There's a good crew up there, but sometimes I am convinced they don't see any need to pay attention to what we tell them. They have done some outstanding work but that does not excuse them from following all the rules, just like any other office."

He seemed ready to terminate the interview but I wanted his approval of what I was planning to do. "Mr. Hoover," I said, "I have made intensive advance preparation and, with your approval, I want to cut down the time in New York from the usual four weeks to three."

He frowned. "All right, but don't take too many short cuts, and if you need to stay longer be sure you do so."

"Yes, sir," I said as he was rising to his feet. "I'll see that you get an inspection report on the New York Office which is as good or better than what you have received before."

He nodded and turned back to the work on his desk. As I walked out of his office, I thought over what he had said, and I knew exactly what he meant. We referred to it in the Bureau as the "New York attitude." That office was bigger, handled some of the most important cases, and had assigned to it some of the most capable and experienced Agents in the service. Perhaps it was not unusual that those Agents sometimes thought of themselves as superior and somehow apart from the rest of the Bureau. Not infrequently, the smaller offices had difficulty in getting the New York Office to cover leads for them. True, there were times when the New York Office had more important work on its hands, but there was no excuse for shunting aside another office. I understood both sides of the problem.

On Thursday, April Fools' Day, the entire staff was ordered back to Washington. The Inspectors were instructed to report on Sunday afternoon, prepared for a three-week inspection assignment, and the word quickly spread that they would be going to either Los Angeles or San Francisco, both customarily requiring that time period. Their hopes were dashed when they arrived at the Justice Department building and saw the Greyhound bus parked outside. This was a clear indication that their destination was to be New York.

When we arrived and had checked into the hotel, I called John F. Malone, Assistant Director and SAC of the New York Office, to let him know that we were in town to start an inspection the following morning. "Where are you?" he asked, after we had exchanged amenities.

"I'm at the Dryden East Hotel. I just arrived."

Sounding pleased, he said, "What are you doing in New York? Is there anything I can do to help?"

"John, I brought the whole inspection staff with me. We are going to start your inspection tomorrow morning."

Obviously less pleased but still friendly, he said. "Oh? When you didn't come in January, I figured you would wait until it was a little warmer. But now is as good a time as any. We're always ready for the Inspectors."

Having been a friend of Malone for many years, I knew he was a Hoover loyalist and that he ran a tight office—too tight, many of the New York Agents believed. I was sure the office would be in good shape and this accounted for Malone's calm. As I hung up the phone, I wondered if I had really surprised the New York Office. If this were not the case, then Malone was a very good actor.

Early the next morning, the Inspectors and their aides

reported to the New York office, a large building on East Sixty-ninth Street which had been converted from warehouse space, and it looked it! However, the facilities were both efficiently laid out and economical. The executive office space left nothing to be desired; it included a large conference room and an elegant private office, built especially for the Director by a liberal General Services Administration. Malone was there to greet us when we arrived and assembled in the conference room. When I introduced him to the staff, he made a few friendly remarks and then left us to begin our work.

One of the first things I noticed as I settled into the executive office was a small closet housing a toilet and wash basin for the infrequent occupants. I learned afterwards that this perquisite had been built after the Director had inspected the new quarters of the New York Office. He had been accompanied by a friend and, of course, Clyde Tolson. Unfortunately for the taxpayers, the friend asked for directions to the toilet and was given an urgent guided tour to the rather Spartan men's room on the far side of the large building. Hoover expressed no concern about this inconvenience, but Tolson did. Out of the Director's presence, he instructed that toilet facilities be installed adjacent to the private office. This was done as soon as possible—an expediture of more than $5,000 in pre-inflation days, which had to be hidden somewhere in the Bureau's bookkeeping. Hoover never visited the New York Office again, and the facility became the private washroom for the SAC.

Bureau officials, both at SOG and in the Field, had ambivalent feelings toward yearly inspections. Most kept their operations as inspection-proof as possible, partly in anticipation of inspections. But they all benefited from inspection and frequently pointed the Inspectors in the direction of problems they had not been able to solve. They also realized that an inspection would provide an in-depth look at each phase of operations in a way that an official in charge would like to do if he were not up to his neck in investigative matters. Unfavorable trends were detected and corrected while they were still minor. Inspections also served another purpose. A SAC, when he had to crack the whip, could blame the possibility of an imminent inspection for his rigorous application of the rules.

The Agents, had they been polled, would have added their own reasons for disliking inspections, which meant a minimum of two weeks of answering questions. In addition, every Agent knew that 25 percent of his case files would be carefully reviewed and, if he was found wanting, this could lead to a letter of censure from the Director.

Inspections did require time and manpower to answer all the questions and prepare all the studies and charts demanded by the Inspector. Probing questions were asked not only for the status of cases but also for plans to solve problems. Detailed statistical information was required to permit comparison with prior years and with other Field Offices of similar size. Financial records were reviewed. Informant programs were evaluated and payments to informants had to be fully justified. All this material would be collected and assimilated by the Inspector, who would prepare a detailed summary for the Director.

Before I arrived in New York, I had carefully studied the material which had been prepared during the last inspection. I tried to look at it from the viewpoint of a harried Field official, at the same time keeping in mind my responsibility to the Director. I made a number of streamlining changes which I felt would be helpful to the Field Office. I also knew from my experience as a SAC and an Inspector that the first two or three days of an inspection involved considerable wheel spinning as the aides became organized and the office adjusted. I resolved to make sure everything was productive from the very first minute. And it was. With Malone's full cooperation, the New York Office moved into high gear immediately, and when the Agents realized that they could be rid of us in three weeks, their efforts became truly amazing. It did not take me long to realize that the office was operating well. Results attested to that.

On April 23 the inspection was completed on schedule, and we managed to finish early enough to ride the Greyhound back to Washington on government time, an unheard of luxury in Hoover days because he preferred that official travel be done on overtime. The streamlined inspection was effective and everyone, including the Director, was pleased.

"Special Projects and Surveys," my other responsibilities, gave the Director an opportunity to evaluate my abilities outside the area of inspection routine. The more I handled, the more Hoover turned to the Inspection Division, and in time he was directing all unusual problems to me. Not all were earthshaking and some were just plain sticky. The stickiest occurred when Hoover ordered me to conduct an inspection of his own office. There had been a slipup over an important piece of mail, a letter marked "Personal," which, like all such correspondence, was sent directly from the Mail Room to Helen Gandy, Hoover's personal secretary.

Miss Gandy, in her sixties at the time, had been Hoover's personal secretary even before he became FBI Director. She was bright and alert and quick-tongued—and completely dedicated to her boss, whose interests she constantly protected. Because she had Hoover's ear, all Bureau officials tried to ingratiate themselves with her. But she had slipped up. Recognizing the importance of the "Personal" letter, Miss Gandy had it carried by special messenger to the Crime Records Division for expeditious handling. Inadvertently, she failed to notify Edna Holmes, the office manager, who would have placed the matter on her "Special List" for day-to-day follow-up. Miss Holmes had also been in the Bureau for many years, and, because of her competence, had risen to a high position.

There was a delay and Hoover demanded an explanation of Miss Gandy, who blamed Miss Holmes. Miss Holmes in turn denied any responsibility. Hoover then instructed me to make a complete inspection of his office to determine what had gone wrong. This put me in a "no win" position. If I sided with Miss Holmes, who was not at fault, I would antagonize Miss Gandy. To have sided with Miss Gandy would have been dishonest. I was between a rock and a hard place.

Searching for something which would please everybody, I made a careful study and analysis of operations in the Director's office, including mail flow, personnel management, and communications. Operations were very efficient, and I was hard-pressed to think of ways of improvement. I made a number of recommendations which were mildly helpful and definitely not critical. The most important area in need of change was the Telephone Room, which handled all incoming and outgoing calls in the Director's office, kept a running log of everything that happened in Hoover's office, and managed and kept track of the Director's commitment calendar. The pressure there was very great and Miss Holmes had been trying to raise the salary level of the Telephone Room clerks, only to be blocked by the Administrative Division. I submitted a recommendation for salary increases and sent it directly to Hoover. He noted, "OK, H."

However, I needed something more impressive than that. The Exhibits Section which ordinarily builds displays and evidence models served me here. The Telephone Room was operating in a make-shift fashion with two desks side by side. The logs, the frequently consulted calendar, and other records were stacked one on top of the other. I asked the Exhibits Section to design a single massive operating desk where all the important material could be put on swinging supports or in special slots for ready access by either clerk. The Exhibits Section outdid itself, and the operations center which it constructed looked like an airline ticket office of the future. Everyone, including Hoover, was extremely pleased. Hoover made no further mention of the error which had triggered the inspection, and I am convinced that all he wanted was to stir things up a bit.

One of the surveys which I handled for the Director led to charges that "in a fit of pique" he had cut off all liaison with other Government agencies. There was some basis for this story, but in fact liaison with other government agencies was not cut off, though changes were made. The incidents which led up to that change were these:

On March 14, 1969, Thomas Riha, a thirty-nine-year-old professor of Russian history at the University of Colorado, disappeared from his home without a trace. The FBI knew of Riha's whereabouts but could not tell local authorities because this might jeopardize confidential sources. However, an FBI Agent confidentially briefed a CIA man, who in turn told

Dr. Joseph R. Smiley, the president of the University. Dr. Smiley made a statement that Riha was "alive and well," but would not disclose his sources. When Hoover learned what had happened, he was very angry and demanded that the CIA identify its FBI source. This the CIA man in Denver refused to do.

Coinciding with the Riha affair, there was a second incident, which had a greater impact on the situation. The FBI maintained a Liaison Section in the Domestic Intelligence Division, and the ten Agents assigned to it were responsible for SOG contacts with all government agencies. Robert Haynes worked full time on White House liaison, and Sam Papich dealt exclusively with the CIA. Papich had an extremely effective working relationship with the CIA, from the lowest supervisor to Director Richard Helms. He shared the concern of his boss, William C. Sullivan, then Assistant Director in charge of the Domestic Intelligence Division, as well as that of Director Helms, that the FBI was not moving aggressively enough against foreign agents in the United States. In 1970, when he retired, Papich wrote a polite but critical note to Hoover urging greater action. Hoover was furious and told me he believed the Papich letter had been drafted by the CIA.

As a result of these two cases, Hoover called me into his office and said, "I want to abolish the Liaison Section. It's costing us a quarter of a million dollars a year, and other agencies obviously benefit more from it than we do. Let the supervisors handle their own contacts with other agencies."

"Let me look into it," I answered. "I think we can work out something which will be effective. What about the White House? Do you want to continue direct liaison there?"

Hoover thought briefly. "Cut it all out except the liaison with the White House."

Clearly, the Director had made up his mind and nothing was going to change it. The old method was more effective though more costly to the Bureau, but it was out. I could only recommend that the FBI handle inter-departmental liaison the way other government agencies did, with individual supervisors dealing with their counterparts in other agencies directly—by telephone, confirmed by correspondence. This in no way ended FBI liaison with other government agencies as has been charged. In 1972, Acting Director Gray reestablished the Liaison Section, though on a smaller scale than it had been prior to the Hoover-ordered change.

My major surveys were designed to streamline various FBI operations. The FBI, for example, was responsible for tracking down military deserters, referred to us by the Pentagon. Investigative leads were sent to the Field from SOG, and one of these was the "barracks bag" check—an inquiry to the military post from which the deserter took his unauthorized departure. In many cases, however, the deserter had returned by the time the administrative process got the investigation under way. The "barracks bag" check therefore ensured that there would be no wasted time and effort by Agents.

The National Crime Information Center had just become operational at FBI headquarters. It consisted of a computer with terminals located in major police departments throughout the country. Local police fed data into the computer, primarily about stolen property and wanted fugitives. The police query would be answered in seconds. When the military began entering data on deserters into NCIC, they would also inform the computer of the return of the deserter. This made the "barracks bag" check valueless. But there were loud cries of anguish from both the Special Investigative Division and the Administrative Division when I recommended that these checks be eliminated. They had no convincing arguments, and their real concern was over the sharp reduction in the case load—several thousand cases at any given time. There was loud and bitter debate over my proposal, but when the pros and cons were submitted to the Director, he noted, "I agree with the Inspection Division." *

In addition to the regular and ordained duties of the Inspectors, there was one other: special assignments in the Field to handle major investigative problems, á la Efrem Zimbalist, Jr., of TV-FBI fame. As far back as the mid-Thirties, Hoover

* Location and apprehension of military deserters by the FBI has since been discontinued.

made a practice of sending Bureau officials to the scene of major cases or anticipated major developments. Hugh H. Clegg was sent to the Midwest in 1934 to take charge of the raid on the Little Bohemia Lodge in Wisconsin, from which John Dillinger, "Baby Face" Nelson and other gangsters escaped after a shootout in which one FBI Agent was killed. Inspector Earl J. Connelly was in almost constant travel status during much of his career and led the squad of Agents which killed the notorious "Ma" Barker and her son in a Florida gun battle. This practice of sending high Bureau officials for on-the-scene direction continued until Hoover's death in 1972.

One of my less successful achievements took place during the summer of 1965 when Salvatore Palma, a "soldier" in the Mafia, was charged with transporting the money from a supermarket holdup in Texas through the mails to Kansas City. Palma, who knew much about Mafia activities, was desperately afraid of being tried in Federal court and ending up in the penitentiary. The Mafia was afraid that, if convicted, Palma would "sing." Early on the day he was to appear in court, his body was found in a cemetery, shot in the head and the back. Mafia leaders, ignoring the shot in the back, said that he had committed suicide. The U.S. Attorney and the FBI knew that Palma had been killed to silence him.

Because I had previously been SAC in Kansas City, Hoover picked me to go to the scene. Gangland slayings go unsolved more often than not and I was not happy with the assignment. And though I stirred up a beehive of investigative activity, we got nowhere. We knew who had committed the murder, but witnesses who feared they would end up in the river if they talked refused to cooperate. Because I had not solved the case, Hoover would not let me return to Washington for five months, after which he relented.

Perhaps my most interesting special assignment resulted from a full-scale revolution in the Dominican Republic in April of 1965 when army insurgents sought to overthrow the ruling civilian triumvirate led by Dr. Donald J. Cabral and to return to power the exiled former president, the leftist Juan Bosch. President Lyndon Johnson was gravely concerned and sent in the Marines, ostensibly to protect American citizens and American property. He demanded thorough and up-to-the-minute information on the fighting—something the Intelligence community could not supply.

On the third day of the revolt, Hoover sent a summary to the President. It outlined specifically what the insurgents were going to do on the fourth day. Events proved the Bureau to be correct, and Hoover continued to supply the President with advance information on the thinking and planning of the insurgents. The President was delighted, and for Hoover it was a feather in the FBI's cap. The information, moreover, was coming in as a result of good investigative procedures.

Bosch was living in Puerto Rico, directing the operations of his forces by long distance telephone. Each evening he talked with his confederates in Santo Domingo for as long as two hours while they plotted their strategy. SAC Wallace R. Estill of the San Juan Office had requested and obtained approval from both Hoover and the Attorney General to plant a wiretap on Bosch's telephone, and every word of the revolutionary strategy sessions was monitored and recorded by FBI Agents. This information was summarized and went to FBI headquarters, then passed on to the President and the Intelligence community, giving Johnson a flow of completely accurate and preemptive knowledge of revolutionary activity.

But after an auspicious start, the value of the Bureau's intelligence began to deteriorate because of delays in transmitting the information from San Juan to Washington FBI Headquarters. Some of the delays were as long as twenty-four hours. A frustrated J. Edgar Hoover called a conference in his office attended by Clyde Tolson; Alan H. Belmont, in charge of all investigative operations; Cartha "Deke" DeLoach, in charge of White House liaison; and me. Hoover cited several examples of extremely slow transmissions from San Juan and stated flatly, "I won't tolerate any more delays like this!" Tolson speculated that the Agents in the San Juan office were "probably going home by five-thirty." Belmont defended them and added that it was a complicated problem. Just then, Miss Gandy entered the room. In her hand was the latest radiogram from San Juan, a fairly short summary of a telephone conversation between Bosch and the insurgents. It had taken place eighteen hours earlier. As Hoover read the radiogram, a flush spread up from under his collar. Knowing the information would be at least nineteen hours old before the President would read it, he turned to me.

"Felt, I want you to go down to San Juan and find out what's the matter. Take whatever steps are necessary to eliminate these inexcusable delays. This information isn't worth anything when it is old."

"Mr. Hoover, I'll leave by the next plane. Possibly they need another encrypter down there. I'll take one with me."

"I want to get this corrected by tomorrow," Hoover said curtly.

As I walked back with Belmont to his office, he said, "Estill insists that the San Juan Office is doing everything humanly possible. Remember, the conversations overheard are in Spanish and this means that every tape has to be translated. Because it's so important, the translation is double-checked by another Agent. They're sending summaries which take time to prepare, but they're long because they resolve any doubt in favor of sending questionable material. And there's further delay because the message has to be decoded when it is received at SOG. Mark, I believe those fellows down there when they say they are working hard. Help them if you can."

When I arrived in San Juan at 3:15 the next morning, I was met at the airport by Wally Estill. We drove directly to the office and on the way he gave me a thorough briefing. The bottleneck was certainly not caused by lack of effort. Estill's overtime was averaging eight hours a day, and this was almost matched by the other Agents. When I surveyed the situation at the office, I decided that nothing further could be done about speeding up the translation of the monitored messages. Another point of delay was in the use of old World War II encoding equipment, secure but cumbersome to use. Even the addition of the second machine I had brought would not solve the problem.

But the greatest single delaying factor was in the method of radio transmission. The San Juan Office had only one transmitter on which the radio operator tapped out the message a letter at a time in Morse code! Two operators were using the transmitter around the clock, but they could not keep up with the traffic.

In the radio room was a large piece of equipment which somewhat resembled a small computer. "What's this?" I asked the radio operator.

"That's our new encoding machine."

"Why aren't we using it?"

He explained that they were waiting for additional equipment to hook it up with the radio transmitter. When that was received, experts from the Laboratory in Washington would come down to install it.

"How does it work?"

"It's a tremendous improvement over the old equipment. You type the message at this end and the machine automatically scrambles it so that no one else can possibly decode it. An identical machine on the other end receives and unscrambles the message as fast as it is being received. It's just like using a teletype."

"Is there any way of using it now?"

The operator thought for a minute. "The only way we could use it now would be to connect it up to a leased telephone line."

"Why don't we do that now?"

"It's against regulations of the National Security Agency. We can't operate it until a special lead-lined room is constructed. There might be a breach in our security. We just can't do it."

Returning to Estill's office, I told him, "If Belmont approves, we're going to order a leased telephone line and connect the new coding machine to it."

Estill frowned. "What about NSA regulations? Where are we going to put it?"

"Wally, we're going to put it wherever you decide is the most convenient place to hook it up to a leased line. I don't care if you put it beside your desk. This is an emergency and we aren't going to worry about regulations."

We called Belmont, and when he came on the line, I explained what I had in mind. He immediately agreed and added that he would make arrangements for the hook-up at his end. I promised him that the new machine would be in operation before the day was over. Late that afternoon the leased line had been brought in and the coding machine was working at full speed. By midnight, the large backlog of summaries had been sent to the Bureau and the messages were going out on a current basis. The coding machine sat in full view for all to see in the center of the Agents' room. There was nothing very confidential about the installation, but I was certain that there was no possibility of any compromise in security. The bottleneck was broken—I had accomplished my objective—and I had done it in one day as Hoover had demanded.

Growing out of the Dominican crisis were the seeds of a rift between the FBI and CIA, which had sole responsibility for intelligence gathering outside the continental limits of the United States. President Johnson was very disappointed with CIA efforts in the Dominican Republic and extremely pleased with the Bureau. Much to the chagrin of CIA, he ordered Hoover to establish an office in Santo Domingo. Hoover did not want this and it took him nearly two years to convince the White House to close the office.

CHAPTER EIGHT

They want you to call on the secure line.

—EDWARD S. MILLER

There had been attacks on the FBI before, but for the most part they had been little more than sporadic sniping. The one frontal assault of any consequence was spearheaded by Max Lowenthal, a Harvard law graduate who had served with various Congressional and Executive Branch Committees and Commissions in the Thirties and Forties. His tedious book entitled *The Federal Bureau of Investigation,* a compilation of virtually every criticism of the FBI and Hoover since the World War I era, was published in 1950 with some encouragement from then President Harry Truman. The Chief Executive had resented J. Edgar Hoover's warnings, ignored by the White House, that Soviet sympathizers in the Government were doing the Kremlin's work. But Lowenthal's book, though purporting to be a scholarly work, was so full of factual errors and distortions that it was quickly discredited by both public and the press.

In the turbulent Sixties the FBI and Hoover were prime targets of the New Left as it rampaged on the campuses and across the Nation. Its paranoid fear of the FBI, which it hysterically equated with the Soviet secret police, seeped into the press and found growing expression among the more bewitched and bothered opinion-makers. The turning point in the FBI's image came when the so-called dissidents were able to create a media-event, late in the evening of March 8, 1971, in a Pennsylvania town, appropriately named Media, when the FBI Resident Agency there was broken into and more than 1,000 classified Government documents were stolen.

The seed from which the Media burglary grew had been planted several months earlier, on November 19, 1970, when Hoover testified before the House Appropriations subcommittee, at which time he asked for additional Agents. Some of his testimony was given in executive session but one item which turned out to be a bombshell, was given in open session.

In describing the extremists then at large, Hoover said, "One example has recently come to light involving an incipient plot on the part of an anarchist group on the east coast, the so-called East Coast Conspiracy to Save Lives. This is a militant group self-described as being composed of Catholic priests and nuns, teachers, students, and former students who have manifested opposition to the war in Vietnam by acts of violence against Government agencies and private corporations engaged in work relating to U. S. participation in the Vietnam conflict.

"The principal leaders of this group are Philip and Daniel Berrigan, Catholic priests who are currently incarcerated in the Federal Correctional Institution at Danbury, Connecticut, for their participation in the destruction of Selective Service records in Baltimore, Maryland, in 1968.

"This group plans to blow up underground electrical conduits and steam pipes serving the Washington, D.C., area in order to disrupt Federal Government operations. The plotters are also concocting a scheme to kidnap a highly placed Government official. The name of a White House staff member has been mentioned as a possible victim. If successful, the plotters would demand an end to U. S. bombing operations in Southeast Asia and the release of all 'political prisoners' as ransom. Intensive investigation is being conducted concerning this matter."

The statement, though accurate and reflecting the results of FBI probing, was gratuitous because Hoover was appearing before the subcommittee in support of more Agents to combat organized crime. Pertinent or not, it made headlines. News stories disclosed that the intended kidnap victim was Henry A. Kissinger, the President's foreign affairs adviser.

The New Left reacted strongly. William M. Kunstler and Reverend William C. Cunningham immediately took up arms against Hoover and branded his statement a "far-fetched spy story." They argued vociferously that if Hoover had "the evidence he claimed to have" his duty would be to see "that the Berrigans and their alleged co-conspirators are prosecuted." Other critics felt that the Hoover remarks constituted prejudicial pretrial publicity which violated the Constitutional rights of the Berrigans. Few noted that it had been the press and not Hoover which had given his statement page one prominence.

Sensitive and unaccustomed to this kind of criticism, the FBI reacted with consternation. Though the background material concerning the Berrigans had originated in the Domestic Intelligence Division, the man who headed it, William C. Sullivan, quickly disclaimed responsibility. He insisted that although he had furnished the information to Hoover, he had warned against its use. Hoover's reaction, however, was to exert greatly increased pressure to bring the case to a speedy conclusion.

Hoover's pressure brought results and on January 12, 1971, Attorney General John Mitchell announced that a Federal Grand Jury in Harrisburg, Pennsylvania, had returned indictments against the Reverend Philip F. Berrigan and five others on charges of conspiring to kidnap Henry A. Kissinger and to blow up the heating systems of Federal buildings in Washington.

The trial actually commenced on February 21, 1972, and was marked by frequent histrionics by the defense attorneys and repeated demonstrations outside the courthouse. On April 5, 1972, a tired jury trooped back into the courtroom to announce that they found Berrigan and Sister Elizabeth McAlister guilty on four counts of smuggling contraband letters at the Lewisburg, Pennsylvania, Federal prison but they were unable to reach a verdict on the charges of conspiracy to kidnap Presidential Adviser Henry Kissinger, blow up Washington, D. C., heating tunnels and raid draft board offices. The defendants and their counsel—Kunstler, Leonard Boudin, and former Attorney General Ramsey Clark—were jubilant, particularly when the Justice Deparment decided not to retry the case.

The Berrigan "victory" was aid and comfort to the extremist left which now saw the FBI as vulnerable and they determined to strike in more damaging ways. I was affected only in an indirect way. Hoover had given me the task of supervising the security of FBI Resident Agencies, in anticipation of revengeful action against the FBI by Berrigan supporters. This is how I became involved in the events at Media.

On Wednesday, March 9, 1971, I was in New York on a routine inspection of the Field Office. I had just started to shave that morning when the phone rang. It was the night supervisor at the New York Office.

"The Bureau wants you to call as soon as possible," he said. "And they want you to call on the secure line."

"What in the world do they want?"

"I don't know," came the expected reply. "They didn't say." They never do. I hurriedly dressed and rushed to the office, picking up the phone at 7:30. The Bureau switchboard operator came on the line right away. "Oh, Mr. Felt, Mr. Miller has been waiting for you to call." Edward S. Miller was then my top assistant in the Inspection Division.

"Mark," he said, "what we feared has finally happened. A group of burglars broke into the Resident Agency at Media, Pennsylvania, near Philly, last night. Apparently they got away with a lot of serials." (Within the Bureau, FBI file documents are called serials.)

Miller explained that a group calling itself the Citizens Commission to Investigate the FBI had called one of the local papers to claim credit for the burglary. Using a crowbar, the raiders had broken the locks on every filing cabinet and made off with hundreds of documents, including many that were extremely sensitive and related to foreign intelligence. Within thirty minutes I was on the Metroliner bound for Philadelphia.

As Ed Miller had said, such a midnight raid had not been unexpected by the Bureau. There had already been several burglaries at draft boards around the country by people opposed to the Vietnam war. Draft records were either stolen or destroyed and in one instance animal blood had been poured over the files by the Berrigan brothers. There had also been an unsuccessful attempt to burglarize the FBI Resident Agency at Babylon, Long Island. The raiding party had attempted to break through the masonry wall, but all they had accomplished was to chip off the plaster, leaving the public corridor in a shambles.

After the bungled incident at Babylon, it was obvious that another break-in would be attempted. It was then that Hoover had put me in charge of a survey to determine what precautionary steps should be taken to insure adequate protection for sensitive FBI material. In conducting the survey, I discovered that only a few Resident Agencies were located in Federal buildings which had twenty-four-hour guard service. Some of these offices had built-in vaults providing good security. Most of the Resident Agencies, however, were located in commercial office space where protection was minimal. The answer was to furnish each office with a combination-lock safe-type of filing cabinet in which confidential FBI documents could be stored. A good burglar-proof cabinet-safe would cost just under $1,000 and of the 536 Resident Agencies, 475 would require cabinet-safes. Some of the Resident Agencies would need more than one cabinet, or at least an outsize model.

Unlike some agencies which casually spend the taxpayers' money, the FBI did not have a half-million dollars to put into cabinet-safes. Some sort of compromise had to be made, and the only workable solution I saw was to pick out the key RAs and recommend them for the added protection. It was something of a calculated risk, but I picked those which were close to colleges and universities where there had been a great deal of activist ferment. My first reaction to the Media burglary, therefore, was to check my memory: Had I picked Media as one of the RAs to receive the new cabinet-safes? When Ed Miller reassured me that I had, I breathed a sigh of relief.

At the Philadelphia Field Office, there was word that Hoover wanted to talk to me as soon as possible. When I called, he told me that a contingent of laboratory and fingerprint experts had been sent from Washington to help with the investigation. He instructed me to confine myself to an inquiry into the breach of security, and I assured him that he would have a memo on his desk when he arrived for work the following morning. When I arrived at the Media Office, the experts were already at work looking for evidence which would help identify the burglars. What I wanted to see, though, was the safe, and there it was—the biggest type of two-door, burglar-proof, fireproof cabinet-safe that money could buy—untouched and unscratched in the middle of the office.

The burglars had apparently not even attempted to jimmy this monster. In fact, I suspect they stole away thinking that they had failed in their mission, that the really secret documents were locked away in the big safe. The regular file cabinets had, however, been destroyed—no match for a determined burglar with a crowbar.

I began my inquiry by asking the Senior Resident Agent, "Okay, let's look at what you have in the safe." Reluctantly he spun the combination dial back and forth several times and swung open the heavy doors. There, in the completely secure interior where the sensitive documents should have been, were several two-way radios, assorted Bureau firearms, handcuffs, blackjack, and a copy of the National Crime Information Center Operation Manual, a public document. The Resident Agents at Media had completely missed the point but the Citizens' Commission to Investigate the FBI had not missed a single important document.

It is sadly significant that the critics of the FBI found ways to distort the facts of the Media raid. In his book, *FBI*, Sanford J. Ungar set the tone when he reported the facts upside down:

> Hoover was enraged and, in FBI tradition, somebody had to be found to serve as the scapegoat. The fact that ———, who was in charge of the Media Resident Agency, had long since requested secure, locking file cabinets for the office, was ignored. ———, declared culpable for this raid,

was suspended for a month without pay and was handed a punitive transfer to the Atlanta Field Office.

Ungar was correct only when he said that Hoover was enraged over the Media burglary—and so was I. The Senior Resident Agent in Charge was responsible for the protection of Bureau documents by putting them in the safe and it was I, as Chief Inspector, who recommended the disciplinary action. This may have been a stern measure but there were no other failures to properly safeguard confidential material.*

For two weeks after the burglary, there were no significant developments in the case. Then, on March 22, Senator George McGovern of South Dakota and Representative Parren Mitchell of Maryland, both outspoken critics of the FBI, received packages of selected material from the stolen files. Both men immediately turned the material over to the Bureau, and McGovern publicly stated that he would not associate himself with "illegal actions of this nature." When the documents were examined by the Bureau, it was found that the Citizens' Commission to Investigate the FBI had selected only those items which put the FBI in a bad light. Contrary, explanatory, or mitigating papers—memoranda rescinding a previous order or censuring a particular action, were excluded. *The Washington Post,* however, described the classified documents taken in the Media raid, and when *The New York Times* and other publications received copies, they printed excerpts from the stolen files. While elected officials had shied away from handling the material, the press showed no such compunction.

In March of 1972, a publication calling itself WIN published

* In direct response to the Media burglary, Hoover ordered that we close as many Resident Agencies as possible. Though he knew that it was desirable to have an Agent as close to the scene as possible, he had always regarded the RAs as something of a necessary evil. I tried to talk Hoover out of this idea, arguing that it would increase transfer and operational costs, and that we would receive angry complaints from citizens of the areas where offices were being closed. Hoover would not listen, and before we were through, the Bureau had closed 100 of its 536 Resident Agencies.

an eighty-two-page large-size pamphlet purporting to be a full reproduction of the more than 1,000 documents stolen from the FBI at Media. It was entitled *The Complete Collection of Political Documents Ripped Off From the FBI Office in Media*—an answer to charges that only damaging documents had been released to the press—but the pamphlet was a repeat performance, a few selected documents. It is interesting to recall that all the media indignation was directed not at the burglars but at the FBI. In comparison, the media's anger focused a few years later on disclosure that the White House "Plumbers" had broken into a psychiatrist's office in search of derogatory information which could be used to discredit Daniel Ellsberg, the man who photocopied and leaked the *Pentagon Papers*.

Publication of those FBI documents which the Citizens' Committee chose to release resulted in a great outcry against FBI practices which were depicted as reprehensible and un-American. That Hoover had over the years been praised by Roger Baldwin, the founder of the American Civil Liberties Union, and Morris Ernst, an ACLU guru, for his care in safeguarding the rights of the citizenry was forgotten, and the charge that the Bureau was a "secret police" was dusted off for use. Also ignored was the fact that in the released documents, the names of those under investigation were carefully excised while making public the names of those who had cooperated with the FBI, exposing them to vituperative attack.

At an earlier time, the Media documents leaked to the press would have been accepted for what they were, but given the distemper of the times, the disclosures were turned into a weapon with which to cripple the effectiveness of the FBI and law enforcement generally.

Much was made of the fact that a telephone operator at Swarthmore College had allowed an FBI Agent to see the long-distance telephone records of a philosophy professor, and this was held up as an invasion of privacy. It was never mentioned that the professor was under suspicion of having harbored several fugitives from justice. There was finger pointing because one of the documents alluded to an investigation of a traveler to East Germany who had visited a number of Communist camps. When it was discovered that the subject was fourteen years old, the FBI had dropped the case. But one pertinent fact was omitted, namely that the FBI had taken up the investigation at the request of United States military authorities in West Germany.

The accusation of "racism" was dredged up because the Media documents showed that the FBI was attempting to recruit informants in the black ghettoes. The FBI directive, however, plainly stated that the purpose of this recruitment was designed to give the Bureau possible advance warning of riots and other outbursts of violence, at a time when the nation's ghettoes were a tinder box. Law enforcement agencies were expecting, and they were correct, serious disturbances in which lives were endangered and property destroyed.

There were loud shouts because among the Media papers was an investigative report on Jacqueline Reuss, the daughter of Congressman Henry S. Reuss, a Wisconsin Democrat. The Bureau's interest was justified, though few would have learned this from reading the papers. Miss Reuss was active in Students for a Democratic Society, an organization which was the seed bed for much of the campus violence of the late Sixties. The FBI's interest, moreover, was not unique. No less than two local police departments and another Government Agency were also keeping tabs on the Congressman's daughter. The accusation was made that the FBI's activities in re Miss Reuss were really a flanking attack on the Congress. Few saw fit to determine what the FBI had in its Jacqueline Reuss file. The file in the Media Resident Office told the story:

MEMORANDUM

TO: DIRECTOR, FBI
FROM: SAC, PHILADELPHIA (100-51799)
SUBJECT: JACQUELINE REUSS
INFORMATION CONCERNING—
SECURITY MATTER

Re Bureau airtels to Alexandra, 10/30/70 and 11/12/70.

MARJORIE WEBB, Secretary to the Registrar, Swarthmore College, Swarthmore, Pa., an established source who requests that her identity be protected, on 11/17/70 advised the files of that office indicate that one JACQUELINE REUSS was born 10/15/49 in Paris, France, and is an American citizen. She listed her residence as 470 North Street, Southwest, Washington, D.C., 20024. She listed her father as HENRY S. REUSS and her mother as MARGARET MACGRATH REUSS, same address as mentioned above. The records indicate that she graduated from Sidwell Friends School, Washington, D.C., and started at Swarthmore College as a freshman in September 1967. The records indicated that she attended the Aiv-Marseilles, Avignon, France. The following two semesters she attended the Paris-X in Nanterre, France. She subsequently returned to Swarthmore College in September 1970 where she is presently attending school. Her major is French and she has many courses in the liberal arts field. Her residence while attending Swarthmore College is listed as 905 South 47th Street, Philadelphia. It was noted that in June 1969 she requested a transcript of her credits be sent to the University of Wisconsin.

It was this file which prompted the charges of "invasion of privacy" and a possible attempt at blackmail of the Congress of the United States!

For the most part, the Media papers simply dealt with routine FBI business. One memo reported on a Rochester, New York, police department program to enlist the Boy Scouts in the war on crime. Another described how FBI offices were linked to the National Crime Information Center so as to be able to trace any firearm, stolen car, person, etc. Memos outlined procedures for handling fugitives, Army deserters, etc. A very precise directive instructed Special Agents on exactly what authorization they needed for the use of wiretaps, spelling out the provisions of the Omnibus Crime

Control Act of 1968. There were transcripts of telephone taps on the then violent Black Panthers, instructions on how to cope with rioters, and a number of investigative reports.

Though with perhaps one exception the Media papers were relatively innocuous, damaging only to confidential FBI work, they were employed by critics of the FBI to revive old stories of a "secret dragnet" and of the "inhibiting" influence of FBI dossiers, previously given wide currency by such writers as Tom Wicker of *The New York Times* and Victor Navasky, a leftist viewer-with-alarm. In 1969, Navasky had written with his flair for the fictional that "a leaked FBI file, a damaging rumor can, of course, ruin a career. When an Attorney General leaves office, his private files go with him, his official files go to the archives, but the FBI files—drenched in 'raw, unevaluated data'—remain. And so the Director—with the FBI files as his private library—is de facto caretaker to the nation's reputations." Wicker carried it a little further.

"When the Bureau broke up a homosexual ring," he wrote, "they found that one of the victims was a member of Congress from an eastern state. Wealthy and a father, he had paid blackmail to keep concealed a homosexual episode with a member of the ring. The FBI has carefully kept his secret; it did not, for instance, call him as a witness; it has let him know that he has nothing to worry about—which guarantees, of course, that he is one of the best 'friends' the Bureau has on Capitol Hill."

Navasky attacked the Bureau because it presumably leaked; Wicker because it did not leak. And in fact, as Hoover replied, the "member of Congress," along with many of the others victimized by the blackmail ring, was not called because his testimony was not necessary to bring about a conviction. "In any case," Hoover added, "the decision was not the Bureau's to make, but the Attorney General's. We did not and do not make the names of such people public. But had we done so, the press would have been the first to condemn us, just as it condemns us now for remaining silent." It was the East Coast Conspiracy which made the FBI files public, but it was the Bureau which received the blame.

The one exception cited above, an interoffice routing slip referring to "COINTELPRO-New Left" opened a door to FBI activities to discover potential and actual violence and subversion in the extremist right and left. This clue, however, was overlooked until March of 1972 when Carl Stern, a bright young reporter for the National Broadcasting Company made a formal request for all FBI documents relating to "COINTELPRO-New Left"—under the provisions of the Freedom of Information Act. When Stern's request was refused, based on certain exemptions in the act, he filed suit in the Federal Courts which ruled that the documents should be made available to him. This opened the floodgates.

Selected for media exploitation was material dealing primarily with the New Left and Black extremist groups. Disregarded was documentation of FBI actions against the Ku Klux Klan and other organizations of the extreme right. As a result, the public was left with the impression that "COINTELPRO" was designed solely to combat leftist political activity rather than to combat violence from both ends of the political spectrum. Ironically, as a result of the Stern disclosures, an anti-Soviet but Communist group, whose leaders were convicted in the Forties of "conspiring to teach or advocate the violent overthrow" of the United States government, was able to file suit for the violation of the civil rights of its members.

The exhaustive investigation to identify the perpetrators of the Media burglary ended in frustration. The Bureau was able to learn who they were, but the evidence to prove it in a court of law was never developed. The greatest investigative problem was that peers and sympathizers of the culprits, wrapped in media martyrdom, refused to talk to the FBI. There was one ironic element in the grinding effort to make a case: Some of the suspects were affiliated with the Catholic left, and if any religion predominates in the FBI it is the Catholic faith.

In the history of the FBI, the Media break-in and subsequent distorted exposure of classified operations was a watershed event. The selective and sustained publication of the stolen documents changed the FBI's image, possibly forever, in the minds of many Americans. With our penchant for overreaction, the pendulum began to swing from blind approval to equally blind rejection. The case is still open, but so are the gaping wounds it inflicted on the Bureau.

CHAPTER NINE

The Bureau can only have one Boss.

—The Author to William C. Sullivan

If the Media burglary marked the turning point in the fortunes of the FBI, the Sullivan Connection was the byway down which the Bureau was led into its state in the public's disapprobation. In the past, the FBI had faced external attack. When William C. Sullivan, who rose to the position of Assistant to the Director the summer of 1970, began his series of maneuvers—working with a White House-Justice Department cabal—the attack was from within. For the first time, there were anti-FBI leaks to the press and to other agencies of Government from a high level in the Bureau and the effect was destructive of morale and efficiency.

Ironically, it was J. Edgar Hoover's move toward procedures which should have gladdened the hearts of civil libertarians and his insistence on the disciplined application of these procedures by Bureau personnel which led Sullivan to connive with Justice officials and the White House to bypass the Director. It also led, in a compounding of the irony, to the creation by President Nixon and his aides of the "Plumbers" unit and the Howard Hunt-Gordon Liddy operations as a means of "protecting" the national security at whatever cost—and, indirectly, to "Watergate." *

To understand Hoover's attitude toward investigative techniques which skirted the Bill of Rights, it is necessary to go back to the New Deal years when he was called in by President Franklin D. Roosevelt and ordered to investigate Communist and Nazi organizations. This was in 1936 and when Hoover protested that he had no authority to embark on this endeavor, the President dug up a Federal Statute which permitted the Secretary of State to sanction such activity. Secretary Cordell Hull was summoned to the Oval office and, in the presence of Hoover, wrote out his authorization which was promptly locked up in the White House safe.

On September 6, 1939, the following statement was released by President Roosevelt:

> The Attorney General has been requested by me to instruct the Federal Bureau of Investigation of the Department of Justice to take charge of investigative work in matters relating to espionage, sabotage, and violations of the neutrality regulations.
>
> This task must be conducted in a comprehensive and effective manner on a national basis, and all information must be carefully sifted out and correlated in order to avoid confusion and irresponsibility.
>
> To this end I request all police officers, sheriffs, and all other law enforcement officers in the United States promptly to turn over to the nearest representative of the Federal Bureau of Investigation any information obtained by them relating to espionage, counterespionage,

* Few remember that it was Hoover who sought to restrain the excesses of the Palmer raids in World War I, and who alone among high U. S. Officialdom opposed the shameless treatment of Japanese-Americans after Pearl Harbor—a treatment strongly supported by such civil libertarians as Earl Warren.

subversive activities, and violations of the neutrality laws.

These directives were repeated almost verbatim by later Presidents.

In the field of foreign intelligence, the FBI demonstrated its capabilities by crippling the German Intelligence apparatus even before Pearl Harbor. Japanese operations were almost non-existent in the United States as a result of FBI effectiveness, as I have already noted. But before the war's end, Hoover had become aware of the activities of espionage agents and sympathizers of our "friendly" Soviet ally. This "friendly" interest was directed particularly toward the United States' capability in the nuclear field. Soviet agents stole our atomic secrets and the technical details of our highly sophisticated proximity fuse, not to mention the wholesale theft of military information.

Passage of the Smith Act, first invoked against the Socialist Workers Party (the Trotskyite branch of Communism which is now suing the Federal Government), and other statutes broadened the scope of FBI investigative authority. The Smith Act, which was passed in 1940, prohibited teaching or advocating the overthrow or destruction of the U. S. Government or of the Government of a state, territory, etc., by force or violence or conspiracy to do so. The Act made no mention of direction by or substantial connections with foreign powers.

Information passed on to President Truman by J. Edgar Hoover in 1945 laid bare a Communist pattern of infiltration into the highest reaches of the U. S. Government, designed not only for espionage but for perverting and misdirecting policy. The Loyalty of Government Employees Program which followed put tremendous new investigative burdens on the FBI.

The FBI continued its domestic intelligence operations throughout the Fifties with the full knowledge and encouragement of both the Executive and Legislative branches and with the strong support of the American people. It was during the Sixties, however, that questions began to arise as to what was the proper role of Government in this area. Numerous violent and revolutionary groups began to form, obliterating the distinction between foreign and domestic operations against the Government and people of the United States. The rise of civil rights groups following the Supreme Court's anti-segregation rulings in 1954 had further intensified both the FBI's mission and its work in the field of civil rights.

During 1957 and 1958, more than 100 bombings and attempted bombings of an apparent racial-hate or religious-hate nature were committed in the United States. Reacting to the growing evidence of such violent outrages, Congress enacted the Civil Rights Act of 1960, expanding the FBI's jurisdiction in such areas as bombings and bomb threats, interference with Court orders and election matters.

The civil rights movement gained added momentum and public support in all parts of the United States in the early Sixties. At the same time, it became the target of vilification by the Ku Klux Klan and other merchants of hate who were inclined to see a Communist behind every banner or sign which urged desegregation and equal rights.

Some Communists did join the ranks of civil rights organizations. Their numbers were small but a few managed to maneuver themselves into positions of influence—positions from which they could wield an influence over the policies and programs of legitimate civil rights groups. Furthermore, a coterie of young demagogues, thirsting for personal power and recognition, were attracted toward the civil rights movements as moths are attracted to a flame. Again, they were comparatively few in number but in the highly charged atmosphere that prevailed in some parts of the United States, their irresponsible rhetoric and actions proved to be dangerous lightning rods.

Given these circumstances, not only confrontation but violence and bloodshed were inevitable. The FBI was called on time and again in the Sixties to *exceed* its authority by providing physical protection to persons engaged in civil rights activities. It refused and was accused of holding back. On the other hand, the FBI also resisted pressures to ignore or neglect its duty to enforce provisions of the Federal Civil

Rights Statutes and for this it earned the enmity of the forces on the opposite side.

The FBI saw its proper role as the prevention of violence and the protection of life and property. It continued its investigations to identify and apprehend bands of terrorists who were jeopardizing the civil rights of other Americans. But increasingly the problem became one of how to distinguish between those persons and organizations which were intent on violence and those that merely employed inflammatory rhetoric. It was also a problem of staying abreast of the plans and activities of the "lightning rods" and others who catalyzed violence. This required both criminal investigation and investigation to obtain intelligence information.

Confronted with this situation, was the FBI to employ those methods sanctioned by higher authority since 1936? Or should it take a safer, but less effective, course and bow to the growing pressures from elements in the media, in Congress, and among civil libertarians to shut down its domestic intelligence operations?

For Hoover, always sensitive to the moods of Congress, a straw in the wind was the hearings held by Senator Edward V. Long of Missouri to investigate the Internal Revenue Service for its electronic surveillance activities in the drive on organized crime during the early Sixties. It was undoubtedly this development which led the Director to call me into his office in mid-1965 to tell me that he wanted a "substantial" cutback in the number of FBI wiretaps. I was directed to review all the case files and to eliminate those wiretaps which were the least productive. Hoover did not offer any guidelines, nor did I ask for any. I simply said, "Mr. Hoover, I'll attend to it."

Hoover knew very well that there would be widespread internal opposition to such a reduction, but it was his custom in those years to toss me the difficult administrative problems and leave the details of solving them up to me. This particular challenge brought into the open my escalating conflict with Bill Sullivan, the man who was soon to engage in a behind-the-scenes intrigue against Hoover which ended with his forced retirement in October of 1971 when it became clear that Sullivan's aim was to unseat Hoover and assume the post of Director for himself.

I had previously confronted Sullivan in matters of lesser magnitude and I knew from these experiences that he could be very difficult to deal with. When thwarted by another FBI official he could be expected to throw a tantrum, followed by the sort of stab-in-the-back techniques which he directed against Cartha D. DeLoach, who was his immediate superior at one time. He directed personal letters to Hoover in which he accused DeLoach of all sorts of machinations against the Director.

Rather than engage in a futile, head-butting contest with this feisty little man over the intensely serious matter of Hoover's instructions to cut back on wiretaps, I went to his superior, Alan H. Belmont, who was at that time Assistant to the Director in charge of all investigative operations. Belmont, one of the most highly regarded of all Bureau officials, with a superb background in intelligence matters, was a pragmatist. A handsome man, he was extremely intelligent and was a very capable administrator. His deceptively mild manner was enhanced by his frequent smiles which, through the years, had carved wrinkles at the outer corners of his eyes. The constant cigar which he alternately chewed and smoked was his trademark. While Sullivan would never have agreed to the cutbacks I was to propose, I knew that Belmont would at least listen and discuss the matter in a rational way.

When I entered Belmont's office less than an hour later, the air had its customary blue haze of cigar smoke. I quickly explained Hoover's instructions to me and requested his support.

Belmont replied forcefully, "Mark, we can't cut back on wiretaps without reducing our effectiveness. The number is at a reasonable level and we have already made cut-backs through the years. You know very well that all wiretap requests are carefully screened and reviewed at every level at regular intervals. Furthermore, I don't recommend a wiretap to the Director in the first place unless I feel it is completely justified and I defy you to find one that is not!"

I was not personally in favor of what the Director had

ordered and I knew what Belmont was saying was true. Ninety-five percent of the wiretap installations were in foreign intelligence cases, and they provided valuable information to assist the Government in its conduct of foreign affairs. But I was new in my position as Assistant Director in Charge of the Inspection Division and I had yet to learn that there were ways in which to subtly influence Hoover without incurring his wrath. This discovery yet to come, I pressed on with my assignment, not to be diverted by Belmont's argument, logical though it might be.

"Al," I said, "that's not the point. The Director wants a reduction and that is what we are going to give him. It would be much better if I had your cooperation."

"I'm not going to help you tear down the effectiveness of the FBI," he said brusquely as he picked up a memorandum from his desk and proceeded to ignore me.

My only course was to begin a review of all current wiretap files to rank them in some order of priority. After a week of twelve-hour days, I was ready to take the first step. I selected the case of an individual suspected of cooperating with the intelligence service of one of the Soviet satellite countries. In my opinion, this wiretap could be discontinued without critical damage to the United States, and the case could be handled by conventional means, albeit somewhat less effectively. I then dictated a memorandum summarizing the case and suggesting that the wiretap phase of the investigation be discontinued. I recommended that the matter be presented to the Executive Conference. These conferences were meetings of all top FBI officials at Bureau Headquarters, usually minus the Director, held at irregular intervals when important policy considerations arose, generally about three or four times a month.

In spite of the public's image of "Hooverized conformity," the Executive Conference was anything but a group of "Yes Men." Arguments for and against a given proposal were aggressively debated before a vote was taken. Associate Director Clyde Tolson, who customarily chaired the meetings in Hoover's absence, encouraged participation by everyone and frequently called for opinions. Afterward, but preferably the same day, the proponent of the matter under consideration would prepare a succinct memorandum summarizing the proposal and the arguments pro and con. The memo was then routed to Hoover for final decision.

Usually he agreed with the majority, but sometimes he took the minority position or even an entirely new position. In any case, the Executive Conference provided Hoover with the dialectical input of all his top assistants, without the necessity of listening to all the wrangling. Under this system, he undoubtedly received many more candid views than he would had he personally chaired the meetings.

When I presented my recommendation for the discontinuance of the wiretap to the Executive Conference, there was a cold silence. Clearly, everyone had strong convictions about the matter and even Tolson opposed me. When the vote was taken, I was the only one voting to discontinue—a minority of one.

The results were sent to the Director and he returned my memorandum with the brief blue-ink notation: "I agree with Felt." Of course, I had expected this because it was his idea in the first place, but it did nothing to increase the popularity of the Inspection Division.

We went through the exercise two more times. In each, I argued alone for the suspension of a wiretap, and each time the Director agreed with the minority of one. My approach was much too slow for what the Director had in mind, and even though the score was now three to nothing, I went back to Alan Belmont. He was the key to the whole issue.

"Look, Al, let's be practical about this. I know very well that you are opposed to further cut-backs. I understand your position, but we can't go on with me chipping away at your wiretaps one at a time. You know perfectly well the Director wants a substantial reduction and that he is going to agree with me. Why don't you accept the inevitable? You are in a much better position than I to decide which taps can be discontinued with the least disadvantage. More importantly, if the initiative comes from you, the Director won't think you're dragging your feet."

Belmont puffed slowly on his cigar. He blew out a big cloud

of smoke and stared at the ceiling. Finally, he gave his full attention to me. He wasn't smiling.

"How many do you want to cut?"

I had already decided on a figure. When my review program started, there were seventy-eight in operation. My efforts, so far, had reduced this number to seventy-five.

"Al, we are going to cut them down to thirty-eight."

Again there was much puffing and a further detailed examination of the ceiling. As the puffing continued, the blue haze in the room grew thicker and after an interminable period Belmont lowered his gaze and said very slowly, "All right, we'll do it."

"Good." I replied, much relieved that the matter could be settled without further waste of time in the Executive Conference. "This is the logical way to handle it."

"You are probably right," he replied, "but Sullivan is going to be absolutely furious."

"I know, I know. It won't be the first time."

The next day a memorandum was submitted by the Domestic Intelligence Division recommending the discontinuance of thirty-seven wiretaps. Each was identified by case title and file number. When it came out of Hoover's office, there was the penned notation, "O.K. H." in the familiar blue ink of authority.

Only a few months later, a disheartened Belmont submitted his application for retirement, effective December 30, 1965, thus creating a vacancy in the Number Three position in the FBI hierarchy. Hoover's choice of a successor to Belmont was a strategic one, Cartha Dekle "Deke" DeLoach, Assistant Director in Charge of the Crime Records Division which handled press relations, research and congressional liaison. Shrewdly playing his cards, DeLoach had insisted upon personally handling all contacts with then Vice President Lyndon B. Johnson and the two hit it off primarily because they were alike in many ways. DeLoach was not without influence for he was a behind-the-scenes power in the American Legion and he had influential friends on Capitol Hill.

Ever the master at charting his way through the bureaucratic shoals of Washington, Hoover trimmed his sails to adjust to the new wind direction in the White House with the selection of DeLoach who was to continue his personal liaison with Johnson in the Executive Mansion. His star was shining brightly and the relationship became so close that the President had a special White House phone installed in DeLoach's bedroom so he would be available for consultations on a twenty-four-hour-a-day basis. There was never any doubt that he was the President's choice to succeed J. Edgar Hoover; but, as in the case of Courtney Evans, events have a way of being unexpected.

The rising tide of resentment against U.S. involvement in Vietnam blasted DeLoach's hopes of becoming Director of the FBI when it forced President Johnson to retire to his Texas ranch on the Pedernales River. Not long after he lost his political mentor, DeLoach retired from the FBI and took a high position with the Pepsi Cola Company.

To replace DeLoach, Hoover selected his personal favorite, the Assistant Director in Charge of the Domestic Intelligence Division—William C. Sullivan, a mercurial little man with a decided Napoleonic complex. He was extremely intelligent and well read. An excellent conversationalist, he could be very ingratiating when it served his purposes. An intellectual, he had expansive writing talent and cultivated Hoover shamelessly with flattering letters. He also made a point of bringing Hoover unusual gifts anytime he had occasion to travel.

Dealing with both Tolson and Hoover was an interesting exercise in psychology, requiring finesse and patience. It was often a good plan, for instance, to plant a seed and later convince them that it was their idea. Sullivan was one of those who understood and made good use of such an approach.

For a full understanding of Sullivan's special status, I should describe how Hoover used names of subordinates. When I was starting out as an Agent, if Hoover had any reason to address me, it would have been as "Mr. Felt." When I was promoted to the position of Assistant Special Agent in Charge and thus became a Bureau official, he started addressing me as "Felt." This was true of all Bureau officials except two, Tolson and Sullivan. While the rest of us were "Nichols," "Mohr," "Rosen," "Belmont," "Felt," and so forth, Hoover addressed Tolson and Sullivan by their first names, "Clyde" and "Bill." It was not unusual that Hoover would call Tolson, his long-time confidante and daily luncheon companion, by his first name; it was unusual, however, that of all the other officials, only Sullivan was granted the honor of this familiarity. It was an indication of the high regard which Hoover had for Sullivan until near the very end.

Even with Sullivan's attributes, it is difficult to explain the favor which he found with Hoover, because he was the complete antithesis of what the Director expected in the way of personal appearance and taste—matters of enormous importance in Hoover's mind. Sullivan was short—barely over the then minimum height of five feet and seven inches. He was pale and drawn and gave the impression of poor health.

What Sullivan lacked in body, he compounded in wardrobe. He dressed in atrocious fashion and always had a rumpled look, as though his clothes had been slept in, as indeed they sometimes were. On one occasion when he was summoned for a conference with Hoover, his aides pointed out that his shoes were covered with mud. He borrowed a pair of shoes from a subordinate which were two sizes too large, and while entering the Director's office, he had to maneuver them like snowshoes.

To sum it up, Sullivan's appearance seemed to the rest of us to be as divergent as possible from what we knew Hoover expected. I can't explain this phenomenon; perhaps Hoover felt sorry for Sullivan. Perhaps he regarded him as a surrogate son, but the fact remains that the Agent who rose to highest favor would have been voted by the rest of us as the least likely to succeed.

Sullivan harbored grudges, and he never forgave Hoover for the reduction of wiretaps or for the directive, issued in 1966, ending surreptitious entries. As head of the Domestic Intelligence Division, Sullivan was genuinely concerned that the FBI was not doing enough to combat and disrupt the violence-oriented segments of the New Left. He sincerely believed that the restrictions placed on him by Hoover impaired the Bureau's ability to protect the citizens of the United States.

At one point, he told me, "The Boss is wrong! We have to get the job done in spite of him!"

"Bill," I replied, "the Bureau can only have one Boss."

"The Director is wrong. You have got to help me convince him."

I drew a deep breath, "Bill, we've talked about this before. I understand your problems but we are going to get the job done in spite of the restrictions—not in spite of the Boss. I am not against you—I am for you but I am also for the Director. He is the Boss. After you have made your position clear, either support him or get out."

I could understand some of Sullivan's frustrations. Calls on FBI manpower for Field Offices in the South, a result of civil rights demonstrations and violence in attempts to counter civil rights progress, had cut down on the number of those assigned to foreign and domestic intelligence matters. What I did not know was that Sullivan was biding his time and waiting for an opportunity to have his own way.

That opportunity came on June 19, 1969, when Tom Charles Huston visited him. Huston, a former Army Intelligence Officer then on the White House staff, had been assigned by Presidential Assistant John Ehrlichman to prepare a report on campus disturbances and New Left violence, a problem deeply disturbing to President Nixon. What Huston wanted was a full FBI report on New Left foreign connections. From this meeting grew a close relationship between the two men which Sullivan skillfully used for his own purposes. Repeatedly Sullivan complained to Huston about the restraints imposed on the FBI by Hoover's refusal to employ wiretaps and surreptitious entries, and about the "question of coordination, the lack of manpower, the inability to get the necessary resources" all presumably attributable to a Director who, in Sullivan's view, had lost his grip and should be relegated to the dust heap.

From June of 1969 until Huston was finally eased out of the White House, he and Sullivan developed what a Senate Committee would later describe as a working alliance to further their ambitions. Huston saw himself as a kind of White House gauleiter over the Intelligence community, riding herd on the FBI, the CIA, the Defense Intelligence Agency, and the National Security Agency, imposing his ideas of how they should move against subversives and dissidents. Sullivan believed that with Huston's backing he could undermine Hoover's position with the President and succeed to the position of Director. If Sullivan did not actually draft the notorious Huston Plan which caused the Nixon White House so much trouble during the Watergate investigation, he certainly inspired it.

A major step toward this plan was the eventual creation by President Nixon, at Huston's urging, of an Interagency Committee on Intelligence (ad hoc) to review and suggest improvements in intelligence-collection procedures against the New Left. It was made up of Hoover for the FBI, Richard Helms for the CIA, Lt. General Donald Bennett for the DIA, Admiral Noel Gayler for the NSA, and Huston representing the White House. It was to prepare a report for the President enumerating the various options which might be open in dealing with the rising tide of violence and terrorism in the country.

By May of 1970, Huston had been promoted to a White House post which made him, in effect, a Presidential adviser on internal security affairs and, as he believed, strategically placed to help Sullivan reverse Hoover's restrictions on wiretaps and surreptitious entries. The crucial month was June of 1970, and lest I be accused of bias, I quote from the Church Committee report on the Huston Plan:

> Huston was responsible for arranging the conference between President Nixon and the intelligence leaders (on June 5, 1970), and had briefed the President in advance. The briefing was based on a two-page working paper that Huston prepared, relying on his conversations with the considerably more experienced Sullivan. As Sullivan's assistant, C. D. Brennan, recalls: "Mr. Huston did not have that sufficient in-depth background concerning intelligence matters to be able to give that strong direction and guidance," and therefore Sullivan was the "principal

figure" behind the preparations leading to the Huston Plan. Sullivan's role seemed to be to tell Huston what were *desirable* changes in the intelligence services; Huston was to try to make what was desirable *possible,* through his position as the White House man charged with responsibility for domestic intelligence.

The result of this meeting was the creation of the Ad Hoc Committee which was ordered to draw up a plan for improving collection techniques. Hoover was named chairman and, at Huston's prompting, Sullivan was appointed chairman of the staff subcommittee. At the first staff committee meeting, Huston made it clear that he and Sullivan would provide the guidelines for whatever recommendations were made by the Intelligence chiefs and would make certain that the "objectives" of the Ad Hoc Committee would include the "maximum use of all special investigative techniques." At subsequent meetings of the working group, Huston found the reports by the member agencies on the elimination of investigative restraints "totally unacceptable" because, he said, "they were not responsive to the President's wishes."

When the final report of the Ad Hoc Committee was drafted, it suggested a series of extreme options: relaxing or eliminating restraints on surreptitious entries, mail openings and electronic surveillance. NSA, CIA, and DIA were all in approval but Sullivan knew this would be distasteful medicine for Hoover, so he added a sugar coating. The report also recommended that Hoover be made the Director of all Domestic Intelligence gathering operations. It did not work. Hoover balked. Wise in the ways of Washington, he told Sullivan that the Ad Hoc Committee would go out of business once the report was submitted. If the report was approved by the President, the FBI would have the "sole responsibility" for implementation in the Domestic Intelligence field. If the plan later backfired, the FBI would be the target for blame. Much to Sullivan's disappointment, Hoover instructed that footnotes be added to the report embodying the FBI's specific objections.

When the working staff reviewed Hoover's footnotes, however, neither Huston nor Sullivan was particularly concerned. Their attitude was that the White House views would prevail in spite of Hoover's objections—and that the FBI would have to play it Huston's way. The Special Huston Plan was signed by the four agency heads recommending precisely what Huston and Sullivan had in mind from the start, except for Hoover's footnote objections.

The Huston Plan was presented to the President on June 26, but was followed by silence from the Oval Office and Sullivan complained that his efforts had been of no avail. Nothing daunted, Huston prepared a memorandum for Presidential assistant H. R. Haldeman—purportedly a "Domestic Intelligence Review." Reflecting Sullivan's thinking, it began with a lashing attack on Hoover. It stated that the Director's objections were "generally inconsistent and frivolous" and that the other agencies had recommended an end to all investigative restraints. Hoover was "bull-headed as hell" and "getting old and worried about his legend." It was "imperative" to move ahead and if it was necessary the President should have a "stroking session" with Hoover. "We can get what we want without putting Edgar's nose out of joint." To this was appended the first Huston Plan which called for the unlimited suspension of investigative restraints with even FBI participants, namely Sullivan, urging that "changes in operating procedures [should] be initiated at once."

On July 14, Haldeman informed Huston that the President had approved of the plan, though he refused to call Hoover in for the recommended "stroking session." A week later, Huston sent the official version by courier to Hoover, Helms, Bennett, and Gayler. It embodied the "most extreme options proposed by the counterintelligence experts," the Church Committee would later report. This caused some surprise among the heads of the other agencies, but Hoover, according to Sullivan, "went through the ceiling." He and "Deke" DeLoach marched into Attorney General John Mitchell's office to repeat their objections and he agreed with them. Hoover's next step was to write a memorandum to Mitchell restating those objections and adding that he would carry out the Huston directive only if ordered to do so in writing by the President and/or the Attorney General.

The rest is history. Mitchell expressed his opposition to the Huston Plan at a meeting with the President who agreed to recall and rescind it. Interestingly, Sullivan, who knew of the Hoover-Mitchell discussion and of Mitchell's impending visit to the Oval Office, called Huston to warn him in advance. Interesting as well was Sullivan's "explanation" of the President's turnabout. "Of course," he said later, implying blackmail, "Hoover had his files." He had done his best to push through the Huston Plan, but while doing so, he had protected his position with Hoover. In a series of memoranda to "Deke" DeLoach, while the plan was under discussion, Sullivan placed the blame for what was for the most part his brainchild on the heads of the other Intelligence agencies and "warned" that there could be "problems involved for the Bureau" if it was implemented. He also urged the FBI to oppose "the relaxation of investigative restraints which affect the Bureau"—and this at a time when he was privately belaboring me and others for not going to the mat with the Director to lift the ban on wiretaps and surreptitious entries.

Sullivan's duplicity in this instance was typical of his method of operation. For example, during an inspection of the Los Angeles Office, the Special Agent in Charge proposed that his Agent complement be increased by forty men. When I asked for justification of this extraordinary request, the SAC produced a communication from the Bureau instructing him to identify every member of every hippie commune in his territory and conduct sufficient investigation of these members to determine whether any had tendencies toward violence.

This was not only completely improper but also very impractical and when I checked the records at Headquarters I found that identical instructions had been sent to eighteen other large Field Offices. I immediately advised all nineteen offices to disregard the instructions until they had received clarification from Washington. On returning to Headquarters, I found that though the instructions had been sent out over

Hoover's name, he had not approved the commune order. It was not unusual for minor communications to be sent to the Field in Hoover's name without his personal approval. But it was extremely unusual and entirely improper for such a sweeping order to have been sent without clearance from a higher level or Hoover's personal approval. The instructions, not surprisingly, had come from the Domestic Intelligence Division—sent directly to the Field by a Sullivan protege. Needless to say, the instructions were canceled.

I had another confrontation with Sullivan when he proposed that the FBI open investigative files on every member of the Students for a Democratic Society. This was an utterly ridiculous proposal. In the first place, only a very small number of members had actually advocated or participated in violence and there was no justification for investigating the others. Secondly, in any event, manpower considerations would preclude opening thousands and thousands of new cases without relocation of Agent personnel. Sullivan argued strenuously but entirely alone for this proposal. I recommended that the matter be discussed at the Executive Conference and an angry Sullivan muttered to himself as his proposal won only two votes, a defeat approved by the Director.

But before his days with the Bureau were to come to an abrupt end, Sullivan was to be embroiled in deep controversy with the Director and with his colleagues. And even prior to that time, he had left his mark on the controversial record of the case involving Reverend Martin Luther King.

CHAPTER TEN

Those sexual things!

—J. EDGAR HOOVER

Probably more mis- and disinformation has surrounded the case of Reverend Martin Luther King, Jr., than any other FBI investigation. Rumor, gossip, conjecture, fact, and malice have all been jumbled together to put the Bureau in as bad a light as possible. Because the major principals—King, Hoover, Robert Kennedy, President Kennedy, William C. Sullivan—are dead, critics have, for various reasons, distorted the facts in their writings and public statements, and setting the record straight becomes a tremendous task. It is worth doing because the story of the King investigation demonstrates the stresses and strains under which the FBI operated and the public is entitled to any additional light which I can shed on the situation.

The account begins in September of 1957, when the Director issued a memorandum to all Special Agents in Charge concerning the Southern Christian Leadership Conference, which was headed by Dr. King. Hoover wrote:

> In the absence of any indication that the Communist Party has attempted, or is attempting, to infiltrate this organization, you should conduct no investigation in this matter. However . . . you should remain alert for public

source information concerning it in connection with the racial situation.

In the years that followed, the FBI compiled information on a number of organizations—including several which espoused the cause of civil rights and/or opposed America's military involvement in Southeast Asia—which had become targets of Communist infiltration efforts.

This was part of the Bureau's responsibility, as mandated by Presidents and Attorneys General since the Thirties. And there was no doubt in our minds, or in the minds of those who kept a close watch on Communist activities, that the CPUSA was making a major effort to gain positions of influence in the civil rights and anti-war movements.

On January 8, 1962, Hoover sent a report to the Attorney General stating that influential members of the Communist Party were, in fact, attempting to infiltrate the SCLC and among King's top advisers was a member of the Communist Party. Some months later Hoover reported to the Attorney General that one of Dr. King's staff members was "a member of the National Committee of the Communist Party." In its final report, dated April 23, 1976, the Select Senate Committee to Study Governmental Operations with Respect to Intelligence Activities set forth the above information and identified the two alleged Communists only as "Adviser A" and "Adviser B," respectively. I shall do the same.

With the written approval of the Attorney General, wiretaps were installed on both the office and home telephones of Adviser A, and in that early period, Bobby Kennedy's concern over possible ties between King and the Communists was much deeper than that of J. Edgar Hoover. Both he and his brother, President Kennedy, were closely tied in the public mind with Martin Luther King and the civil rights movement. It was no secret that Bobby realized what political damage could result for the Administration if it became known that King was working with Communists. It was imperative that the Attorney General have the facts and then, if necessary, bring pressure on King to sever such damaging ties. Therefore, directly and through his aides, he not only authorized but also pressed for an in-depth investigation, including telephone taps.

Both he and the White House, moreover, were anxious to know what Dr. King was up to and the FBI reports which gave information about King's meetings with his advisers, details of his strategy, and the attitudes of civil rights leaders were welcomed by the Kennedy Administration. For the Kennedys, it was a fine arrangement until King and Hoover began to feud.

In the autumn of 1962, Dr. King picked up a false charge made by the Southern Regional Council—that the FBI was deliberately dragging its feet in civil rights cases—and compounded its falsity. "One of the great problems we face with the FBI in the South," King said in a *New York Times* interview, "is that the Agents are white Southerners who have been influenced by the mores of the community. To maintain their status, they have to be friendly with the local police and people who are promoting segregation."

This was patently untrue, as I know firsthand. The majority of the Agents working in Southern offices were born and raised in the North. Furthermore, the Bureau's ranks were as open to qualified blacks—from either the South or the North—as they were to everyone else. The Bureau was actively trying to recruit qualified Agent applicants from minority groups to prevent just this sort of criticism. The number of black FBI Agents has always been small—and probably will be for some time to come—because those with the necessary qualifications have chosen to move into better paying or more prestigious jobs. Bobby Kennedy tried to force Hoover to accept unqualified blacks, but the Director stood firm. He was not going to lower standards just to please the Kennedy Administration.

Always sensitive to criticism of the Bureau, Hoover reacted strongly to King's charges. At his instruction, two calls were made to King so that he would have the facts—one by "Deke" DeLoach and the other by the SAC in Atlanta. In both instances, a SCLC secretary took the message and promised that the Reverend would return the call. He never did, which convinced FBI officials that King "does not desire to be told the facts."

The Bureau's memoranda about Adviser A and Adviser B had badly shaken Bobby Kennedy and one of his first steps was to have Assistant Attorney General Burke Marshall, who was in charge of the Civil Rights Division of the Justice Department, speak to Dr. King about the problem caused by his associations. King flatly refused to cease contacts with Adviser A, who was a close personal friend as well as adviser, but he did promise Marshall that he would drop Adviser B because of his being on the National Committee of the CPUSA.

King's promise to Marshall was nothing more than window dressing to placate the young Attorney General, for in June of 1962, the Bureau intercepted a telephone conversation between King and Adviser A during which they worked out a small deception. King would continue to use Adviser B as an unofficial assistant, but without formal connection with the Southern Christian Leadership Conference. "No matter what a man was," King said, "if he can stand up now and say he is not connected, then as far as I am concerned, he is eligible to work for me."

There followed a series of memoranda from the Bureau to Attorney General Kennedy, reporting the continued association between Dr. King and his suspect advisers, in spite of his promise not to have further dealings with Adviser B.

On a memorandum from the Bureau dealing with a secret meeting of King, Adviser A, and Adviser B, Kennedy penned a notation to Marshall: "Burke—this is not getting any better." Once more Marshall was dispatched to Atlanta to urge King to break off the worrisome relationship. It had little effect and in June of 1963, Hoover directed a memorandum to top officials in the FBI in which he detailed a conversation with young Kennedy:

> The Attorney General called and advised he would like to have Assistant Attorney General Burke Marshall talk to Martin Luther King and tell Dr. King he has got to get

rid of [A and B], that he should not have any contact with them, directly or indirectly.

> I pointed out that if Dr. King continues this association, he is going to hurt his own cause as there are more and more Communists trying to take advantage of the movement and bigots down South who are against integration are beginning to charge Dr. King is tied in with the Communists.

Marshall did talk to Dr. King once more and he summed up the conversation in a memorandum to Hoover.

> I brought the matter to the attention of Dr. King very explicitly in my office on the morning of June 22 prior to a scheduled meeting which Dr. King had with the President. This was done at the direction of the Attorney General, and the President separately. [I] strongly urged Dr. King that there should be no further connection between [Adviser B] and the Southern Christian Leadership Conference. Dr. King stated that the connection would be ended.*

Apparently as a result of these conversations, the civil rights leader wrote a letter to Adviser B stating that he had been cleared by the FBI, but that nevertheless his permanent resignation from the SCLC was necessary because "the situation in the country is such . . . that any allusion to the left brings forth an emotional response which would seem to

---

* Hoover told me that the President did talk with Dr. King and, while the two were strolling through the White House Rose Garden, he attempted to dissuade King from further questionable contact with the two advisers. There are different versions of this conversation because Dr. King told Andrew Young, then one of his associates and now United States Ambassador to the United Nations, a completely different story, quoting the President as saying that "There was an attempt by the FBI to smear the movement on the basis of Communist influence" and adding, "I assume you know you're under very close surveillance."

indicate that SCLC and the Southern Freedom Movement are Communist inspired." Whether intended or not, this allowed the Attorney General to respond to queries from Congressional leaders about King's contacts with the formulation that there had been attempts to infiltrate the civil rights movement, which Dr. King had successfully resisted.

Attorney General Kennedy, however, was not fully satisfied that Dr. King had truly severed his connections with Adviser B. At one point he suggested that the FBI subject Dr. King to "technical surveillance" which could have meant either wiretaps or microphones. Hoover agreed but insisted that the request be in writing. Kennedy pulled back from this.

There was continuing debate inside the Justice Department over the King problem. On one occasion, Courtney Evans, who was liaison between the Attorney General and the FBI, wrote that although the Civil Rights Division was not concerned, "Andrew Oehmann, the Attorney General's Executive Assistant, has counseled him [The Attorney General] that in his judgment there is ample evidence there is a continuing relationship with [Adviser B] which Martin Luther King is trying to conceal."

Again Kennedy brought up the subject of electronic surveillance. Hoover at first demurred, warning of the political consequences if such coverage became known and questioned the feasibility, since Dr. King was moving about the country much of the time. For telephone taps of King's home and office, authorization by the Attorney General was required and Kennedy put his signature to the order in October of 1963. What convinced him of the necessity for this kind of surveillance was the knowledge that King had broken his word and was still consulting Adviser A and Adviser B.

Beginning three months later, microphones were placed in various hotel and motel rooms occupied by Dr. King in his travels about the United States. The controversy is still going on as to who authorized and who knew about the microphones.*

---

* I cannot produce hard evidence that Attorney General Kennedy knew of these microphone surveillances—as distinguished from the telephone taps—

The microphone surveillances and the telephone taps on Dr. King and the SCLC demonstrated conclusively that the civil rights leader continued his contacts with Communists contrary to his promises and that he attempted to keep this knowledge from the Attorney General with whom he had been less than candid. But there was still another consequence. When the puritanical Director read the transcripts of the tapes disclosing what went on behind Dr. King's closed hotel doors, he was outraged by the drunken sexual orgies, including acts of perversion often involving several persons. Hoover referred to these episodes with repugnance as "those sexual things."

The tapes and the transcripts have been sealed by court order and turned over to the National Archives for safekeeping. Some may argue the propriety of this, as others have argued the propriety of recording Dr. King's more intimate moments in the first place. What the tapes recorded was a running account of his extramarital sex life. On his journeyings about the country in quest of civil rights, he had been visited in his hotel rooms by a parade of white females, and it was all there to be heard, right down to his outcries in the throes of passion. Frequently his male visitors joined in the festivities.

It is not my purpose to pass judgment on Dr. King's moral conduct and there may even be some who would envy his sexual exploits. The point I am trying to make is that it was his personal private conduct, more than the attacks on the Bureau and his association with Communists, which inflamed Hoover and led him to embark on a campaign to discredit

---

but I am convinced that he did. Both Nicholas Katzenbach, Robert Kennedy's successor as Attorney General, and President Lyndon Johnson knew of them, as FBI records clearly show. Some of the last of the microphones were authorized by William C. Sullivan without prior consultation with Hoover or any other of his superiors. On the memorandum, written by Sullivan, noting installation of these microphones, Associate Director Clyde Tolson wrote, "Remove this surveillance at once," and Hoover wrote, "yes." A further note by Tolson said, "No one here approved this. I have told Sullivan again not to institute a mike surveillance without the Director's approval." Hoover noted, "Right!"

Martin Luther King, whom he regarded as a hypocrite who was not fit to lead the civil rights movement. Hoover was an extremely straitlaced man who did not tolerate even the appearance of alcoholic or sexual irregularities involving Bureau personnel. He was incensed that a man preaching morality to the Nation should comport himself as Dr. King did.

These three factors: Dr. King's continued involvement with Communists despite his promises to Attorney General Kennedy, his unfounded attacks on the Bureau, and his marathon adulteries, led to what the media seized upon as a "feud" between King and the FBI. Charges were made by various reporters that Hoover had offered to play the King tapes to them but when asked by Attorney General Katzenbach to "confront" Hoover with these allegations, they declined, preferring not to challenge the old lion while he was still alive.

This brings me to the case of the composite tape sent anonymously to Dr. King in November of 1964. The known and verifiable facts are that William C. Sullivan sent an FBI Agent from Washington, D. C., to Miami, Florida, with a package to be mailed from there to Dr. King. The package, according to Sullivan's later testimony, was one which he had prepared containing a composite of the microphone surveillance tapes. Sullivan testified that the order to prepare the tape and send it to Dr. King came to him, indirectly, from Hoover and Tolson.

Included in the package with the composite was a letter reading as follows:

> King, look into your heart, you are a colossal fraud and an evil vicious one at that. But you are done.
>
> King, there is only one thing left for you to do. You know what it is. You have just 34 days to do this. There is but one way out for you. You better take it before your filthy fraudulent self is bared to the nation.

Sullivan denied knowledge of this letter, but in 1975, four years after his retirement from the FBI, a copy of the letter was found in Sullivan's private files which had been sealed at the time of his departure. Sullivan claimed that this was a "plant." The only explanation which seems logical to me is that the project had been Sullivan's brainchild and carried out without the knowledge or authorization of the Director. There is nothing to indicate that Hoover was aware of this action.

As the conflict between Hoover and King heated up, some civil rights leaders called for an open confrontation. But as one of King's legal counselors warned with astonishing frankness, this could be the "beginning of an Alger Hiss-type dilemma." It was the Director, however, who brought the matter to a head at a meeting with a group of women reporters. In response to a question, Hoover cited some of King's accusations, demolished them, and said for the record that the civil rights leader was "one of the most notorious liars in the country" and "one of the lowest characters."

In the uproar that followed, King suggested that Hoover was "faltering." In a telegram, he said that he was "appalled and surprised at your reported statement maligning my integrity. What motivated such an irresponsible accusation is a mystery to me." He suggested a meeting with Hoover but added that he had "sought in vain" for a record of any attempt by the Bureau to arrange a meeting—an assertion which could have been true only if his associates had deceived him.

There are several versions of the Hoover-King meeting, differing mainly in emphasis. Andrew Young's account stresses the long lecture that Hoover delivered on the FBI's work. "Deke" DeLoach's notes highlight a conciliatory speech by King in which he lauded Hoover and the Bureau—"a love feast." *Time* magazine published two accounts. The first quoted Hoover as saying:

> King was very suave and smooth. He . . . said he never criticized the FBI. I said to Mr. King, stop right there, you're lying. He then pulled out a press release that he said he intended to give to the press. I couldn't understand how he could have prepared a press release even before we met. Then he asked me if I would go out and

> have a photograph taken with him, and I said I certainly would mind. And I said, if you ever say anything that is a lie again, I will brand you a liar again. Strange to say, he never attacked the Bureau again for as long as he lived.

The second *Time* account reads:

> Hoover, *Time* learned, explained to King just what damaging private detail he had on the tapes, and lectured him that his morals should be those befitting a Nobel Prize winner. He also suggested that King should tone down his criticism of the FBI.

On the basis of my knowledge of Hoover, the true account probably lies somewhere among the contradictions but I am sure he warned Dr. King. It is true that King never publicly attacked the Bureau again. As a result, the controversy died down, although the FBI interest in all phases of the civil rights movement, both pro and con, was still present.

The case of Martin Luther King, Jr., continued to receive widespread publicity as a result of the House Special Committee to investigate the assassinations of President John F. Kennedy and Dr. King. Irresponsible allegations were made that the FBI participated in some way in a conspiracy to assassinate the black leader, but no thinking American will place any credence in these charges. In fact, the FBI was often able to protect King from personal injuries and possible death even though it had no authority for protective intervention. When the FBI learned from informants of planned violence against civil rights demonstrators, it was a simple but effective tactic to let the planners, as well as the local police, know that the FBI knew of their plans and this action was generally enough to defuse tense situations.

In 1976, Attorney General Griffin Bell appointed a Department of Justice task force to review the FBI's handling of the entire King case, including the security investigation as well as the assassination investigation. After an eight-month intensive review of FBI files and the interview of numerous witnesses, the task force submitted a 149-page report covering all aspects of the matter.

In a press release dated February 18, 1977, Attorney General Bell announced that "The FBI conducted a painstaking and successful investigation of the 1968 assassination of King in Memphis, Tennessee. The task force also found no evidence of FBI complicity in the murder." According to the release, the task force found sufficient basis for the FBI to initiate a security investigation of Dr. King but concluded that it should have been terminated in 1963. Carefully overlooked was the fact that most of the impetus for the investigation came from Attorney General Robert Kennedy at that time.

FBI actions to drive Dr. King out of the civil rights movement, such as the above-described letter and composite tape, were described as clearly improper—and with this I agree.

As I have noted, there is no way at this late date to determine exactly which of the actions by William C. Sullivan were cleared, or even known, by high FBI officials, including Hoover and Tolson. I do know that Sullivan, as head of the Domestic Intelligence Division, had ready and frequent access to top officials of the Nixon Administration and used those connections to feed the growing White House fears of the New Left. Sullivan ingratiated himself with Henry Kissinger, then National Security Adviser to President Nixon, with Alexander Haig, Kissinger's Deputy, and with Assistant Attorney General Robert Mardian, who headed the Internal Security Division at the Justice Department and claimed to have direct contacts to the Oval Office. Sullivan was also in constant touch with the CIA and other branches of the Intelligence Community.

Under Sullivan's aggressive guidance, intelligence summaries emanating from the FBI's Domestic Intelligence Division, particularly those relating to the threat of the New Left, went beyond factual reporting to include highly inflammatory editorializing. When Sullivan appeared before the President's Intelligence Advisory Board, his comments on FBI operations tended to emphasize his personal frustrations at restrictions imposed by Hoover and his complaints at what he saw as

Hoover's conservatism. In my opinion, Sullivan's actions were responsible for much of the over-reaction of the White House and the FBI as to the scope of intelligence operations.

That these scare tactics and this backbiting, as well as Sullivan's anomalous—to put it mildly—role in the developments leading up to the Huston Plan reached Hoover is a certainty. But in spite of this, Hoover held back and there was no specific point of conflict until October of 1970, when Sullivan addressed a group of newspaper officials at a meeting in Williamsburg, Virginia. During the question and answer period, Sullivan was asked about the current threat of the Communist Party USA and possible Communist connections with the New Left. He answered that the Communist Party had been greatly contained through the years and that he did not feel the current threat was serious.

Even though Sullivan "waffled" in his answer, it made headlines across the nation. A high FBI official, the press reported, had minimized the Communist threat. Hoover was furious. For years he had emphasized that the CPUSA was "an integral part of the international Communist conspiracy." It was, moreover, Hoover's very defensible contention that the CPUSA, however circumscribed by the FBI, was still giving secret aid and comfort to the New Left and to its terrorist off-shoots.

It is more than possible that Hoover, because of the intrigue of the efforts on imposing the Huston Plan, had been informed by Tolson of what Sullivan was up to—and he may have decided to use this incident to clamp down hard on a rambunctious subordinate. Sullivan might have salvaged the situation by protesting that he had been quoted out of context—which was true—but he refused to give in. Having watched his machinations, I am convinced that he decided to come out in the open in his bid for power. Already, one of his aides was saying that Sullivan would be the new Director within a few months, placed on the throne by friends in the White House and the Justice Department.

Hoover, who had fought the bureaucratic wars for years, did not make an issue of every point of difference, but Sullivan did. An example of this occurred in connection with the investigation of Daniel Ellsberg, who had turned over the Pentagon Papers to the press. It was proposed that FBI Agents interview Louis Marx, a toy manufacturer with considerable influence in Washington, who was the father of Barbara Ellsberg, Daniel's wife. Because Marx was a friend of Hoover, a memorandum was submitted requesting authority to conduct the interview. In one of his blue-ink notations, Hoover wrote, "No. H." The memorandum was routed to Assistant Director Charles Brennan, a member of the Sullivan faction, who later claimed that he misread the notation and thought it said, "OK. H." In fact, however, the interview had been conducted before Hoover's permission was sought.

When Hoover discovered this, he was livid. This was deliberate insubordination, and knowing that Brennan was Sullivan's right-hand man made him doubly angry. He ordered Brennan demoted to SAC in Cleveland. Two days later, the Director received a telephone call from Attorney General John Mitchell indicating White House displeasure. Mitchell asked Hoover to cancel the transfer. Whether it was a "request" or "an order," Hoover decided to go along with it. To those of us in the Bureau, it was clear that Sullivan had used his White House contacts to force Hoover to capitulate.

There followed in short order a number of newspaper pieces by columnists Robert Novak and Rowland Evans, among others, directly attacking Hoover and openly stating that he was no longer able to control the FBI because of advancing age. The details of these articles made it clear that they had come from within the Bureau, and they implied a revolt against his authority by both officials and the rank-and-file. They also built up Robert Mardian as an idol of FBI Agents, which was sheer fiction. (In fact, he was cordially disliked for his abrupt and overbearing manner.) The language of these newspaper columns, moreover, gave away the source, namely Sullivan.

Points of difference between Sullivan and Hoover became an almost daily fact of life for us in the Bureau. As another example: In the spring of 1971, President Nixon personally requested Hoover to expand liaison coverage in foreign countries. He told Hoover that government officials returning from overseas trips repeatedly told him that at the various embassies, the only personnel who really seemed to know what was going on were the Legal Attachés—the FBI Agents. They did no investigative work but maintained liaison with foreign intelligence and police officials in several major countries. Hoover did not want to expand FBI operations abroad; but since the President had requested it, Hoover went through the formality of taking it up with top Bureau officials who agreed that because of the source of the request, compliance was the only course.

Sullivan, who had gone along with the rest of us, suddenly reversed his field and came out in strong opposition, perhaps because he knew that his friends in the CIA, who resented what they considered FBI incursions into their jurisdiction, would be pleased by his stand. His memoranda became increasingly bitter and insubordinate. The lines had been drawn, however, by Sullivan himself and he found himself to be a minority of one.

Immediately after Hoover approved the requested expansion of FBI personnel in foreign posts, the FBI again came under attack from Evans and Novak for seemingly trying to force its way into a field which would normally be the responsibility of the Central Intelligence Agency. And again, the arguments advanced and the language used were exactly the same as Sullivan had used within the Bureau.

Sullivan had to go!

CHAPTER ELEVEN

> The greatest mistake I ever made was to promote Sullivan.
>
> —J. Edgar Hoover

Hoover reacted against Sullivan in true bureaucratic fashion—by a realignment of channels of authority which nudged Sullivan to a lower rung on the Bureau's promotional ladder. I learned of this when Hoover called me in to his office, on July 1, 1971. He rose to his feet as I entered, and I saw something I had never seen before: the Director looked tired.

Not wasting any time on amenities, Hoover informed me of his plan. "Felt," he said, "I am creating a new position in the chain of command. I am calling it Deputy Associate Director, and it will be the number three position in the Bureau. You are the one I have selected for this assignment."

This surprised me. While I was sure I had been handling my job in a way that would please the Director, it had never occurred to me that such high responsibility was so close.

"Mr. Hoover, I am extremely gratified—more than I can say. I will try to do a good job for you."

"Felt," he continued, "I need someone who can control Sullivan. I think you know he has been getting out of hand. You have been the only one to curb him."

"Yes, sir," I replied. "He and I have been bumping heads very frequently. I know what the problem is."

"Watch everything that comes out of the Domestic Intelligence Division very closely," Hoover warned. "I want to slow them down. They are going too far."

"Mr. Hoover, I'll do the very best I can. I understand the problem and I know what to do about it."

Hoover waved his hand, and the interview was terminated. "Keep me informed," he added, "and let me know what the problems are."

Neither of us had touched upon the most critical point of all—the health of Associate Director Clyde Tolson, which had continued to deteriorate rapidly. While he was still mentally sharp, he did not have the physical stamina to give Hoover needed support. He was not able to come into the office every day, and he had difficulty reading because of strokes in the retinas of his eyes. He simply could not keep up with the pace of the day-to-day operations in the FBI. It was obvious to me, therefore, that my promotion was more than a pressure device to serve notice on Sullivan that he was no longer in favored status. Someone was needed to begin taking over Tolson's functions.

The space I was to occupy had been vacated by Rufus R. Beaver, who was retiring. He and a second Inspector, William B. Soyars, Jr., assisted Tolson out of a cubby-hole office, just to the left of the spacious reception room—quite a change from the excellent space I had occupied in the Inspection Division. The reception room was crowded with three secretarial desks. One was occupied by Mrs. Lillian Brown, an administrative assistant to Tolson. Miss Carol Tschudy, my Administrative Assistant, occupied another, and the third was occupied by a secretary. Opening off the reception room to the right was a small office occupied by Mrs. Dorothy Skillman, Administrative Assistant and Personal Secretary to Tolson, whose drab private office was immediately adjoining hers.

The four-room suite was not only overcrowded, but maintained in Spartan simplicity. Beaver and Soyars had managed to obtain a few small pictures to adorn the walls of their room, but the long and high walls of the reception room were mostly bare. The faded gray carpeting was spotted with stains accumulated through many years and so worn in places, that the backing showed. The condition of his offices was a reflection of Tolson's personality of frugality and negativism. He would not permit the installation of new carpeting even though by strictest Government standards, it was eligible for replacement many years past.

A slightly built man of medium height, he looked tired and weak and far older than his seventy-two years. His face, always thin, had become wrinkled and drawn. Burdened with the debilitating effects of a series of strokes and other serious medical problems, and battered by the demands of the perfectionist Hoover, Tolson was a difficult man to work for. It required a lot of tact, finesse, and patience to get along with him, but knowing of his physical problems helped me to cope with him.

I truly felt sorry for this old man, who was ashamed to let anyone know how seriously disabled he was. However, working with him so closely, it was impossible for him to hide it from me. A stroke left him crippled in one leg, and while he could move about in the privacy of his office, I noticed at lunchtime, he could not keep up with Hoover's usual brisk pace. Instead of the customary one or two steps to the rear, which was his mark of deference to the Director, it became twelve or fifteen steps. Hoover confided to me one day that he purposely kept up the pace to force Tolson to greater effort, in the hope this would speed his rehabilitation—or at least keep him alive.

When younger and in good health, Tolson was a very tough and capable administrator. Much like Hoover, Tolson spent most of his adult life with the FBI. He came to Washington when he was eighteen years old and worked in the War Department while he went to night school at George Washington University, receiving a B.A. degree in 1925 and a Law degree in 1927. He became a Special Agent of the FBI in April of 1928 and held various important positions at FBI Headquarters before being promoted to Associate Director, the Number Two position, in 1947, a position created by Hoover to give Tolson more authority.

Tolson wielded this authority with an iron hand, functioning more as a buffer than as an innovator; and it became his all-consuming passion to protect the Director from mistakes, criticism, and the pressures from strong, dynamic officials at FBI Headquarters who were pushing the interests of their respective divisions. Everything that went to Hoover first passed through Tolson's office and his tendency to react negatively considerably reduced the pressure on the Director. Tolson also enjoyed the role of Hoover's confidant. Hoover needed someone with whom to discuss high level personnel problems and other administrative considerations.

The location of Tolson's office in relation to that of the Director was indicative of the relationship between the two men. Both offices were located on the fifth floor of the Justice Building at the corner of Ninth Street and Pennsylvania Avenue. Hoover had a long suite of offices extending down the Ninth Street side, but his private office was back-to-back with Tolson's, the two being separated by a small vestibule which opened onto the corridor and the elevator lobby.

Tolson could leave through his rear entrance and with a few steps be at the back entrance to Hoover's private office. Both always arrived and left through these rear doors. It was convenient for Tolson to respond to Hoover's requests for personal conferences.

Not only did I have to please both Tolson and the Director in my new job, but the volume of work was enormous. There were memoranda on major cases and about policy matters to be handled. But I also had to review important letters addressed to persons outside the Bureau, appointment letters to new Special Agents, FBI TV scripts, and hundreds of other papers. Some of the more routine matters were screened out by the Administrative Assistants, but most of the work came to me. I cut off some of the flow, but a heavy volume of material still went to Tolson who in turn passed it on to the Director. I quickly found out the hard way that I should not initial a memorandum, or any other material going to Tolson or Hoover, unless I could anticipate and be prepared to answer any questions which either one of them might raise, and they usually made very probing inquiries.

One of my responsibilities was to be sure that Tolson was fully briefed on any action taken by the Director and submitted during the morning between 11:30 and lunchtime, which was always at noon sharp. Hoover always expected Tolson to be right up to the minute on any actions taken and this was part of their mealtime discussion.

The new job also carried with it the requirement of "Saturday duty." Hoover rarely came to the office on Saturday or Sunday, nor did Tolson; but the Director wanted to know what was going on and crime never takes a day off. My responsibility was to be at the office on Saturday, no later than 11:00 A.M., to review the accumulated material and decide which should be sent to the Director and which could wait until Monday morning. Frequently, I would add explanatory comments and recommendations. When I had completed my review, which took from two to three hours, I would put the documents in "The Pouch"—an old and worn briefcase—and take it to Miss Gandy who was always there waiting. Miss Gandy then handed the pouch to Tom Moton, who was invariably standing by, and he drove out to the Director's house to deliver it. Hoover skimmed through the material on Saturday, and on Sunday he carefully studied it all. The first thing each Monday morning, all the material would come back from the Director's office with his notations and instructions where necessary.

I was also in charge of the preparation, for Tolson, of all recommendations for promotions and transfers of top-level personnel, both in the Field and at Headquarters. I could make a contribution in this area in view of my six years as Assistant Director of the Inspection Division, where service on the staff was a necessary step on the promotional ladder. For this reason, most of the Special Agents in Charge, the Assistant Special Agents in Charge, and those eligible for promotion to such positions, had worked for me at one time or another. Previously, in many instances, these selections were made by officials who could only be guided by the written record in the personnel file. Another factor which worked in my favor was that as he gained confidence in me, Tolson came to accept my recommendations and actions without question. He was frequently unable to come to the office at all and on those days, I acted for him.

Along with adapting to the demands of these new responsibilities, I set about the other task Hoover had assigned me, that of restoring order and morale to the Domestic Intelligence Division and putting the reins on Sullivan. My first major accomplishment was to soften the rhetoric of the Intelligence Letters which were being sent to the White House and agencies in the Intelligence Community.

Sullivan did not fail to recognize the point of my promotion over him, and my first directives to halt the literary license of the Domestic Intelligence Division were a signal that his uncontrolled activity was over. On August 28, 1971, two months after I was appointed over him, Sullivan wrote a letter to Hoover in which he spilled out all his resentment and frustration, and in doing so, inadvertently provided Hoover with sufficient cause for requesting his retirement. Hoover called me in to read Sullivan's letter and I was shocked by the vicious tone and rambling text. Sullivan typed the letter himself and submitted it replete with mistakes and smudges. Hoover called me again later the same day. "I showed the letter to the Attorney General. He told me I had no choice but to get rid of Sullivan and that's what I'm going to do."

(Much later, there was a mysterious development with regard to Sullivan's letter to Hoover. Some time during the Gray tenure, the letter disappeared from Sullivan's personnel file without a trace.)

On September 3, 1971, Hoover wrote a formal letter to Sullivan stating, "Submit your application for retirement after taking the annual leave to which you are entitled." Indicative of Hoover's determination, he appointed Alex Rosen, the Assistant Director in charge of the General Investigative Division, to succeed Sullivan. Sullivan did not respond, but he did take annual leave and there ensued a period of uncertainty as we waited for the next development.

During this hectic period, there was another episode which did nothing to quench the flames. With Sullivan and Hoover at odds and with Brennan the Assistant Director in charge of the Domestic Intelligence Division solely because of White House interference, something had to be done. I decided on a plan that would remove Brennan from leadership of the DID which could not be objected to by his White House supporters.

I reminded Hoover, "The White House ordered you not to transfer Brennan because he was so important to the Ellsberg case. Why not set up a separate unit to handle that case and put Brennan in complete charge with no change in salary? This would permit him to devote full time to the case, giving the White House exactly what it asked for."

Hoover thought about this for a minute. If he appreciated the poetic justice of my proposal, he didn't give any indication.

I went on. "We've got to do something. Morale under Brennan is deteriorating badly. He is not a popular leader. Many of his employees still resent his having been promoted at Sullivan's request over the heads of others who had served longer and he does not know how to assuage them. He exerts his authority unnecessarily. His removal is a necessary step to bring the Domestic Intelligence Division back under control."

Hoover stroked his chin. "Whom do you recommend to replace Brennan?"

I was ready for this. "I recommend Inspector Ed Miller. He has handled the last three inspections of the Domestic Intelligence Division and is thoroughly familiar with its operations." Edward S. Miller was Inspector and Number One Man in the Inspection Division. I knew his capabilities well because he had served under me in the same capacity.

Hoover paused for a minute and then said, "I'll think about it."

It did not take him long to make up his mind. His conference with me had been in the late afternoon of September 9, 1971, and in the first mail delivery the following day, Brennan received a letter from Hoover notifying him of his new position. Miller received a letter advising that he was being promoted to the position of Assistant Director in Charge of the Domestic Intelligence Division.

Miller confided to me later that all this came as a complete surprise. He had scarcely finished reading his letter when he received a call from the Telephone Room—the Director wanted to see him right away. While he was with Hoover, the entire time was spent in emphasis on the restraints and curbs which had to be applied to the operations of the Domestic Intelligence Division. Miller knew from his inspections of the Division and from conversations with me what the problems were.

It was an excellent move. Miller had the trust and confidence of the Agent Supervisors and morale began to improve rapidly. His first step was to institute a complete overhaul and redrafting of the Manual of Instructions for the handling and supervision of internal security matters. Many investigations which could not be fully justified were closed. Things began to move in the right direction.

Several days before Sullivan's last day on duty, I learned of the files in his possession relating to wiretaps which the FBI had conducted for the White House. Indicative of the degree of secrecy with which these operations had been carried out, only Sullivan and a few of his confidants knew all the details. They were never indexed as is normally the case.

These wiretaps later became known as the "Kissinger Taps," but with all the denials and fingerpointing which have gone on, it is impossible to fix specific responsibility within the White House. At the time, Dr. Henry Kissinger was Director of the National Security Council and the wiretaps were placed on members of his staff suspected of leaking information and on members of the press suspected of receiving it.

When I was first alerted to the existence of these sensitive files, I immediately sought a conference with Hoover to discuss this development, which was entirely new to me. He showed no particular reaction and simply told me to obtain the files from Sullivan and maintain them in my office. I became aware later that Hoover knew all about the mysterious wiretap files and had instructed Sullivan to maintain them in his personal possession rather than place them in the general files; but he never made any mention of this to me. Apparently, he did not intend to take any action, trusting Sullivan to pass them along to his successor.

Recovery of these files sounded like a simple assignment at first, but it didn't turn out to be, because the files were nowhere to be found. I asked Miller to set up and supervise an extensive search; and with a trusted aide, Thomas J. Smith, he searched all the file cabinets in Sullivan's office and all other logical places they could think of, with no success. As a safety precaution, I ordered the combinations on the locks of these cabinets changed and this led to the newspaper accounts that Sullivan found himself locked out of his office when he returned from annual leave.

The search by Miller and Smith expanded throughout the entire Domestic Intelligence Division and did result in the location of six file cabinets chock-full of confidential FBI research material. These cabinets had been maintained in Brennan's office and all were marked "Sullivan–Personal." This material was returned to its proper place in the regular files.

But no wiretap files!

When Sullivan returned from his annual leave during the last week of September, he found Rosen occupying his office. In spite of this, he made no move to retire and on September 30, Hoover wrote another letter telling Sullivan that he was being relieved of all duties and placed on annual leave status pending his application for retirement. This time Sullivan gave up and on October 6, he submitted his application for retirement effective as soon as possible.

When I confronted Sullivan about the missing files, he said he had given them to Brennan with instructions that they be delivered to Assistant Attorney General Robert Mardian. Brennan confirmed this story but denied that he knew what was in the files. None of us believed him.

Sullivan refused to discuss the matter further. He kept repeating, "If you want to know more, you'll have to talk to the Attorney General."

While this was going on, Sullivan was cleaning out his personal effects. He very pointedly left behind only his autographed picture of J. Edgar Hoover. He seemed edgy and upset that we would not let him get into the locked file cabinets. There was no way by which he could get the new combinations and his reaction was perfectly understandable because we now know they contained the only copy of the so-called suicide letter to Dr. Martin Luther King.

Sullivan's last day was a memorable one. All the FBI officials were glad to see him go, but we were also worried about how he would next attack the Bureau. I accused him of being a "Judas" and he challenged me to a fist fight. He was like a little banty rooster and I think he really would have fought me had I accepted his challenge, although I am half again his size.

Later in the day, after I briefed Hoover about these developments, there was a long pause before he slowly shook his head and said thoughtfully, "The greatest mistake I ever made was to promote Sullivan!" Then he turned and looked out the window overlooking Pennsylvania Avenue.

A full minute passed without a word being spoken and then I rose and said, "Mr. Hoover, I'll go back to my office now and get a memo into preparation summarizing developments."

He turned back from the window and looked at me as though he had forgotten I was there. He said curtly, "That will be fine, Felt."

As I was leaving his office I saw him turn again to the window and I left him alone with his thoughts.

It is very strange that Hoover did not explain the entire situation to me because he must have known I was groping in the dark. He knew the whole story—Attorney General Mitchell knew, President Nixon knew, as did his close White House confidants; but there was no written record and I asked Miller and Smith to reconstruct what had happened and reduce it to writing. Inside the Bureau, only a handful were aware of all the details. Naturally, those employees essential to arranging for the installation of the wiretaps and those who had to do the monitoring knew what was going on, but only a few had been entrusted with all the background.

My investigative team was able to learn that the wiretaps were first instituted at the request of Dr. Kissinger. Kissinger has denied it was his idea, but the record shows that he called Hoover three times from Key Biscayne, Florida, on May 9, 1969, and the first tap was placed on Morton H. Halperin, one of Kissinger's principal aides on the National Security Council, who was suspected of leaking information to *The New York Times*.

Because we did not think it desirable to consult the telephone company at that late date, it was impossible to check the dates on which various taps were placed or their chronological sequence, but on the basis of the recollections of those who had been involved, it was determined that taps were also placed subsequently on Helmet Sonnefelt, Daniel I. Davidson, Richard M. Moose, Anthony Lake, and Winston Lord, all of whom worked for Kissinger on the National Security Council. When the source of the leak was not disclosed by this coverage, it was expanded to include John P. Sears, Deputy Counsel to the President; Colonel Robert Pursley, aide to Melvin Laird, Secretary of Defense; William H. Sullivan, Deputy Assistant Secretary of State for Asian Affairs; Richard F. Pederson of the State Department; William Safire, a Presidential speech writer; and James W. McLane, Executive Assistant to Robert H. Finch, Secretary of Health, Education, and Welfare. Newsmen tapped were Henry Bradon of *The London Sunday Times;* William Beecher and Hedrick L. Smith, both of *The New York Times;* and Marvin Kalb, a correspondent for the Columbia Broadcasting System.

Some of the Agents also recalled that cooperation of French authorities had been obtained by Sullivan to arrange for a wiretap on Joseph Kraft, the syndicated columnist, who was writing and broadcasting from Paris at the time. Subsequently, questions have arisen as to whether this was telephone or microphone surveillance.

On the basis of the information garnered by Miller and Smith, I prepared an informal memorandum dated November 2, 1971, to send to Hoover. It had one serious omission; the name of Richard L. Sneider of the National Security Conference was not included among the group of tappees simply because no one remembered it. Also, two of the names were misspelled.

Actually, eighteen persons were involved but my memorandum only referred to seventeen since we didn't know about Sneider. The largest number of taps in operation at one time was believed to be eight. The last request was made on December 14, 1970, and all of the coverage was discontinued around the end of May or the first part of June, 1971. Following discontinuance of the coverage, instructions were issued by an unidentified Presidential aide that all memoranda reporting on results of the coverage be retrieved from the White House and kept in a secure place at the Bureau. All known copies of the material were returned to Sullivan who retained them in his personal possession.

Indicative of the secrecy in which this entire operation was held, I did not learn of it until Sullivan's retirement.

On November 12, 1971, Hoover addressed the following to me:

> With reference to your memorandum of November 2, 1971, which I am returning herewith in order for it to be placed in the Confidential Files. In conversation with the Attorney General on November 1, 1971, he advised me that the Sensitive Files which W. C. Sullivan had, without my authority, turned over to Assistant Attorney General Mardian had not been destroyed, but had been sent to Mr. John Ehrlichman at the White House to be kept there. The Attorney General states this was done in view of the fact that should any Congressional inquiry be made and a subpoena issued to the Department of Justice or the FBI, we would not have such files in our custody and the White House, under Executive Privilege, would be in a position to refuse availability to the files since they were in the possession of the White House, namely, Mr. Ehrlichman.
>
> I expressed to the Attorney General my concern about this whole matter and the way in which it had been handled rather surreptitiously between Mr. Mardian and Mr. Sullivan. I stated that I hoped that the *full contents* of the Sensitive Files had actually been turned over to Mr. Ehrlichman and that no one had retained any copies, either original or photocopies. The Attorney General indicated he believed this had been done.

This is the story as it was reconstructed inside the FBI from information furnished from Bureau personnel who worked on the wiretaps.

Because the wiretap files were maintained personally by Sullivan, they were never indexed in the General Files or in the Electronic Surveillance (ELSUR) Index, and these factors compounded the unfortunate damage resulting. The purpose of the ELSUR Index which was started in October, 1966, was to permit the Bureau to advise the Justice Department quickly if any person had ever been overheard on a wiretap, whether the tappee or a third party.

On July 1, 1971, the Department of Justice submitted a routine inquiry to the Bureau to determine whether Daniel Ellsberg had ever been the subject of a wiretap or overheard on a wiretap. Sullivan routinely referred the inquiry to the Special Investigative Division which maintained the ELSUR Index. Ellsberg had been a house guest at the home of Morton Halperin, an employee of the National Security Council, and one of the seventeen individuals covered by the "Kissinger Wiretaps." Ellsberg was overheard while using the Halperin telephone on fifteen separate occasions, but of course, there was no record of this in the ELSUR Index.

This is when Sullivan first approached Mardian about the secret wiretap files. Sullivan saw that he was losing out in his confrontation with Hoover and seeking to promote his own interests, he attempted to ingratiate himself with Mardian and the White House. He told Mardian about the wiretap files and said he was worried that Hoover would use them to blackmail President Nixon. Mardian reacted as expected and notified the White House. He was instructed to fly to San Clemente for instructions and did so the same weekend.

In the meantime, another ELSUR check request was received from the Department. This time the request was regarding Morton Halperin. Again, Sullivan referred it to the Special Investigative Division. A check of the indices was negative as Sullivan knew it would be.

When William D. Ruckelshaus came to the FBI as a temporary caretaker, one of his first official steps was to order an investigation to recover the Kissinger Wiretap Files. I knew the files were at the White House and consequently, the order appeared to have strong political overtones. I was out of town on a speaking engagement at the time and was not consulted by Ruckelshaus.

One of the first to be interviewed at the White House was John Ehrlichman. He calmly surrendered the files to Ruckelshaus, who then held a press conference disclosing with great fanfare what he had done. The only possible explanation for this unusual action is that it was an attempt by the Administration to offset the adverse effect of the disclosure in *Time* Magazine of the existence of the wiretaps and the files.

Sullivan first raised the question of blackmail and the allegation has been frequently repeated that Hoover used the information in his possession to pressure Presidents or Members of Congress. Never, during my thirty-two years with the FBI, did I know of, or hear of, a single instance where any proof of this has been offered.

Shortly after Sullivan's retirement an Evans-Novak column dated October 11, 1971, reported the event. It stated that Hoover was displeased with Sullivan's thesis that the Communist Party no longer was a threat to our security and had absolutely nothing to do with terrorist groups. The column referred to restrictions on Domestic Intelligence, imposed by Hoover, to the detriment of counterintelligence work of the FBI. It referred to Hoover's objections to the speech which Sullivan made at Williamsburg, Virginia. The column stated that, in frustration, some of the FBI top officials began dealing, behind Hoover's back, directly with the chiefs of the Nixon Justice Department, and that furious, "Hoover struck back with a reign of terror."

Subsequent columns by Evans and Novak were equally critical of Hoover and later of Gray. Those of us on the inside were convinced that the information in the columns was supplied by Sullivan.

Later, to placate Nixon, who was desperately worried about radicals and violent anti-war groups, White House Aides came up with a scheme to create an Intelligence Evaluation Committee for the purpose of pooling intelligence information from various agencies concerning radical groups.

In the FBI, we knew that the Committee was nothing more than window dressing to pacify the President. Actually, a similar organization had been in existence in the Justice Department since 1967. At that time, then Attorney General

Ramsey Clark created in the Department the Interdivisional Information Unit, the purpose of which was to coordinate information about extremist groups advocating violence. The Intelligence Evaluation Committee was nothing more than a new name for an old unit, but there was, however, one significant change. Previously, the FBI disseminated data directly to various members of the Intelligence Community. Under the new plan, all dissemination of information was to be made first to the Committee which would, in turn, pass it along to interested agencies. Approximately 95 percent of the information which the Committee received came from the FBI and after a few weeks of the new arrangement, FBI officials in the Domestic Intelligence Division realized the only real effect of the Committee was to delay transmittal to other agencies from twenty-four to forty-eight hours. Because of this, the FBI resumed direct dissemination in addition to sending material to the IEC. Justice Department officials never knew this.

During the summer of 1972, Sullivan received a telephone call from Attorney General Richard G. Kleindienst, offering him a position as Director of the newly established Office of National Narcotics Intelligence, within the Justice Department. The new office would serve as a computer clearinghouse for intelligence information gathered by Government agencies relating to the narcotics problem. Sullivan accepted, and by August, 1972, less than a year after his departure from Washington, he was back in a prestigious position. Mardian confided to Edward S. Miller that Sullivan had been given the high-paying job to keep him from writing a book about what he knew.

Sullivan offered advice to L. Patrick Gray III on several occasions but was given a cold shoulder. When Gray's candidacy for the permanent appointment as Director of the FBI appeared to be foundering, Sullivan renewed his efforts to take over the FBI Directorship. He inundated Robert Mardian with letters about the FBI, commenting on its budget, its management, and many other topics. Mardian, who had moved over to the Committee for the Re-election of the President, encouraged the letters, hoping to keep Sullivan quiet until after the November Presidential elections. Sullivan also wrote repeatedly to Attorney General Kleindienst about how he would change the Bureau.

The White House was not only anxious to keep Sullivan quiet about abuses of the Nixon Administration, it also wanted to use him as a source of information as to abuses of the FBI by prior Administrations. Both Nixon and his Chief Counsel, John Dean, saw this as a possible way out from under the enormous pressure of Watergate which was building up. If Nixon could prove other Presidents had abused the FBI, perhaps this would tend to reduce criticism of him.

In February, 1973, Nixon discussed this possibility with Dean. "Hoover was my crony. He was closer to me than Johnson, actually, although Johnson used him more. . . . I think we would have been a lot better off during this whole Watergate thing if he had been alive. Because he knew how to handle the Bureau. He would have scared them to death."

Nixon and Dean then explored the allegation that Johnson directed bugging operations against him in the 1968 Presidential Campaign. Nixon said, "We were bugged in sixty-eight on the [campaign] plane. God Damnedest thing you ever saw."

This approach bogged down when "Deke" DeLoach told John Mitchell that Nixon's plane had not been bugged but that the FBI had traced toll-call records from telephones near the Agnew plane when it was parked on the ramp at Albuquerque in 1968. Dean then suggested Sullivan, who was disgruntled and "has a world of information," as a source for this material.

Eager to approach Sullivan, Nixon asked, "You think Sullivan is basically reliable? . . . Why would he want to play ball?"

Dean explained that Sullivan badly wanted to get back into the FBI and Nixon replied, "That's easy."

Dean said, "He might tell everything he knows . . . he's a bomb!"

Dean called Sullivan to the White House and asked him point-blank to prepare a memorandum listing examples of political use of the FBI by previous Presidents. Sullivan still nurturing his ambition to be the Director of the FBI, saw this as a chance to further ingratiate himself with the President.

He prepared two memoranda, which Dean later turned over to the Senate Watergate Committee. In the first, he offered "to testify in behalf of the Administration" and the facts, he said, "would put the current Administration in a very favorable light." The second memorandum was four pages in length and detailed specific instances of questionable use of the FBI by previous Presidents. Both documents were typed personally by Sullivan in his familiar rough style.

The longer memoradum read in part: "To my memory, the two Administrations which used the FBI the most for political purposes were Mr. Roosevelt's and Mr. Johnson's. Complete and willing cooperation was given to both. For example, Mr. Roosevelt requested us to look into the backgrounds of those who opposed his Lend-Lease Bill. . . . Mrs. Roosevelt would also make some unusual requests. The contrary was also true in that the Roosevelts would indicate to the FBI they were not interested in the FBI pushing certain investigations too far if the subjects were ones the Roosevelts did not want derogatory information on." Sullivan cited as an example of the latter Roosevelt's lack of interest in pursuing allegations that Sumner Welles, the Under Secretary of State, had made homosexual advances to a porter on a railroad train.

Sullivan said that President Johnson, "would ask the FBI for derogatory information . . . on Senators in his own Democratic Party who were opposing him, which he would leak to Everett M. Dirksen, the Republican Leader of the Senate, who would use it with telling effect against President Johnson's opponents."

Sullivan also disclosed Johnson's use of a special FBI squad at the 1964 Democratic Convention in Atlantic City, which bugged the hotel room of Dr. Martin Luther King, tapped the storefront office used by black groups and set up a network of informants to infiltrate various factions at the convention. From all these sources, a steady stream of information kept flowing to President Johnson.

Sullivan dealt with political pressure in the handling of the case of Walter Jenkins, the Johnson aide who was arrested on a morals charge in a YMCA men's room. He cited alleged bugging of Agnew's campaign plane, which he knew to be untrue, the wiretapping of the South Vietnamese Embassy, and the surveillance of Anna Chennault—believed by Johnson to be a contact between Republicans and the South Vietnamese to delay peace negotiations until after the 1968 elections, thus giving a political advantage to Nixon.

While Sullivan's memorandum contained some truth, much of it was sheer fiction, and he produced neither proof nor documentation to support any of his charges. It was therefore of no value to Nixon, and when later John Dean turned it over to the Senate Watergate Committee, it was set aside as a basis for inquiry because of its "personal cheap shots" which had little or no substantiation.

But these shotgun blasts at the Bureau served one purpose. They became the basis for allegations and attacks on the Bureau in the media, in various anti-FBI books, and in the reports of the Senate Intelligence Committee. Ironically, though the committee commented on his obvious bias and his attempts at getting back at Hoover, the reports nevertheless leaned heavily on Sullivan in the case it constructed against the FBI. So Sullivan had the "revenge" he sought, but at a heavy cost to the internal security of the United States and the future effectiveness of the FBI.

CHAPTER TWELVE

Scare the Bastards!

—RICHARD M. NIXON

For many Americans, the FBI is a collection of Efrem Zimbalist types, implacably tracking down bank robbers, kidnappers, espionage agents, and other lawbreakers, all in TV thriller fashion. Recently, however, some members of Congress and antagonists within the media have added to that concept the idea that the FBI stays up nights thinking up ways to deprive Americans of their civil rights. Few realize that no organization could be what the FBI has always been acknowledged as being—the "world's greatest law enforcement agency"—by devoting itself solely to the cops-and-robbers game. Even fewer know that until recently, the FBI received high marks from the American Civil Liberties Union.

As I knew when I was an Agent in the Field and learned fully during my rise to the position of second man in the Bureau, the FBI is a complex organization with a multiplicity of activities and responsibilities. The actual pursuit of lawbreakers is but one of the many aspects of FBI work. There has been extensive cooperation with local law enforcement in such areas as the Identification Division which provides fingerprint indentification services to every law enforcement agency just as the Laboratory provides scientific crime detection expertise. The Training Division has provided training classes for tens of thousands of police officers from all over the United States and from many foreign countries. The National Crime Information Center provides a computerized network for local police where they may store notices concerning stolen property and wanted fugitives. The FBI is responsible for defending the Government and the people of the United States from foreign and domestic enemies and for containing, as far as legal restraints permit, the organized crime empire. It sends accountants into banks and corporate entities to uncover "white collar" crime and is frequently called upon by the White House to investigate the backgrounds of men and women being considered for appointment to high Federal office. The above are but a few of the areas of responsibility of the FBI.

This far-ranging effort has been accomplished by the creation of a highly disciplined and strictly organized structure, where every individual's duties are carefully defined. The chain of command is fast and clear and particular functions are specifically categorized and assigned. Under J. Edgar Hoover, moreover, human fallibility was reduced to the minimum by tight supervisory methods. All of these factors contributed to morale and esprit de corps and with few exceptions FBI personnel were proud of their jobs and willing to give unstintingly of their time and loyalty—the kind of dedication which is rarely found in civilian Government agencies.

The FBI can best be described as a hierarchical Pyramid with the Director at the top and the Agents and clerks in the fifty-nine Field Offices at the base. At the time of my transfer to Washington in 1962, a movement up the side of the Pyramid for me, the Bureau looked like this. At the top, in the command center, were Hoover and Clyde Tolson, his Associate Director. Below them was John P. Mohr, third in command with the title of Assistant to the Director in charge of administration.* Under Mohr were Assistant Directors in charge of the Identification Division; the Training Division, which not only handled the indoctrination of new Agents but also maintained the high level of competency among those

* A short time later Mohr was relegated to Number Four in the chain of command when Deke DeLoach replaced Belmont.

already in the ranks; the Administrative Division; the Files and Communications Division; and the Crime Records Division, which under Louis "Lou" Nichols, DeLoach, and others through the years, also served a public and press relations function.

On the investigative side, there was Assistant to the Director Alan Belmont, Number Four in the chain of command. He was responsible for the operations of the Domestic Intelligence Division, headed at that time by Sullivan; the General Investigative Division under Al Rosen who held that position for more than thirty years; the FBI Laboratory; and Courtney Evans's Special Investigative Division, among whose functions it was to maintain liaison with the Attorney General. Though there were personnel changes from time to time, the basic organization of the Bureau remained the same until 1971.

The Bureau for years had an Agent in the Training Division responsible for legal research but in 1971 Hoover set up the Office of Legal Counsel to handle the proliferating legal problems faced by the Bureau. Several years later, Dwight Dalbey, the Legal Counsel, was given the title of Assistant Director.

The FBI had been the first Government agency to computerize its payroll operations, and when Hoover inaugurated the computerized National Crime Information Center, all these functions were consolidated in a New Computer Systems Division in 1972.*

The Bureau was not only a self-contained pyramid but the hub of a wheel whose spokes moved out to other Government agencies with which the FBI worked in tandem. There was liaison with all Government agencies, some on a daily basis and some infrequently. Summaries were furnished to the Central Intelligence Agency, the National Security Agency,

---

* Since Hoover's death, new Directors have reshuffled and renamed some of these Divisions, but the basic functions, with the exception of Domestic Intelligence, which has been almost completely phased out, have remained the same. Gray, for example, abolished the Crime Records Division because he suspected some of its staff members were leaking information to the media. He himself took over the responsibility of relations with the media and other duties were divided among various Divisions.

the State Department and the intelligence arms of the military services. Reports and memoranda went directly to the White House for the eyes of the President or his aides. Hoover personally reported annually to the Appropriations Committees of the House and Senate and supplied national legislators with such information as the law required or as the President authorized him to disclose.

When Hoover appointed me Deputy Associate Director, in effect the second man in the Bureau since Associate Director Tolson was frequently too ill to hold the reins of authority or to keep abreast of the many activities of the FBI, it became my job to supervise the routine of this great organism. A heavy and never-ceasing flow of work crossed my desk, and I was expected to keep Hoover and Tolson fully informed of developments in fast-breaking cases and in the daily routine. I was therefore on tap from very early morning to 10:30 at night—the hour at which Hoover was no longer accessible except in the case of a tremendous emergency.

More than one phone at home became a vital necessity if I was to handle my responsibilities, so a "hot line" was installed which connected directly with the FBI switchboard. The extension to that phone in my bedroom had a red light which went on when I was called and remained on if the call was unanswered. There were times, however, when I was needed immediately though I was neither at home nor at the Bureau. To maintain constant contact, I provided myself with a "Page Boy"—a small radio receiver about the size of a package of cigarettes which gave a high-pitched signal when Headquarters needed me. I would then call in from the nearest telephone.

The "Page Boy" could also be a nuisance. Frequently there were calls from the White House from assistants to H.R. Haldeman, President Nixon's chief of staff, from John Dean, the legal counsel, or from other staff members which were of little significance and no urgency and I would rush to the phone only to be asked some routine question. To make matters worse, some of the calls which purported to be from the White House came from individuals who used that exalted switchboard to make themselves seem important. One such person was Assistant Attorney General Robert Mardian who liked to give the impression that he practically lived in the Oval Office. On very rare occasions I had direct calls from President Nixon himself such as during the afternoon of the attempted assassination of Govenor George Wallace.

On a Saturday morning, July 24, 1971, at 9:30 A.M., I received a call on the "hot line" which gives an idea of the many different kinds of assignments that were passed on to the FBI. The caller was Hoover. "Felt," he said, "I just received a call from Egil Krogh at the White House. The President is gravely concerned about a story which appeared yesterday in *The New York Times*. Walter Beecher, a *Times* reporter, wrote the story which completely sets forth the U.S. back-up position in the SALT talks. The President is furious."

"Mr. Hoover," I answered, "I don't blame the President for being mad. That's like playing stud poker with your hole card exposed."

"The President is bound and determined to find out who the leaker is, and Krogh has been designated to handle the inquiry. Krogh has requested FBI assistance in providing polygraph equipment and operators to assist in the interrogation of suspected leakers. I agreed to this request and told him you would attend a meeting at the White House at 2 P.M. today to discuss details."

"I'll be there," I said.

"Very good, Felt," he said in his usual abrupt manner. "Goodbye."

I realized that he had not brought up the fact that on his specific orders the FBI had not used the polygraph for more than seven years. Since this is what the White House wanted, Hoover had committed himself and it was up to me to work out the details.

The first step was to call up the Saturday Supervisor at the Bureau and to have the *Times* story read to me. It was headlined U.S. URGES SOVIET TO JOIN IN MISSILES MORATORIUM and it discussed at great length the Strategic Arms Limitation Talks and the U.S. negotiation position. Then, in devastating detail, the article described the American back-up position—the minimum the United States would settle for if its initial proposals were rejected. This put our negotiators in the position of being able to expect only the least they had hoped for, since the Soviets were now informed of our negotiating strategy.

This was not the first time highly sensitive information dealing with foreign policy matters had leaked, and the President was, I have been told, "climbing the walls." It was in an early attempt to stop these leaks that the FBI was ordered by the White House to place the "Kissinger Wiretaps" on staff members and on certain newspaper reporters. These leaks, moreover, were what caused the White House to form "the Plumbers" unit, bypassing the FBI which John Ehrlichman and other Nixon aides thought was being too dainty about civil rights.

Having listened to the text of Beecher's story, I next called Assistant Director Ivan Conrad, who headed the FBI Laboratory. Conrad had been in charge of the polygraph equipment and had trained the Agents who operated it. Conrad had been very disappointed when use of the polygraph was discontinued. He had great confidence in it, as did many of us in the FBI. Though it is less than 100 percent accurate, it did help weed out the innocent and allowed us to focus our investigative efforts on those whose readings had been doubtful or who had refused to take the test. Hoover had banned use of this lie-detection technique at the same time as he had put a stop to other FBI investigative methods which were arousing the ire of highly vocal civil libertarians.

Conrad was more than a little upset when I spoke to him. "Mark," he said, "we just can't do it. Our equipment is covered with dust in the warehouse at Quantico. The Agent operators haven't had any practice for seven years. This is a terrible mistake."

"Ivan," I told him, "we're going to do it anyway. Start getting the instruments back to Washington and lining up the best operators. We may have to do some tests as early as tomorrow. On Monday, we will probably have to be ready to go all out. The Boss said the President was very upset about it. We will know better when we get back from the White House."

"What do you mean by 'we'?"

"I'd like to have you go, too. There may be some technical questions." But here Conrad put his foot down. "If you agree, Mark, I would rather spend my time in the Lab. If I am going to do the impossible, at least let me be here to do it." Instead, he sent a qualified assistant. And by the time I reported at the White House, Conrad had begun to do the "impossible." Several machines had been dusted off and were on their way from Quantico and because Conrad had not been sure of the Bureau's long-inactive equipment, he had arranged to borrow some machines from the New York City Police Department, which were being brought to Washington in Bureau cars.

We were the first to arrive for the White House meeting—or so I thought. A balding little man, dressed in what looked like work clothes and dirty tennis shoes, was shuffling about the room, arranging the chairs and I took him to be a member of the cleaning staff. He turned out to be Robert Mardian, who had been reached on the tennis court with orders to attend the meeting.

Egil "Bud" Krogh chaired the meeting. Others attending were David R. Young of the White House staff, who seemed to be assisting Krogh; General Alexander Haig, at that time Kissinger's chief deputy; E. Howard Hunt, a nondescript man who said practically nothing; and two representatives from the Office of Legal Counsel of the Defense Department. It was the first time I had met any of them, although I had talked to Mardian on the phone.

Krogh explained the President's great concern over the growing number of leaks of national defense information—and he made it clear that he had received some forceful instructions! It was an article by Beecher, on May 9, 1971, which had reported the secret bombing of Cambodia, triggering student protests and the "Kissinger Wiretaps." On June 13, *The New York Times* had begun publishing the stolen Pentagon Papers which, at the very least may have enabled other countries to break the U.S. diplomatic code. According to Krogh, the principal suspect was an expert on strategic weapons at the Defense Department, on leave from a large university, who was known to have had recent contacts with Beecher.

We were informed that the suspect's office would be

searched that afternoon by Pentagon authorities, and in due course the FBI would give him a lie-detector test. Mardian then argued forcefully for the use of wiretaps. I pointed out that though there had probably been violations of the Espionage Act, use of National Security authority would nevertheless bar use in court of any evidence obtained. I suggested that if wiretaps were to be used, it would be better to obtain a court order under the provisions of the Omnibus Crime Control and Safe Streets Act of 1968. But Mardian brushed this aside, stating that the act could only be applied against organized crime. He was wrong, but he would not listen to the facts.

Confident that the case was solved, Krogh told me that he would be in touch about the use of the polygraph. All of this I reported to Hoover. I have since learned that after the meeting adjourned, Krogh immediately reported to the President and to John Ehrlichman that "we've got one person that comes out of the Department of Defense, according to Al Haig, who is the prime suspect right now. He had access to the document and apparently he has views very similar to those which were reflected in the Beecher article. And it would be my feeling that we should begin with him and those immediately around him before going to a dragnet polygraph."

"Polygraph him!" the President ordered. And he added, "I want that to be done now with about four or five hundred people in State, Defense, and so forth, so that we can immediately scare the bastards."

The following Monday, I received a terse phone call from Krogh. "We have decided to let the 'Agency' [CIA] handle the polygraph interviews," he said, and apologized for causing the Bureau any difficulty. Obviously, John Ehrlichman had decided to "punish" the Bureau for what he saw as its lack of cooperation and its refusal to get involved in the work which the "Plumbers" later undertook. Krogh seemed embarrassed, but he could not have known that the Bureau was relieved rather than angry at being brushed aside. I immediately called the Director to tell him of the White House turnabout. He merely thanked me for calling. I'm sure he was relieved, too.

There is a sour postscript to this. Under Krogh, a full-scale investigation was conducted to determine the source of the SALT leak. The suspect was given a polygraph examination by CIA, but it was inconclusive. The investigation was broadened to include others at the Pentagon and the State Department, conducted by the CIA. But the media blamed both the investigation and the polygraph interviews on the FBI.

It was on August 19, 1971, at 6:45 P.M., just as I was getting ready to go home, that I received another phone call from the Director. "Felt," he said, "I have just received a long distance phone call from Lawrence Higbee, who is with the President at San Clemente. He wants a full-field investigation of Daniel Schorr. I don't know what position Schorr is being considered for, but the White House is in a hurry. Get the investigation started at once and set a short deadline."

All I knew about Schorr was that he was a newsman. *Who's Who* listed him as a reporter and broadcaster for CBS News. Had I checked with other newsmen, I would have learned that he had been conducting a vendetta with the Nixon Administration, that he had a waspish temperament, and that he was disliked by his colleagues at CBS and elsewhere in the media. That the White House had given us no clue as to what Government post he was presumably slated for was not unusual. In fact, the Bureau preferred it that way. Sometimes secrecy was wanted, and if there were leaks we could not be accused of them. I immediately called Lorenz H. Martin, Chief of the Special Inquiry Section responsible for investigations of this nature, and briefed him on the call I had received from Hoover.

"What's the deadline?" he asked.

"Larry, the Director said the White House is in a hurry and that means pull out all the stops."

"He's been a reporter for many years and was assigned abroad for a long time," Martin objected. "This guy has written millions of words and God knows what all he has said. We'll have to interview hundreds of people—and we'll have to send leads to Europe to see if he was ever arrested or if there is anything else the White House should know in deciding whether to hire him."

We agreed that it would be a tough assignment, which

possibly could be completed in three days, but not without leaving a dangerous number of loose ends. Then Martin set the wheels to turning, which meant getting Agents in the field to drop other investigations in order to get the job done.

Agents hated these "short deadline" cases, and they were known as "no-win." They were, in effect, a contest between the Bureau and the news media. The FBI was required on a crash basis to look into a person's entire life history to uncover all information which might have a bearing on the wisdom of appointing the subject to an important Government position. If, after the appointment was announced, a reporter was able to dig up something the Bureau had missed, it made headlines. The Agent responsible for missing this information was censured and the Bureau looked bad. If the investigation missed nothing the Agents were merely considered to have done their job and received no credit for it. Investigations of media people, moreover, were particularly sensitive because if an Agent did anything that might be criticized, it always ended up in print.

It was the established precedure in the investigations of Presidential appointments to go directly to the candidate. He could furnish background information better than any one else and thereby expedite matters. In most instances, candidates did not attempt to conceal any part of their background. It was also important to go to the candidate at the outset so as to let him know why he was being investigated. This was done in Schorr's case, and he helpfully furnished information on his past employment, past residences, close associates, references, names of relatives, and everything else that he was asked about. He also expressed his pleasure to the Agent who interviewed him that he was under consideration for a high Government position.

Among those at the top of the list of interviewees was Richard Salant, president of CBS News and Schorr's boss. Perturbed because Schorr seemed to be looking for other employment and with our full-field investigation barely under way, Salant called the New York Office of the FBI. He said that he had just talked to Schorr by telephone and quoted him as saying that he was not considering taking any position with the government, that he did not know anything about it, and that he did not want to be investigated by the FBI. When this was relayed to the supervisor in charge at Headquarters, he called Alexander Butterfield's office at the White House. (Butterfield was appointments secretary and would later achieve fame or notoriety during the Watergate hearings by disclosing that the Oval Office was wired for sound and that President Nixon taped all his conversations.) The supervisor also instructed all Field Offices to hold the Schorr investigation in abeyance. An hour later, Butterfield's office called back with instructions to drop the investigation.

Two dozen individuals had been interviewed prior to Salant's call to the New York Office, and the inquiries concerning Schorr had lasted a very few hours before they were discontinued by the notice, at second-hand, that Schorr did not want to be investigated. Had he not given tacit approval, when he was interviewed, the investigation would have ended there and then.

When I learned of this turnabout I was shocked. Obviously someone had made a serious mistake. Could I have misunderstood Hoover when he ordered the full-field investigation? I called him right away and said, "Mr. Hoover, possibly Higbee was confused and only intended to ask for a file search on Schorr."

"No," the Director told me. "Higbee was very definite about it. He specifically asked for a full-field investigation. Let him worry about it."

The facts, as we know today, are that someone at the White House, angered by what Schorr had been broadcasting, hoped to find something derogatory about Schorr in order to silence him. Perhaps Higbee did not know the difference between a file check and a full-field investigation. But in either case, the White House had attempted to use the FBI for its own purposes, the discrediting of an antagonistic newsman. This was bad enough, but this act was compounded by subsequent floundering.

Ron Zeigler, the White House press secretary, denied any attempt at intimidating Schorr. The CBS broadcaster, he said, had in fact been considered for an appointment in the "environmental area"—which no one believed. Zeigler added that the idea had originated in the office of Frederick Malek, a Nixon aide. Later, reporters were told that Schorr was being considered for a job as assistant to Russell Train, then chairman of the Council on Environmental Quality. Then Malek went through the comedy of interviewing other newsmen for the "environmental" position. Ron Nessen, later to be President Ford's press secretary, was quoted by Schorr as saying, "I got the impression that Malek was not so much offering me a job as trying to get me to spread the word that there was a Schorr job."

The White House had been wrong, first in attempting to go after Daniel Schorr and then in dragging the FBI into it. It was foolish in giving Schorr the opportunity to pose as a martyr. In an article for *Harper's,* he claimed that he was harassed by the FBI and that the few hours of interviews had an "impact" on his life—his "relations with employers, neighbors, and friends"—where in truth it had gotten him much favorable publicity. The fact is that Schorr's case was no different from thousands of applicant investigations conducted by the FBI. For years the Bureau was requested to make thorough inquiries concerning individuals being considered for top Government jobs, including Supreme Court Justices, Cabinet officers, and even in the cases of Gerald Ford and Nelson Rockefeller, of appointees for the Vice-Presidency.

Ironically, what brought Schorr down was not the efforts of the Nixon Administration—or any other Administration—but his own action when in February, 1976, he furnished classified data from the House Intelligence Committee on classified CIA operations to the *Village Voice.* At first, Schorr denied that he was the source of the report or that he had passed it on to the *Village Voice.* Colleagues at CBS were incensed because they felt Schorr had tried to divert suspicion to another correspondent. He was suspended with full pay by CBS, and on September 18, 1976, resigned because "the polarizing effects within CBS News of the controversy involving me" had made it impossible for him to "function effectively."

His explanation reminded me of his failure to inform CBS back in 1971 that he had expressed no objection to being investigated by the FBI for a Government post when he was first contacted. He had been less than candid on the first occasion—in 1971—and emerged as a martyr in the minds of most observers. When he tried the same tactic in 1976, it didn't work.

CHAPTER THIRTEEN

Tell him the request came from the White House!

—JOHN WESLEY DEAN

The FBI Laboratory was J. Edgar Hoover's pride and joy. Its technicians were—and are—skilled in scientific detection; its equipment was probably the best in the country, if not the world; and it served not only the Bureau but police departments throughout the United States. The FBI Lab's achieved goal was complete objectivity in the analysis of criminal means and methods, from forged documents to ballistics. But even the Laboratory felt the pressures of the Nixon Administration to make it a political arm of the White House. That Hoover and the rest of us resisted those pressures won the Bureau few friends in the White House and the Justice Department, and the fact that no recognition came from the "watchdog" press is one of the sad ironies of the pre- and post-Watergate eras.

The case of Dita Beard, ITT, and the Justice Department is an example of the pressures to use the FBI for political purposes and it began when John Mitchell resigned as Attorney General to take over direction of President Nixon's reelection campaign. To replace Mitchell, Nixon nominated Deputy Attorney General Richard Kleindienst and Pat Gray, then Assistant Attorney General in charge of the Civil Division, to move up into the Kleindienst slot. Confirmation hearings before the Senate Judiciary Committee began in February of 1972, with Gray acting as unofficial counsel for the Attorney General-designate. The only serious question raised by committee members was an allegation that the Justice Department had been improperly influenced in the settlement of a major antitrust suit against International Telephone and Telegraph Company. Kleindienst denied any pressures or influence, and the hearings were closed.

A few days later, on February 19, columnist Jack Anderson exploded a bomb by publishing the text of a memorandum purportedly written on June 25, 1971, by Dita Beard, an ITT lobbyist, to one of the company's vice presidents, W. R. Merriam. The memorandum baldly implied that there had been a payoff in the anti-trust settlement. If Dita Beard was to be believed—and the more cynical in the Washington press corps saw the memo as an effort on her part to make herself important—Attorney General Mitchell had told her that the suit would be settled favorably in return for a $400,000 contribution of ITT cash and services to the Republican National Convention, then scheduled to be held in San Diego where the company's Sheraton subsidiary owned a hotel. The following day, Anderson charged that Kleindienst had been an "outright" liar when he testified about the ITT case.

It is not my purpose to go into the veracity of the Dita Beard memorandum. She was one of Capitol Hill's more flamboyant characters—hard-drinking, hard-swearing, and not above giving her employers an exaggerated sense of her importance and effectiveness.

The memorandum did raise some serious and legitimate questions about the probity of the Nixon Justice Department, the White House, and Richard Kleindienst. If believed, it could cause a scandal that might do considerable damage to the President's reelection campaign. The FBI was in no way involved and we saw no chance of being dragged in until Robert Mardian called me.

He called from the office of Senator Eastland, chairman of the Judiciary Committee. "A subpoena has been issued by the committee ordering Mrs. Beard to appear and testify but she has disappeared. Senator Eastland has requested the FBI to locate her and serve the subpoena. I am instructing you to do it." Ironically, the hearings had been reopened at Kleindienst's request, contrary to White House wishes, so that he could clear his name.

I did not like the idea of having the FBI serve the subpoena because it smelled of politics. But Hoover cleared Eastland's request without question. It was no great job to trace Mrs. Beard, however, and FBI Agents quickly located her at the Rocky Mountain Osteopathic Hospital in Denver, where she was being treated for a heart ailment. With permission from her doctor, the subpoena was served, but this did not help the committee. Mrs. Beard's doctor said that she would not be well enough to travel to Washington for some time. But since her testimony was crucial, some committee members traveled to Colorado. The interview did not produce any positive results.

What followed was a series of events which I carefully recorded for FBI files. They involved the Justice Department, the White House, and the FBI.

On March 10, I recieved an urgent telephone call from Pat Gray. I had never met him before, nor had I ever talked to him on the telephone. He explained that he had a very important matter to discuss about which he had to see me immediately. A few minutes later, he was in my office. Almost six feet tall, his hair closely cropped, his face weather-beaten—he had been a submarine commander during World War II—he was a strong and vigorous-looking man. He took no time in getting to the point. After explaining that he was managing the reopened hearings for Kleindienst, he gave me a brief rundown on the uproar that was raging. Then he handed me a large manila envelope and said, "The original Dita Beard memorandum is inside. The Judiciary Committee got it from Jack Anderson. It is very important to know whether it is authentic. I would like the FBI Lab to identify the typing, check the paper for watermarks, and determine if there have been any erasures."

"We can do that," I assured him.

"We don't want any examination made which would in any way alter the memorandum," he ordered.

"All right," I answered, "but that may limit what tests we can do."

"I understand that, but we must not alter the document in any way," he insisted.

I agreed and after Gray had left, I got clearance from the Director and sent the document to the Lab by special messenger. Less than an hour later, Gray's office called, frantically asking that the memorandum be returned immediately. I explained that the Lab could not have had the time to complete the examination requested by Gray, but that made no difference. The document had to be returned at once. I notified a startled Ivan Conrad at the Laboratory who retrieved the memorandum and sped it on its way back to Gray. Conrad called later to tell me that they had been able to photograph the memorandum but that all they would be able to determine from the copy was the probable make and model of the typewriter on which it had been prepared. On March 11, we informed Gray of just that.

Four days later, Gray was on the phone again to tell me that he was returning the Beard memorandum together with six pages of typewritten notes made by Britt Hume, an investigative reporter for Jack Anderson, who had interviewed Mrs. Beard. Gray wanted the memorandum and the notes examined, but with no tests made on either that might alter them.

"Mr. Gray," I said, "I am sure you realize that what we can do is very limited without access to the typewriters in question and without known typing specimens for comparison."

"I know, I know," Gray answered, "but that's the best I can provide. Tell them to do what they can."

Again, the documents were turned over to the Lab—and again, within the hour, Gray's office was calling to inform me that it was very urgent that the Beard memorandum be returned immediately. This backing and forthing troubled me but I relayed the message to Conrad who was becoming more than a little annoyed.

"Look, Mark," he said, "with such limited access to the memo and no material for comparison purposes, there is nothing we can do except to say that the Beard memo and the Hume notes were not typed on the same machine."

The next day, Gray called me still again. He was sending me copies of Mrs. Beard's initials, he said. He explained that she had denied that the intitials on the original memorandum were hers. By this time, I was becoming a little exasperated myself and I said to Gray, "You are asking us to compare copies with copies and this will make any positive conclusion impossible."

"Please check them anyway," he insisted.

I was not surprised when Conrad called to say that the Lab could arrive at no positive conclusions and this was reported to Gray. My hope was that this would be the end of the FBI's participation in what seemed to be some kind of game. But I was wrong. Twenty-four hours later, John Dean, the White House counsel, called me. He explained that private document examiners working for ITT had obtained three sets of documents typed on the same machine as the Beard memo, but at different periods between June 2, 1971, and February 18, 1972. According to Dean, ITT's experts had concluded that the Beard memo had been typed during January of 1972 instead of June 25, 1971, as it was dated. If true, this would conclusively prove that the memo was a forgery. He said he would have the original memorandum delivered to me from the Senate Judiciary Committee and the typing specimens from the Washington ITT office. But he would not permit chemical analysis to test paper, ink, and so on—which left the Lab nowhere, though Conrad did the best he could.

On March 17, Mrs. Beard issued a statement which was released simultaneously by her attorney and by Senate Republican Leader Hugh Scott. It read, in part: "I did not prepare it [the memo] and could not have . . . I have done nothing to be ashamed of and my family and I—and in a sense, the whole American Government—are the victims of a cruel fraud." Against this there would be Jack Anderson's testimony that Britt Hume, his assistant, had gone over the memo line by line with Mrs. Beard before he had published it and that she had confirmed its authenticity.*

* A bizarre sidelight: The White House sent E. Howard Hunt, of "plumbers" and Watergate fame, though this came later, to interview Mrs. Beard in Denver. Mrs. Beard's son, Robert, told newsmen, "The man refused to identify himself. He seemed to have inside information about what would

At 9 A.M. on Saturday, March 18, I called John Dean to advise him that the findings of the FBI Laboratory disagreed with those of the ITT experts and raised the strong presumption—though no positive conclusion—that the Beard memo was typed at or about the time it was dated. Dean sounded annoyed and argued that because no positive conclusion had been reached, the FBI Lab report should be modified so as not to conflict with the findings of the ITT analysts. That, I told Dean, would be completely out of the question. When he realized that I would not "budge," as he put it, he asked that I check with Hoover.

"Tell him the request comes from the White House," he stressed. When I told Hoover of my conversation, he exploded. "Call Dean right back and tell him I said for him to go jump in the lake! I want to cooperate when I can, but this request is completely improper!"

I did not quote Hoover exactly to Dean, but I let him know that Hoover had very firmly refused. It was obvious that Dean was very angry at our refusal to "cooperate." But the White House would not give up. At 1:30 P.M. on the same day, Mardian called me—from the White House, he said—to notify me that he had just dictated a memorandum directing the FBI to conduct whatever investigations and Laboratory examinations were necessary to determine the authenticity, or lack of it, of the Beard memorandum. He said Senator Eastland had insisted on this. Mardian's memorandum set a 10:00 A.M. Monday deadline for our report. Agents were immediately sent to the ITT office, where they took typing specimens from the typewriter used by Mrs. Beard's secretary and obtained other memoranda typed on that machine on or near the date of the original document.

Pat Gray got the Lab's report well before the deadline. Though the findings were not categorical, they made a strong case that the original Beard memorandum was prepared on or about June 25 and that it was authentic. The known speci-

---

happen next . . ." The visitor was "very eerie, he did have a red wig on cockeyed like he put it on in a dark car. I couldn't have identified my brother if he was dressed like that." Hunt's visit was subsequently verified. The red wig was borrowed from the CIA.

mens and the original memo were returned to Dean by courier at his urgent request. The following day, Gray personally returned the Lab report to me, advising me that Senator Eastland wanted the substance of the memorandum incorporated in a letter to him.

At 7:30 P.M. that day, John Dean called me. "Has the final Lab report gone to Senator Eastland yet?" he asked.

"No," I said. "But it is on the Director's desk for his signature."

"I must talk to the Director before it is delivered," Dean said with urgency.

"John, I'm sure he'll talk to you but be sure to call as soon after 9:00 A.M. tomorrow as possible."

Shortly after nine o'clock the next day, Hoover had me on the intercom.

"Felt, the White House wants to have some document examiners hired by ITT to have a chance to look at the original memorandum and to talk to our examiners before we send the final report to Senator Eastland. The memorandum actually belongs to ITT, so I saw no objection and I told Dean it would be all right. Tell the Laboratory."

I immediately made arrangements with Ivan Conrad and let John Dean know where the examiners should report. They did not arrive until 5:30 P.M.—a group consisting of Martin Tytell, a typewriter expert from New York; his wife, Pearl, who was a specialist in document examination; Walter McCrone, a spectogram expert from Chicago; and a lawyer representing ITT. I could not help but be wryly amused at the Nixon White House's sponsorship of ITT's experts. Tytell had been hired by Alger Hiss, after his conviction for perjury involving espionage, to construct a typewriter which would prove the FBI's typewriter identification false. At a cost of $7,500, Tytell had built a machine for the Hiss defense but it did not have the characteristics of the typewriter on which the classified documents which helped convict Alger Hiss were written. The contention that Whittaker Chambers, with the probable connivance of the FBI and Richard Nixon, had committed "forgery by typewriter" was never sustained—and Hiss went to prison.

Now Tytell and his associates were trying to prove that the

original Beard memorandum had been written in January of 1972 and was therefore a forgery. But their arguments were hardly convincing, and the FBI Laboratory experts stuck firmly to their opinion that the memorandum was written on or about the date it bore and was probably authentic. The ITT people then asked for permission to cut certain letters from the memo, to be taken to Chicago by McCrone for testing in his own laboratory. When Ivan Conrad refused, the ITT lawyer asked for the use of a private phone from which he called the White House. Within fifteen minutes, Conrad received a call from Hoover directing him to comply with the ITT request to mutilate the document. Later, Hoover told me that he had given his permission after receiving a call from John Ehrlichman who argued that ITT was entitled to do what it wished to the document since it was the company's property. He had yielded to this White House pressure.

Still stalling, the ITT experts did not return to the FBI Lab until 1:45 the following day, March 23. They cut the fifteen letters from the Beard memo and departed. At 3:45 P.M. the formal FBI Laboratory report was delivered to Senator Eastland. At 7:00 P.M. Dean called me.

"Has the formal report been delivered to Senator Eastland?" he asked. I told him that it had been delivered that afternoon.

There was a long pause, and then Dean asked, "Did you change it or was it in its original form?"

"It was in its original form."

Another long pause, then, "I see," Dean said curtly and hung up without another word. He was furious that I had not, bowing to White House pressure, changed the report.

Ten minutes later, Mardian called to say that Senator Eastland was complaining about a leak: Senator Edward M. Kennedy had called him to see the report before it had reached the Senate.

At 10:45 on the following day, Dean appeared at my office. "Mark," he said, "we have just received a spectographic report on the memorandum made by Walter McCrone in his Chicago laboratory. He is convinced the Beard memo is a forgery. I want him to talk with your Lab people."

I wondered why McCrone had called the White House

instead of the Bureau, but all I said was, "Oh?" Then I added, "Okay, John. I don't believe our Lab men have much confidence in McCrone—not after what he told them before. But I'll ask the Director. I'm sure he'll approve."

"I'd appreciate that," Dean answered. "You can reach me in the Attorney General's office during the next hour. After that, I'll be back in my office."

"Where's McCrone?" I asked.

"He's here in Washington. We'll make him available on short notice." The White House was still in the act.

"That's fine," I said. "I'll call within the hour. I'm sure we can arrange the meeting for today."

"We will appreciate that," Dean said huffily, and with no further comment he left my office.

When I explained the situation to the Director, he remarked, "They are persistent, aren't they? Go ahead and set up a meeting between Conrad and McCrone. Let me know promptly what the results are."

"Okay," I answered. "I don't know what McCrone has to present but I doubt very much that our Lab is going to change its position." I knew how meticulously Conrad worked. He was not given to snap judgments.

The Director laughed and said, "No, I don't think so either."

At 1:00 P.M., McCrone was at the Lab. After the meeting, Conrad called to say that McCrone had nothing new to offer and was, in fact, rather apologetic in his presentation. I sent a short note to the Director, giving him the facts and then I called Dean. He was not in his office so I left a message with his secretary describing the outcome of the meeting. Dean did not return my call.

Several days later, Pat Gray came by to discuss the affair. He told me that Senator Eastland had learned of all the wheeling and dealing, the pressure to get the FBI to declare the Beard memorandum a forgery. In a worried tone, Gray said, "Senator Eastland said that it might be enough to block my own confirmation as Deputy Attorney General." But Gray's difficulties with the Senate Judiciary Committee did not begin until a year later during the confirmation hearings on his appointment as permanent FBI Director.

The White House manipulations over the Dita Beard memo,

however, were only one phase of an ITT case which was the undoing of Attorney General Kleindienst. He had testified originally that "I was not interfered with by anybody at the White House. I was not importuned. I was not pressured. I was not directed." The Beard memorandum and White House documents subsequently made available contradicted this. On May 16, 1974, he pleaded guilty to a misdemeanor charge that he had not testified "accurately and fully" about the handling of the ITT anti-trust settlement and admitted concealing his communication on the case with President Nixon about not proceeding further against the company. Kleindienst was fined $100 and given a thirty-day suspended sentence.

I was sorry for Dick Kleindienst. But looking back, I am glad that the FBI was able to resist White House pressure to take part in a cover-up which in some ways was a prelude to Watergate.

CHAPTER FOURTEEN

Mr. Gray, why don't we go over and look at the files in Mr. Hoover's office?

—AUTHOR

Tuesday, May 2, 1972, began like any other day since I had become the third man in the FBI. I was up at 5:45 A.M. and not long after I was having breakfast and scanning the headlines of the *Washington Post* so as to be briefed on the key stories because I would have to answer Hoover's questions about them later in the day. At 6:45, I was on the way to the office, arriving there well before the official work day had begun in order to review all the teletypes and memoranda which had accumulated during the night and were on my desk awaiting action.

At 9:00 A.M., official life began. There were conferences, phone calls, and discussions with other Bureau officials. Ahead of me lay the FBI day, which would not end until 6:30 or 7:00 P.M., when the Director left. It was a Bureau tradition that the Director would be the first to leave and there was always much to be done which kept us at our desks anyway. There were many nights when I was at my desk long after this.

Shortly before 9:00 A.M. the two administrative assistants, Tolson's and mine, and the two secretaries came in. Messengers came in with large bundles of Bureau communications. Dorothy Skillman, Tolson's assistant, told me that he would not be coming in—no surprise because his increasing battles with minor strokes often made it impossible for him to be at his desk. I made the necessary decisions for him, hoping that he would not later disagree. Then, at 9:45 A.M., John P. Mohr, the Assistant to the Director in Charge of Administrative Operations, walked into my office. I was surprised because he would usually communicate with me on the intercom.

"He is dead," John said, enunciating each word carefully. I was sure that he was talking about Tolson.

"Did he have another stroke?" I asked.

"Hoover is dead," Mohr said.

I was stunned. Tolson's death would not have surprised me because I was well aware of his steadily deteriorating physical condition, but I could not grasp the reality of Hoover's death. I had talked with him several times the day before and he had been his usual vigorous and energetic self. It seemed impossible. Of course, I knew that a seventy-seven-year-old man could go at any time, but it just did not seem possible that Hoover could leave the scene so suddenly.

Mohr stood there silently watching my reaction and he saw my expression change from one of disbelief to one of shock.

"He died sometime last night or early this morning. Annie, the housekeeper, found him," John said. Dr. Choisser had been there and said it was a heart attack. Miss Gandy called me shortly after nine and I went up to see her. I talked with Tolson at Hoover's house and he asked me to handle funeral arrangements and to notify the Attorney General. Tolson is taking this pretty hard."

"What was Kleindienst's reaction? What did he say?"

"Not very much at first," John replied. "I told him that Miss Gandy and I had been instructed by Tolson to handle the funeral arrangements and I asked him if he wanted me to notify the White House. He said no. He wanted to call the President personally and he was sure the White House would want to announce the death."

I was relieved to have someone else handling funeral and other business arrangements because I knew how difficult the days ahead were going to be. I said, "That's fine, John. Tolson won't be coming in and whatever you and Miss Gandy decide will be okay with me."

John turned to leave the room and said, "I'll fill you in on more details later but I want to tell all the Assistant Directors before they hear the news by the grapevine."

I jumped from my desk and went into the next office to tell my two Agent Assistants. They were as stunned as I. Then, I went into the next office to advise my Administrative Assistant and the two secretaries. They were dumbfounded and one of them started to cry. As I entered the next room to bring the sad news to Dorothy Skillman, she was talking on the telephone and I could tell by the expression on her face that she was learning the story from someone else. The look on her face was one of shocked disbelief.

She hung up the phone and said, "That was Miss Gandy. She told me what happened."

I said, "This is going to be very rough on your boss."

"I know," she replied. "I don't know how long he'll last without Mr. Hoover's support."

"Don't worry about it today," I said. "We'll have plenty of other things to keep us occupied for the next few days."

As I turned to leave the office, her tears were starting to flow.

Although the formal announcement of Hoover's death did not come from the White House until a few minutes before noon, the news leaked to the press well in advance. Word spread through the FBI and the Justice Department. Wives and friends were called and, of course, there were leaks to the press. I was so busy it didn't occur to me to call my wife and it was she who called me at mid-morning. She had just received the news from our stockbroker who had read the story on the wire-service tape. News photographers were in front of the Hoover home well in advance of the White House announcement.

Looking back in retrospect at those first hours, it is hard to assess my exact feelings. I felt no sense of personal loss, because my relationship with Hoover had been restricted to the office. Hoover had once fraternized on a limited basis with some of his top officials, but during his later years, Tolson was the only Bureau official who had any social contact with the Director.

Hoover turned to me in 1971 because he was aware that Tolson's weakened physical condition left him unable to cope with the many daily problems which arose. He knew I had no designs on his job because I had never given him the slightest indication of this—and I truly did not. I am positive I had his complete confidence because he paid careful attention to my advice and recommendations on investigative as well as personnel matters. He enjoyed talking with me, sometimes at considerable length, about current topics of interest. I feel that he respected me as much as I respected him.

This is not to say he was an easy man to work for. He was tough and irascible. He would not accept even 98 percent perfection. He was extremely bright and had an amazing memory about even the smallest of details. Allegations that he had become senile are completely baseless. I know, because I had to deal with him on a day-to-day basis, and he would recall details of a memorandum he had seen days before.

He was a ruthless fighter for causes in which he believed and was as fierce and tough as the bulldog he was said to resemble. I had tremendous admiration for the man. I was and am proud of the FBI and it was Hoover who built it into the finest law enforcement agency in the world. It may never again be the same.

All I could do was to keep the FBI as nearly intact as possible. I knew Tolson would retire, and being next in the chain of command, it would be up to me to keep the FBI on course. I had to set the example—make sure there were no breakdowns in any phase of operations and take every possible step to prevent morale from sagging. I was sure this could be done because of the excellent FBI staff. It did not cross my mind that the President would appoint an outsider to replace Hoover. Had I known this, I would not not have been hopeful about the future. There were many trained executives in the FBI who could have effectively handled the job of Director. My own record was good and I allowed myself to think I had an excellent chance.

As the day went on, I reconstructed what had happened on

the Director's last day by questioning the various people involved. It was May Day, and it began very routinely. Tom Moton, who chauffeured Hoover's bullet-proof Cadillac limousine, drove it into the courtyard at the Justice Department building at three minutes past nine, slightly behind schedule, and took his passenger to the special parking space in the basement immediately adjacent to the lobby of the elevator bank at the corner nearest 9th and Pennsylvania Avenue. These elevators were almost directly in back of the Director's office on the fifth floor and it was but a few steps from car to elevator in the parking area and only a few more from the elevator lobby on the fifth floor to the private rear entrance to Hoover's office which he always used.

Hoover usually had his limousine pick up Clyde Tolson at his apartment and they would arrive together, Tolson a few steps to the rear as was his custom. On this day, Hoover was alone as he left the car and strode briskly to the elevator bank.

When Hoover left the limousine, parked but a few steps from the elevator lobby, Moton always went to a special phone and called the Director's office to alert everyone. "He's on the way up." This resulted each time in a flurry of activity and if there were any relaxed employees there before the call, there were none after.

Nothing unusual happened this day—I saw Hoover and talked with him several times on the intercom. He was alert, forceful, typically aggressive, and, so far as I could tell, completely normal in every respect.

He left the office shortly before six o'clock and was driven to Tolson's apartment, where he had dinner. Later, Moton drove him home, where they arrived at 10:15 P.M. Annie Fields, the housekeeper, did not hear him come in which was not unusual because she spent evenings in her apartment located in the basement.

Annie said Hoover customarily let his two shaggy Cairn terrier dogs run in the back yard after coming home late, and there was no evidence on the newspapers spread near where they slept to indicate they had not relieved themselves outside as usual. The two dogs were very attached to Hoover and the older, a male called "G Boy," died a few weeks after his master's death; the other, a female called "Cindy," moped, refused to eat and died a few months later.

The next morning, Annie had breakfast ready promptly at 7:30 A.M. in accordance with Hoover's strict routine. This day was an exception, because Hoover did not come down and as the minutes passed with no sound of activity from the bedroom upstairs, she began to worry. At exactly 7:45 A.M. Moton arrived with the limousine, several minutes early as always, ready to drive the Director to work. A few minutes later, James "Jimmy" Crawford arrived. Crawford had been Hoover's chauffeur for many years but he retired in December of 1971 after major surgery. Since his retirement, he had been hired by Hoover for odd jobs around the house. This morning he had come to plant some rose bushes which had arrived the day before from a west coast nursery with which Hoover did frequent business. Crawford had come early because he knew the "Boss" would want to mark exactly where each bush should be planted.

The three of them discussed the situation and together they decided that Annie should go upstairs and knock on the Director's door. This she did, gingerly at first, and then much louder. Still getting no answer, she tried the door. It was unlocked, which was very unusual, and slowly entering the bedroom Annie saw the man whom she had served for so many years stretched on the floor near the bed. She raced downstairs to get Crawford. He picked up Hoover's hand which was stiff and cold. He let the hand drop to the floor and then took a blanket from the bed to cover the body, certain that Hoover was dead. Crawford phoned Tolson and then sent Moton, with the limousine, to pick him up. Annie called the Director's office and advised Mrs. Metcalf who, in turn, called the Director's private physician, Dr. Robert Choisser, giving him the task of pronouncing Hoover dead when he arrived a short time later.

Shortly before eleven, John Mohr called Joseph Gawler's Funeral Home at Wisconsin Avenue and Harrison Street, N.W., which was close to the Hoover residence. As is customary in the case of dignitaries, Gawler's dispatched an unmarked car, specially constructed without a rear seat, so that a stretcher bearing a corpse can be placed in the rear and strapped into place. When the car approached the house, news photographers were so numerous that it was decided to enter the alley and go into the house from the back.

Because the coroner's representatives would not permit the body to be removed until the formal announcement from the White House had been made, it was not until 12:15 P.M. that the body was placed on a stretcher and carried through the back door, across the back yard and through the garage to the waiting car. Gawler's car left the house at 12:30 P.M.

John Mohr and Helen Gandy had been considering a Masonic funeral, but at 2:05 P.M. the White House called to advise that the President had decided upon a state funeral with full military honors. The body would lie in state in the Rotunda of the Capitol on May 3, and memorial services would be on May 4.

Mohr was in charge of coordinating the services but the military took over the ceremonial arrangements with precise efficiency and the combination produced one of the most impressive state funerals ever seen in Washington.

May 3, 1972, dawned gray and dismal and the light mist drifting down from the low-hanging clouds set a somber mood for the services in the Capitol Rotunda. The heavy casket was to be placed on the catafalque originally built for President Abraham Lincoln and used by only twenty-one American heroes and statesmen before Hoover. The hearse arrived in front of the Capitol building promptly at 11:30 A.M. The group of eight military pallbearers was ready. They lifted the casket out of the hearse and preceded by the Reverend Edward L.R. Elson, pastor of the National Presbyterian Church and Chaplain of the United States Senate, laboriously carried their burden up the long steps, where it was placed upon the catafalque in the center of the Rotunda.

Mohr confided to me later that he and Miss Gandy had not given any thought to the problem of carrying the casket up the Capitol steps and the one they selected was lead-lined and weighed well over 1,000 pounds. It must have been an incredible strain for the young men, two of whom suffered ruptures as they struggled up the long steps.

Services in the Rotunda were impressive. Hundreds of dignitaries were present to do homage to a great man. All the members of the FBI Executive Conference were there as honorary pallbearers and many others from the Bureau also attended. Chief Justice Warren E. Burger of the United States Supreme Court, whom Hoover had always regarded very highly, gave the eulogy. He said:

> From modest beginnings, he rose to the pinnacle of his profession and established a world-wide reputation that was without equal among those to whom societies entrust the difficult tasks relating to the enforcement of the laws. . . . He was a man of unyielding integrity and his standards of personal conduct pervaded the entire organization so that its incorruptibility matched its efficiency . . . his high standards produced the institution that is, in a very real sense, the lengthened shadow of a man. . . .

Thousands came to pay their final respects during the afternoon and evening. The closed casket led a few sensation-seeking writers to assume that Hoover died from some mysterious foul play, and to put an end to such speculation, once and for all, let me point out that the casket was open for all to see the preceding evening during visiting hours at Gawler's and there was not the slightest indication of foul play.

Late in the afternoon, as Mohr sat at his desk thinking of the heavy strain his lack of attention to detail had placed upon the military pallbearers, a visitor to his office was announced. It was L. Patrick Gray III.

Gray announced that he was there at the direction of the Attorney General to review the "secret" files. Mohr patiently explained that the FBI had no secret files he knew of and after a few remarks by both about the man whose body still lay in its casket on the catafalque in the Rotunda, Gray left, apparently satisfied.

The next morning, May 3, Gray returned to Mohr's office in a very agitated state, demanding to know where the secret files were kept. Again, Mohr, himself becoming somewhat agitated, firmly assured Gray there were no secret files. The conversation grew heated and the language became less and less formal. Mohr said later, "I guess I did cuss at him a little."

At this point, Gray stood, thrust out his chin and said, "Look, Mr. Mohr. I am a hard-headed Irishman and nobody pushes me around!".

Mohr also rose to his feet and in a loud voice, claimed to have been heard several doors away, said "Look, Mr. Gray, I am a hard-headed Dutchman and nobody pushes me around either."

Gray turned on his heel and left. Less than three hours later, Gray was appointed Acting FBI Director by Attorney General Richard Kleindienst. Within thirty minutes of the announcement of Gray's appointment, I received a telephone call from Tolson.

He said, "I want you to arrange for my retirement effective today!"

I asked, "Do you want to dictate the letter to Mrs. Skillman over the telephone?"

"No," he said, "I want you to write it. Make it short, nothing fancy. Have Mrs. Skillman sign my name to it."

"All right," I said. "I'll get it to Gray this afternoon and see that it is processed right away."

I wrote the letter and couched it in much softer terms than Tolson would have, had he dictated it himself. Having had considerable contact with Gray during the Kleindienst confirmation hearings, I didn't hesitate to call him directly. I told him what had happened and he was not surprised.

He said, "Write him a warm letter accepting his application for retirement. Commend him for his many fine years of service. Write it for my signature. Date it today." He paused for a moment and then went on, "I want to have a talk with you after the funeral and I'll sign it then."

"Fine," I replied, "I'll be available. Do you want me to come to your office over there or are you going to come here?"

"I'll come over there. There is something I want to ask about and also I want to look at the space in the Director's office."

"Glad to cooperate fully," I said. "I'll be here."

"Good," Gray replied, and hung up the phone.

I knew of Gray's encounter with John Mohr about the so-called secret files and I was sure he wanted to talk about this. Also, it was only logical that he would want to survey a new office which he had never seen.

All of this occurred on May 3, while Hoover's body lay in state in the Rotunda. There it remained through the night of the third. Early on the fourth it was removed by Gawler's and the military pallbearers to the National Presbyterian Church on Nebraska Avenue for the memorial services.

The services were a television spectacular, designed more to aggrandize the President than to honor the departed Director. Seating arrangements became a matter of critical concern because of television coverage. Original plans called for President and Mrs. Nixon and Acting Director Gray with his wife, Bea, to sit in the front pew on the left-hand side. The honorary pallbearers, consisting of myself, as Acting Associate Director, John Mohr and Alex Rosen, the two Assistants to the Director, and all the Assistant Directors to occupy the first two pews on the right.

Late in the afternoon of May 3, the newly appointed Acting Director Gray, bypassing Mohr, the "hard-headed Dutchman," called James Adams, Mohr's Assistant, and instructed that the seating assignment for Attorney General Kleindienst be changed. Originally scheduled to be sitting in the second row, left, with Vice President Spiro Agnew, Kleindienst wanted to sit in the first place in the first row, right, directly opposite the President, and, incidentally, directly in front of the television cameras. In view of Gray's new authority, his instructions were carried out and during the service the Attorney General sat with the honorary pallbearers.

In his eulogy, President Nixon said, "J. Edgar Hoover was one of the giants. His long life brimmed over with magnificent achievement and dedicated service to this country which he loved so well. . . . He became a living legend while still a young man and he lived up to his legend as the decades passed. . . . The greatness of Edgar Hoover will remain inseparable from the greatness of the organization he created and gave his whole life to building, the Federal Bureau of Investigation. He made the FBI the finest law enforcement agency on earth, the invincible and incorruptible defender of every American's precious right to be free from fear. . . . The United States is a better country because this good man lived his long life among us these past seventy-seven years. Each of us stands forever in his debt. In the years ahead, let us cherish his memory. Let us be true to his legacy. Let us honor him as he would surely want us to do, by honoring all the men and women who carry on in his noble profession by helping keep peace in our society. . . ."

After the service, we waited outside for the alignment of the funeral procession which was to take the body to Congressional Cemetery for graveside services and interment. The people who had not been able to be admitted to the church crowded around for a view of the casket. The procession was to consist of ten cars with a police motorcycle escort.

As we left the church grounds and turned onto Nebraska Avenue, there was an amazing sight. As far as the eye could see, there were solid lines of uniformed police officers on each side of the avenue. Many were from the Washington Metropolitan Police Department but others had come from surrounding areas. It was an unforgettable scene and I later learned it had been arranged by the military authorities.

Uniformed officers had been stationed at all intersections on Constitution and Pennsylvania Avenues. In Southeast Washington, the procession turned north on Potomac Avenue which led directly to the cemetery where Hoover's parents were buried. The neighborhood is residential and householders had come to the sidewalks to see the procession go by.

Later in the day when I went back to the office, I waited, curious to see what my new boss would have to say. He called a few minutes after three o'clock and asked if it would be convenient for him to come to see me.

I said, "I'll be glad to come to your office. Are you sure you wouldn't prefer that?"

"No," he replied, "I would rather come over there." He knew where my office was because of our conferences about the Dita Beard memorandum.

A few minutes later, he came in, extended his hand for a firm, cordial handshake, and sat down in the chair beside my desk.

I said, "Congratulations on your appointment as Acting Director. Frankly, most of us were hoping that the President would select an insider but I can assure you that all of us will do everything we can to help you." I was completely sincere but I don't believe Gray trusted the FBI officials at SOG.

He smiled and said, "Thank you, Mark. I'll need all the help I can get. I am greatly flattered by the appointment. I have always had an enormous respect for the FBI." (I know that Gray really came to love and admire the FBI and subsequent failure of his confirmation was a terrible disappointment to him.) Gray went on, "We will have a lot of things to talk about later, but today, the first thing I want to know about is the 'secret' files."

"Mr. Gray," I said, "the Bureau doesn't have any secret files. There are thousands and thousands of files with derogatory information in them, some of which was obtained through investigation of FBI cases and some of which was volunteered. There are files with extremely confidential and sensitive information about espionage investigations. Many of our files are classified 'Top Secret' or 'Confidential' under rules that govern all Government agencies."

"Mark, I'm not talking about the regular files. Everybody knows that Hoover had his own secret files containing derogatory data on important people."

"The FBI has files on many important people," I said. "A few may have been investigated for violation of some Federal statute but thousands have been investigated for high office in the Federal Government. The FBI has been requested by various Presidents to conduct full-field investigations on persons who may be considered for appointment, for example, to the Supreme Court or Cabinet positions. Some files involving important people might contain information that was unsolicited by the FBI. For instance, someone writes concerning a Congressman and complains about questionable activities which do not involve the violation of any state or Federal law.

The information would be retained in view of the possibility that the Bureau might be requested by a future President to investigate that particular Congressman for a high position. The questionable information, which did not previously concern the Bureau, would then become very important for Presidential consideration."

Gray stopped me. "I know all that, but what about the files that Hoover kept in his office?"

I tried hard to keep from becoming impatient. "He had hundreds of personal correspondence files which I have never viewed. He also sometimes kept Bureau files in his office which were so sensitive that he felt they should be kept on a 'Need-to-Know' basis so as not to be available to the curious eyes of any Agent or clerk who might come across them by chance."

Gray interjected, "Would he follow this practice if the information involved a high-placed person?"

"Sure, or the Bureau file might involve an extremely sensitive and delicate espionage investigation. We have a special file room where access is tightly limited and the cases there are mostly of a foreign intelligence nature. But, you see, all other files are kept in the Files Section and because every Bureau employee is cleared for 'Top Secret' access, there must be some exceptions and these are the files that might be in the Director's office."

Gray moved his head from side to side, thoughtfully. Obviously, he still had doubts.

"Mr. Gray, why don't we go over and look at the files in Hoover's office?"

Gray smiled and said, "Okay, let's go."

Both of us rose to our feet. I called one of the secretaries to let my office know where we would be. I escorted Gray to his new office and we talked pleasantly on the way over. When we arrived, I introduced him to the receptionists and then took him directly to Miss Gandy's office where I introduced him to Hoover's personal secretary of fifty-three years and to Erma Metcalf who shared the space. Gray was extremely charming and gracious to the two women.

I explained why we were there, namely that Gray wanted to see the so-called Hoover files and to have a tour of his new space.

Miss Gandy smiled and said, "Well, there they are," pointing to the ten five-drawer file cabinets which completely filled two walls of the small office. "Most of this material is Mr. Hoover's personal correspondence—some of it going back to when he first became Director. I am planning to pack up the personal correspondence in cardboard file boxes and ship it out to his house. Mr. Tolson instructed me to do that. He also said that all the Bureau files should be sent to Mr. Felt."

Gray looked casually at one open file drawer but made no further reference to these files. There was no indication that he was not completely satisfied with what Miss Gandy and I had explained. I then gave Mr. Gray a complete tour of the Director's space, starting with the private inner office which had been occupied for so long by Mr. Hoover.

"Mr. Gray," I said, "this furniture was obtained by Mr. Hoover when he first became Director. It is almost fifty years old. You may want to replace it."

"No," he replied. "I'd like to keep it just as it is."

We next walked through the large conference room. Gray instructed that the desk at one end of the room where Hoover posed for pictures with visitors and employees on their anniversaries of service be removed and I made a mental note to be sure that it would be done.

Walking through the space, we again came by Miss Gandy's office and Gray moved through the doorway to ask, "Miss Gandy, how much time will you need to clear out all of Mr. Hoover's things so that I can move in? I don't want to rush you."

"I think one week would be sufficient," she replied. "I don't want to keep you out of your new office any longer than I can help."

Gray paused a moment and then said, "Are you sure one week is enough? I'll plan on moving in on Friday the twelfth or Monday the fifteenth."

She replied, "That will be fine and I'll keep Mr. Felt posted on my progress."

We continued walking through the space and I introduced Gray to each staff member as we went along. He was extremely gracious and cordial to all.

When we had completed the tour, Gray said, "I am going to need at least one more room. Miss Gandy and Miss Edna Holmes have indicated that they intend to retire but I will be bringing four staff members with me and the two extra people will need space. See what you can do."

"I'll handle it. It should be contiguous space and I think I know where to get it."

"Fine," he replied. "Now, the next thing is that I want to address the Executive Conference this afternoon. It will just be a short meeting."

I looked at my watch; it was three-thirty. "How about four o'clock?" I asked.

"Four will be fine."

I said, "Okay, I'll set it up and I'll meet you in the Director's reception room exactly at four and take you to the Conference Room and introduce you."

We parted just outside the Director's reception room, Gray on his way back to his office in the Justice Department and I on my way back to my office to put wheels in motion to set up the Conference. Because of the tight time schedule, I instructed the secretaries to divide up the necessary calls and to ask all members of the Conference to be in the Director's Conference Room at 3:55 P.M.

Everything went smoothly and at three minutes to four, I was waiting outside the door to the reception room. Soon I could see Gray striding forcefully down the long corridor. My feelings were mixed. I was resentful that an outsider was taking over, yet at the same time, I was impressed with the strength and sincerity of this man. I determined to do everything I could to help him become a successful Director. My purpose was to preserve the FBI as I had known it for so many years and I felt this could best be done by helping the new Chief.

Greeting Gray at the door, I escorted him through the reception room, down the long corridor, past all the raised and curious female heads and into the Conference Room where the FBI officials were seated at the long conference table.

As we entered the room, everyone rose to his feet and I led Gray to the head of the table. I said simply, "Gentlemen, this is Mr. L. Patrick Gray III, the newly appointed Acting Director of the FBI." There was a round of applause before the officials resumed their seats waiting to hear what their new Boss would have to say.

Gray is an excellent speaker and his remarks on this occasion attested to that fact. He anticipated hostility and orchestrated his appearance toward this possibility. He praised the FBI as the "finest law enforcement agency in the world" and he complimented the dedication of the FBI officials who helped make it that way. He expressed sympathy and understanding of our feelings about the loss of a great leader and said he would not be surprised if we felt some misgivings about an outsider coming in. He explained that he would make changes and had to administer the FBI according to his own views but he was careful to say, "I want to maintain the FBI as an institution."

He said, "I intend to run the Bureau with patience, understanding and compassion." He appealed to us to help him meet the "serious challenges in the months ahead" and concluded by saying, "Thank you, gentlemen." Then he walked from the room alone.

As the group broke up there was considerable discussion and everything I heard was favorable to our new Boss.

CHAPTER FIFTEEN

> As long as I am Director of this Bureau, any attack upon an FBI employee who is conscientiously carrying out his official duties will be considered an attack upon me personally.
>
> —J. Edgar Hoover

Right after Pearl Harbor, the United States was seized by a kind of hysteria—and it was used by cynical or misguided Americans to perpetrate one of the most vicious and unnecessary acts in American history: the "relocation" of loyal Japanese-Americans—citizens all—to concentration camps. This action, which was accompanied by the seizure of their property—farms and shops and small business—at distress prices, was ordered by President Franklin D. Roosevelt and supported by such staunch liberals as Earl Warren, then California's Attorney General; Secretary of the U.S. Treasury Henry Morgenthau, Jr.; Walter Lippmann, a preacher of civil liberties; and the more vocal among the exponents of civil rights in both Congress and the press.

Charges by the United States Army that "more than 60,000 rounds of ammunition and many rifles, shotguns and maps of all kinds" had been found in raids on the Nisei were found to be based on "evidence" taken from one sporting goods shop and one warehouse. It was also widely reported that ships leaving one west coast port were attacked by Japanese submarines receiving their information from Nisei—which after careful investigation by the FBI was conclusively shown to be sheer fiction.

The one man of high rank in the Federal Government who sought to prevent this rape of the Constitution and of human rights was FBI Director J. Edgar Hoover. In discussions with Morgenthau and in a memorandum to Attorney General Francis Biddle, Hoover stated his opposition to any "dragnet" or "round-up" of people whose only offense was that their parents had emigrated from Japan and he vigorously argued that no action should be taken against them "unless there were specific actions upon which criminal complaints could be filed."

This is one side of the Director which, in his last days, was forgotten, if they ever knew it, by those who belabored him for his reputed insensitivity to civil liberties. They did not know and would not have cared that Hoover jeopardized his relations with the Nixon White House by categorically barring "black bag jobs" and drastically reducing the number of wiretaps and electronic surveillances, even in national security cases.

What this tells us about J. Edgar Hoover is that he was a very complex man. The media, whether it was building him up in the Thirties as the great gangbuster or tearing him down as a storm trooper in the late Sixties and early Seventies, were never able to see more than one side of this man. His associates and subordinates in the FBI saw him from a completely different perspective. People who met him socially took away still another impression. FDR was "delighted" by what Hoover accomplished and Attorney General Biddle, although admittedly ambivalent, felt something akin to affection for Hoover. Reflecting on what Biddle had written about the Hoover of the Forties, William Ruckelshaus would say in the Seventies, "Really, the man had only one motive. That was to make the FBI the finest investigative organization in the world."

I can only testify to the J. Edgar Hoover I knew as I moved up the FBI pyramid. One of the first things I learned about him during the years when I saw him daily was that he was

FBI Academy at Quantico, Virginia, as it looked when the author attended training school in 1942. *Official FBI photograph*

FBI Academy at Quantico, Virginia. *Official FBI photograph*

The author on the firearms range of Salt Lake City, Utah.

Deseret News, Salt Lake City, Utah

Standards of weight, height and build under Hoover, since greatly relaxed by Gray.

HEIGHT	SMALL FRAME	MEDIUM FRAME	LARGE FRAME
5'4"	117-125	123-135	131-148
5'5"	120-129	126-139	134-152
5'6"	124-133	130-143	138-157
5'7"	128-137	134-148	143-162
5'8"	132-141	138-152	147-166
5'9"	136-146	142-156	151-170
5'10"	140-150	146-161	155-175
5'11"	144-154	150-166	160-180
6'	148-158	154-171	164-185
6'1"	152-163	158-176	169-190
6'2"	156-167	163-181	174-195
6'3"	160-171	168-186	178-200
6'4"	169-180	178-196	188-210
6'5"	174-185	182-202	192-216

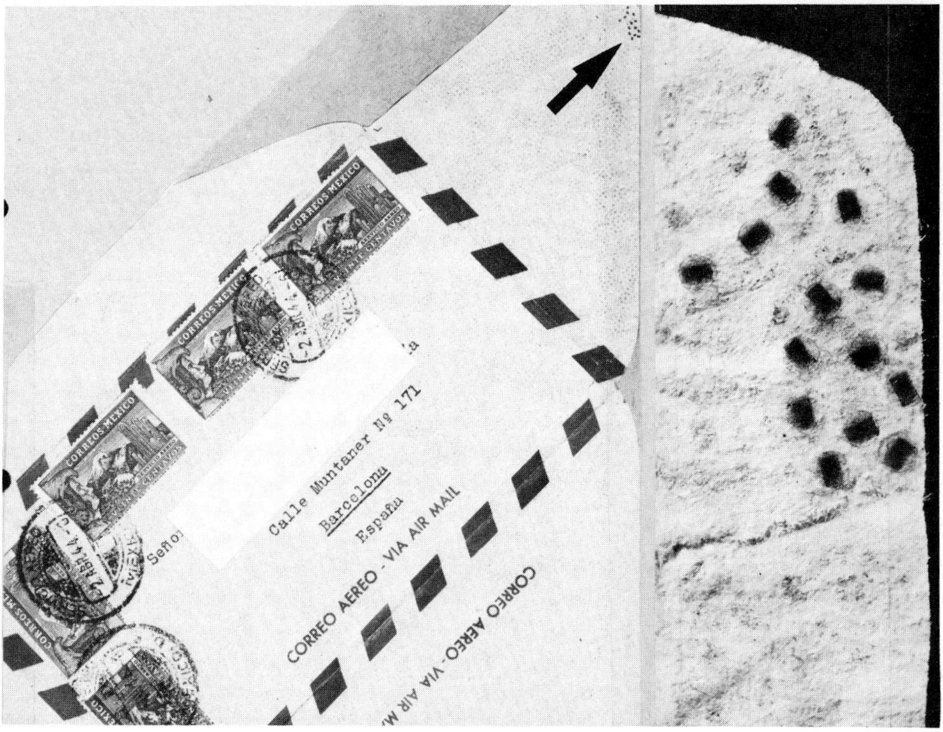

Actual photograph of German microdot letter.

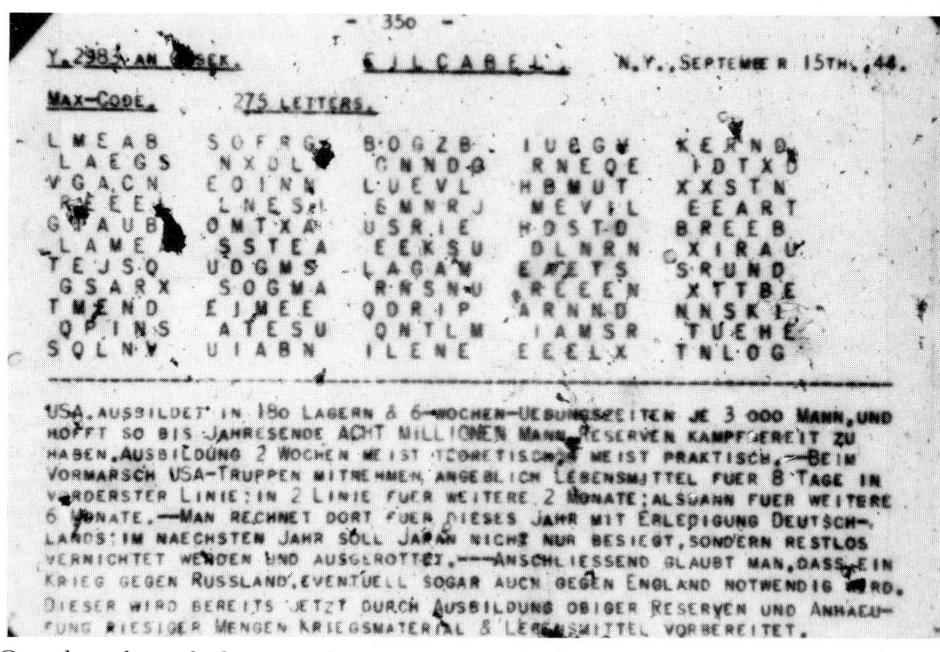

\- 350 -

Y. 2983 AN [illegible]. [illegible]. N.Y., SEPTEMBER 15TH, 44.

MAX-CODE. 275 LETTERS.

LMEAB SOFRG BOGZB IUBGW KERND
LAEGS NXOL[illegible] CNNDQ RNEQE IDTXD
VGACN EOINN LUEVL HBMUT XXSTN
[illegible]EEE[illegible] LNES[illegible] EMNRJ MEVIL EEART
G[illegible]AUB OMTXA USRIE HOSTO BREEB
LAME[illegible] SSTEA EEKSU OLNRN XIRAU
TEJSQ UDGMS LAGAW E[illegible]ETS SRUND
GSARX SOGMA RNSNU RECEEN XTTBE
TMEND EJMEE QORIP ARNND NNSKI
QPINS ATESU QNTLM IAMSR TUEHE
SQLNV UIABN ILENE EEELX TNLOG

USA. AUSBILDET IN 180 LAGERN & 6-WOCHEN-UEBUNGSZEITEN JE 3 000 MANN, UND HOFFT SO BIS JAHRESENDE ACHT MILLIONEN MANN RESERVEN KAMPFBEREIT ZU HABEN. AUSBILDUNG 2 WOCHEN MEIST TEORETISCH, [illegible] MEIST PRAKTISCH. — BEIM VORMARSCH USA-TRUPPEN MITNEHMEN, ANGEBLICH LEBENSMITTEL FUER 8 TAGE IN VORDERSTER LINIE; IN 2 LINIE FUER WEITERE 2 MONATE; ALSDANN FUER WEITERE 6 MONATE. — MAN RECHNET DORT FUER DIESES JAHR MIT ERLEDIGUNG DEUTSCHLANDS; IM NAECHSTEN JAHR SOLL JAPAN NICHT NUR BESIEGT, SONDERN RESTLOS VERNICHTET WERDEN UND AUSGEROTTET. — ANSCHLIESSEND GLAUBT MAN, DASS EIN KRIEG GEGEN RUSSLAND, EVENTUELL SOGAR AUCH GEGEN ENGLAND NOTWENDIG WIRD. DIESER WIRD BEREITS JETZT DURCH AUSBILDUNG OBIGER RESERVEN UND ANHAEUFUNG RIESIGER MENGEN KRIEGSMATERIAL & LEBENSMITTEL VORBEREITET.

Greatly enlarged photograph of a German microdot. *Official FBI photograph*

Loyalty

If you work for a man, in heaven's name work for him; speak well of him and stand by the institution he represents.

Remember -- an ounce of loyalty is worth a pound of cleverness.

If you must growl, condemn, and eternally find fault, why -- resign your position and when you are on the outside, damn to your heart's content -- but as long as you are a part of the institution do not condemn it, if you do, the first high wind that comes along will blow you away, and probably you will never know why.

Elbert Hubbard

J. Edgar Hoover had a copy of this framed and hanging in every field office.

Author while serving as Special Agent in Charge of the Kansas City FBI Office. Assistant Agent in Charge Paul Stoddard standing by.

Author and Inspection Crew during inspection of New York Office.

January 26, 1967. Author and his wife were photographed with J. Edgar Hoover following the presentation of the author's 25-year Service Award Key.

October 22, 1971. Author with J. Edgar Hoover at cocktail party preceding dinner in Hoover's honor given by the Washington, D.C., Chapter of the Society of Former Special Agents of the FBI.

Author and Mrs. Felt with J. Edgar Hoover at same occasion.

J. Edgar Hoover

Author with his two assistants in the Office of Associate Director. Left to right, Inspectors Harold N. Bassett and Wason G. Campbell.

Author's appearance on Firing Line.

Southern Educational Communications Association

Author (center) greeted by 1,200 agents and former agents on steps of United States Court House, Washington, D.C., on day of his arraignment.

Washington Post

not the insensitive and irascible man that antagonistic writers painted. When crossed or aroused, he could indeed be scorching and even vindictive, but on most occasions his compassion made it necessary for him to screen himself from subordinates in his FBI world. He was, as I quickly discovered, a soft touch to the right personal approach—and knowing this he insisted that most of his official contacts be in writing since it was much easier for him to be firm that way. This is undoubtedly one of the reasons why he kept his personal life completely separated from his office life.

Hoover was protective not only of the Bureau but of Bureau employees. An example occurred when former Governor Grant Sawyer of Nevada criticized an FBI action. When Hoover reacted sharply to set the record straight, Sawyer stated that he had not intended to attack the FBI or Hoover personally. He said that his remarks had been intended only for the local FBI office. Hoover quickly responded, "Let me reiterate my oft-stated position that as long as I am Director of this Bureau, any attack upon an FBI employee who is conscientiously carrying out his official duties will be considered an attack on me personally."

Hoover led a life closely circumscribed by the set schedule patterns which he had developed during the years. He seldom left his desk and on his few vacation trips he kept in constant touch by telephone, including weekends. I know from personal observation at close quarters that he was always fully aware of all the workings of the complex FBI machine which he directed—something his successors have not been able to do. This is not to say that Hoover had no sense of humor or that he did not fully appreciate the pleasures of good dining and visits to the race track in which he indulged himself.

Hoover loved his house, his yard and garden and his dogs. The house was maintained with meticulous care. All of the modest collectors' items and memorabilia were always carefully dusted and in their proper places. Well aware of his collector's tastes, Sloan's Auction House on 13th Street, Northwest, in downtown Washington, frequently alerted him to sale items in which he might be interested—and usually he was. Hoover's home did not look ornate—it looked lived-in, as indicated by the lounge chair on the decking off his bedroom where he took sun baths when Sunday weather permitted.

He took great personal interest in his yard and garden and personally selected the numerous shrubs which were planted there from time to time. He even had a small garden plot, about seven by ten feet, and he took great pride in the tomatoes which his gardener helped him to grow.

Hoover was very fond of his two Cairn dogs and indulged them to the extent that their careless toilet habits occasionally required new linoleum on the kitchen floor and finally artificial turf in the back yard. Detractors have claimed that taxpayers paid for the artificial turf but this is not true. Hoover paid for it and also put up with a lot of kidding about it from his friends.

J. Edgar Hoover was one of the most self-disciplined men I have ever known and he expected the same degree of control from those who worked for him. This insistence that others measure up to the standards which he set for himself gave him a reputation for being an inflexible martinet. But he was not the humorless bureaucrat that some believed him to be. He could and did tell stories about himself in which he was the butt. One of the best of his stories was his account of a visit to Alcatraz prison in which he bought a canary from the Bird Man, one of the prisoners, as a present for his mother. It turned out to be a sparrow dyed yellow—and Hoover always laughed the hardest when retelling the story.

The truth is that with his close personal associates, Hoover was known as a prankster. He liked to play tricks on friends and sometimes went to great lengths, even to the extent of using FBI personnel to help set the stage. In earlier days, he joked and kidded with close FBI associates but as the years went by he became more and more distant from his staff. I was present on one occasion when he played a joke on one of the top Bureau officials who had some difficulty meeting Bureau weight standards. The occasion was at an FBI reception for an official of the Royal Canadian Mounted Police held at the Army-Navy Club. The affair was attended by twenty Bureau officials and the guest of honor. After a thirty-minute period to allow everyone an opportunity to take advantage of the open bar, Hoover and Tolson arrived. They were served drinks—Jack Daniels and water for Hoover and Johnnie Walker Red Label scotch and soda for Tolson—while they chatted with the guest. Drink consumed, Hoover took the center of the floor and made a short speech of welcome to our friend from the North to which the guest responded with a few appropriate words of his own. Hoover and Tolson thereupon left the scene and all felt free to return to the open bar and to partake of the hors d'oeuvres.

Among the first to reach the table of food was the slightly heavy FBI official who proceeded to make himself a large sandwich. Then an unheard of thing happened. Hoover and Tolson returned to the room and made directly for the food area. Accosting the official who stood frozen with the sandwich halfway to his mouth, Hoover said, "Ahha! I knew that when I left the room you would be the first to reach the food." With that, he turned and strode from the room, Tolson at his heels. After a few seconds of shocked silence, everyone roared with laughter.

Personally and officially, he was a frugal man and this allowed him to build up an estate which was appraised at more than a half-million dollars, including his house and personal property. His investments were conservative and he was primarily concerned with the amount of dividends paid. This, of course, is little compared to what he could have earned had he left the Government. The offers were there, from the corporate heads who courted him. But repeatedly, he turned down fabulous executive positions including one from the late Howard Hughes, who told Hoover he could name his own salary.

He had political opportunities which he scorned. On October 12, 1955, Joseph P. Kennedy, father of former President John F. Kennedy, wrote Hoover as follows:

Dear Edgar,

You sent me a personal note on June 7 which I saw on my return to the United States a week or so ago. I gave my office hell for not sending it to me but they said my final instructions were "not to bother you with any mail or messages for three months." So that's what happened. I want to thank you for your most kind and generous remarks.

I think I have become too cynical in my old age but the only two men that I know in public life today for whose opinion I give one continental both happen to be named Hoover—one John Edgar and one Herbert—and I am proud to think that both of them hold me in some esteem. I am all even on all the rest.

I listened to Walter Winchell mention your name as a candidate for President. If that should come to pass, it would be the most wonderful thing for the United States, and whether you were on a Republican or Democratic ticket, I would guarantee you the largest contribution that you would ever get from anybody and the hardest work by either a Democrat or Republican. I think the United States deserves you. I only hope it gets you.

My best to you always.

Sincerely,
JOE

Hoover respected the taxpayers from whose pocket FBI funds were appropriated. The FBI budget was one of the most tightly controlled in the Government and Hoover was perhaps the only administrator in Washington history to return unexpended funds to the Treasury at the end of the fiscal year. "I must explain every item in our budget and how the money is used," he once said. "I never want any secret fund, a lump-sum appropriation for which I don't have to account. I want to account for every cent because an unexplained fund is dangerous." Hoover's economies resulted in an atmosphere at every level of the Bureau which produced respect for the taxpayers' money.

Hoover was the complete Director—self-assured and totally in command. He had no ambition to rise politically and repeatedly fought off attempts to expand the FBI's jurisdiction beyond what he knew were its capabilities. He knew the political game and played it to the hilt in his relations with

Presidents, Attorneys General, and the Congress, but his goal never went beyond greater independence for the FBI—and for himself as its creator and Director. He basked in the power and the adulation which his position brought and in the perquisites which went with it. I am sure he was proud and pleased to be the only official besides the President to have an armored limousine. This extra protection for Hoover was provided when he personally led raids against gangsters in the Thirties and as a result received numerous threats against his life. He was continually a recipient of threats.

Critics of J. Edgar Hoover forget that he was called in to clean out a corrupt and politics-ridden Bureau of Investigation. This was not only because of his reputation for efficiency and administrative ability but also because of a moral streak in him—a morality which was basically puritanical. He would tolerate no financial or sexual looseness among his subordinates—once firing a male clerical employee who had allowed his girl friend to spend the night with him. But he carried his morality well beyond this. His difficulty in adjusting to the Kennedy Administration stemmed partly from his scorn of JFK's philandering. Personality differences set up a barrier with Attorney General Robert F. Kennedy, and Hoover's refusal to accept the alleged affair with Marilyn Monroe added to the antagonism. The famous confrontation with Dr. Martin Luther King was a direct result of Hoover's disgust when he learned of the civil rights leader's marathon sexual and drunken exploits.

One of the Director's outstanding assets was his practice of making up his mind quickly and decisively. Because of the energy with which he pursued all official business, he frequently moved abruptly—and major changes, policy decisions, and high-level transfers were made with sometimes terrifying speed. Many of Hoover's directives, as well as some of his outbursts, were written in bright blue ink in his angular hand at the bottom of memoranda and correspondence which crossed his desk. The language of these commentaries was always perfectly proper but it could be nonetheless blistering. These outspoken expressions of Hoover's views were never meant to be seen outside of the FBI but they are coming to light under the sweep of the Freedom of Information Act which is destroying all the confidentiality of the Bureau's business and operations. For outsiders who had invited his wrath, Hoover would use such words as "jackal," "scurrilous," or "mental halitosis." Insiders could be put in their place by having their ideas branded as "ridiculous" or "atrocious." On one Hiss case memorandum, at a time when one Congressman Richard M. Nixon seemed to be going in both directions, Hoover wrote, "I wish this young man would make up his mind."

When FBI veterans tried to cope with Hoover's use of marginal notes by planning their controversial memoranda so that there was little space on the sides and bottoms on which he could make his caustic comments, Hoover would then resort to his memo pad to be sure his views were fully and succinctly set forth.

Another characteristic of Hoover was that he had a "memory like an elephant." He never forgot or forgave what he regarded as a "cheap shot" at himself or the Bureau. He explained this to me one time saying, "It depends on whether something comes from the heart or the head." He could rail against a mistake but once convinced it was an honest error of judgment or even a stupid action repented, he could forgive. He would never forgive what he regarded as a malicious attack.

To be sure, Hoover had his idiosyncrasies and there was no other way for insiders but to learn to live with them. For example, he would not tolerate tardiness. Outsiders could expect appointments at a specific date and time and would be received with great punctuality. But for Agents desiring to see him, Hoover would seldom set a time and they were merely placed on the "appointment list" which was open-ended. Hoover would see them at his convenience and it was up to them to be available near a designated phone of their choosing in Bureau Headquarters. To insure they did not miss their appointments, the Agents came in to the office no later than the Director, ate lunch when he did, and waited until he had left in the evening before ending their vigil. This stand-by alert could last for several days and did nothing for the nerves of those who wanted to see him. One Field official was unavailable when Hoover called for him. He was unmoved by the young man's explanation and apology and ordered him passed over for promotion—although, as in the case of many of the Director's more Draconian moves, he later relented and placed the young man back on the promotional ladder.

Questions have been raised as to Hoover's soundness of mind in the last years of his tenure. Having seen him at work until the very end, I can say flatly that he was bright, alert, and vigorous right until the day of his death. I never saw any sign of mental or physical weakness—or of any flagging in the energy and uncanny memory for details in memoranda which had crossed his desk days or years before. One reason for this was that he took very good care of himself. He had regular annual physical examinations and every morning Valerie Stewart, the chief nurse of the FBI Health Service, gave him an injection of multiple vitamins. He also kept abreast of medical developments and I recall several occasions when he mentioned articles which he had read relating to such matters. He insisted that I eat one banana each day as an excellent source of potassium which, he assured me was "good for your heart."

The idea that Hoover was brisk in his manner and always to the point in his conversations with FBI officials was not entirely true. Once I had gained his confidence, he would sometimes digress from the business at hand to chat at length about other matters. He was particularly worried about the health of his closest friend and associate, Clyde Tolson, and he often discussed this with me. Once he told me that he had suggested to Tolson that he set up a punching bag in a corner of his office so that he might hit it when he felt tense and wanted to relieve his frustrations, He wasn't really serious but he said to me, "I can leave my problems behind when I leave the office at night. Tolson can't and he needs to get rid of his tensions." In the talks we had, I got the impression that Hoover was lonely and wanted someone in whom he could confide.

As the attacks on the Director mounted and became increasingly shrill and unfair, that loneliness grew—and one of its concomitants was a fear that his life's work, the FBI, was being destroyed, His sense of public relations, which had been among the best, sometimes deserted him and he lashed out as he never would have done in the past. Yet in his day-to-day work he remained as methodical as ever. He never relaxed the demands on himself or on the Bureau.

To the very end, his charm and graciousness with women and children remained with him. Wives left his office all aglow when they were received with Agent husbands who had been congratulated by the Director for an anniversary or for a job well done. This happened to my wife, Audrey, on three occasions. She accompanied me to Hoover's office for a short picture-taking ceremony on both my twenty-fifth and thirtieth anniversaries of Bureau service. At both times he was highly complimentary of me but he spoke to her when I was out of hearing distance. In October of 1971, when Audrey and I attended a private reception before the Silver Anniversary Dinner-Dance of the Society of Former FBI Agents, Hoover kissed her on the cheek and, as she later told me, said, "Your husband has been of tremendous help to me."

Another of those captivated by the Hoover charm was Martha Mitchell, wife of the then Attorney General, and their relationship was one of mutual admiration. (She called him "Jedgar.") At her invitation, Hoover made one of his rare public appearances, at the American Newspaperwomen's Club in May of 1971. In her introduction, Mrs. Mitchell paid tribute to Hoover's many years of service by quipping, "When you have seen one FBI Director, you have seen them all." There followed a standing ovation.

Hoover, whose caricature had just appeared on the cover of *Life* magazine as a Roman emperor, replied, "I know that those of you who regularly subscribe to an alleged national magazine may have had some difficulty recognizing me in the conventional clothes I am wearing this evening. But like ordinary people we 'emperors' do have our problems, and I regret to say that my toga did not get back from the cleaners on time."

I have often heard Hoover talk at informal gatherings of Bureau officials and foreign liaison representatives and was always impressed by his impromptu wit and fluency. I later learned that like other famous men—including comedians such as Bob Hope—he carefully prepared these off-the-cuff remarks and memorized them for "spontaneous" delivery.

There is no point in avoiding the allegations that Hoover was a homosexual. These innuendoes were based on his confirmed bachelorhood and his close association with Clyde Tolson. A New York newspaper, which for years had aimed a steady fire at Hoover, assigned reporters to "prove" the charge but after failing to find any corroboration, it dropped the story and circulated that it had done so because of threats from the Bureau. I never heard of any such threats and I never saw any indication of homosexual tendencies in Hoover. To my knowledge, neither did any of my colleagues in the FBI. Hoover was married to his job—the FBI and his home were his all-consuming interests. He could have retired on full pay but he chose to remain. He did have a close association with Tolson. They conferred frequently during the day and they invariably ate lunch together, most often at the Mayflower Hotel. On Wednesday they had dinner at Tolson's apartment, on Friday at Hoover's house. Their only vice was going to the races on Saturdays when the horses were running and where Hoover almost consistently lost his two-dollar bets.

That association was not without its rifts. As he did with all other high-level subordinates from time to time, Hoover occasionally became displeased with Tolson. Other officials in the Hoover "dog house" had to put up with being bypassed in the daily business of the Bureau until he cooled off. With Tolson the strain was much more severe because he was constantly in direct contact with Hoover "letting off steam."

I know from my talks with Hoover that he was genuinely fond of Tolson, as an older brother might be. He looked after him and worried about his precarious state of health.

An aggressive and energetic man, Hoover could keep several feuds going at once—and he enjoyed it. He was certainly stubborn. In matters of internal Bureau discipline, his own blue-inked notations in personnel files often refreshed his recollection of unpleasant things past—but in most instances he forgave and forgot. With me, Hoover was always fair and even-handed, and I have no bad memories of the years, even though exhausting, I spent working for him. But with some others, there were times when he overreacted, sometimes over trivial matters. He would insist on disciplinary action even when the Administrative Division cautioned that it might be reversed on appeal to the Civil Service Commission or the courts, depending upon the status of the employee.

There was, for example, the case of the young clerk who refused to cut his hair to meet Bureau standards. After repeated instructions to the clerk brought no results, Hoover's patience wore out and he ordered the clerk's dismissal. The clerk took the matter to court which ordered him reinstated with back pay—and long hair. Hoover took this in stride. Fortunately, Hoover was no longer there when the clerk refused to wear a necktie in an area visited by the public.

Attempts to go over Hoover's head for any personnel action short of dismissal were, however, most foolhardy. In Hoover's eyes, this marked a malcontent to be watched and distrusted forever. On the other hand, acceptance of disciplinary action in good spirit was a decided plus and could actually help an employee's standing with him.

Hoover was an absolute tyrant on three points. An error of any sort, even a typographical mistake, in an outgoing communication was a sin punishable by censure. A second inviolate rule was that all incoming communications from outside the Bureau had to be acknowledged within twenty-four hours. This seems like an unduly harsh rule but Hoover explained, "It is like a clock. It can run on time or it can run slow but the number of hours in the day will always be the same." He was right. Once the twenty-four-hour rule was in effect it was just as easy to handle the mail on time as to handle it late—perhaps easier. The third point was that Hoover insisted on courtesy and promptness in answering telephone calls from the outside. The calls had to be answered before the fourth ring. Never was an operator to inquire, "Who is calling?"

This chapter would not be complete without mention of the allegations of corruption in the FBI under J. Edgar Hoover. Hoover was the primary target of these allegations that he used Bureau materials and Bureau personnel for work at his home. Unfortunately, Hoover is no longer here to defend himself and the Bureau in his own inimitable and very vigorous fashion.

This all began when an employee of the FBI Laboratory reported that the FBI favored the U.S. Recording Company of Washington, D.C., by purchasing equipment from that company at higher prices than would have been paid had the Bureau gone directly to the manufacturer. When the matter first came up, internal FBI inquiries determined that such use of a "cut out" was not only proper but commonplace when the purpose was to conceal for security reasons the type of electronic equipment being purchased by Government Intelligence agencies.

The matter would have rested there had it not been that former Congresswoman Bella Abzug was not satisfied with responses from former FBI officials who testified before her Congressional Subcommittee on Government Operations. According to my sources, Mrs. Abzug carried her complaint to Attorney General Edward H. Levi and informed him that if he did not reopen the investigation into alleged FBI corruption she would do so before her Subcommittee. Thus pressured, Levi hastily reimbursed the Bureau for the cost of installing locks on doors at his residence by FBI Agents and then reopened the corruption probe.

No improprieties were found in connection with FBI purchases from the U.S. Recording Company or any other company. The Department neglected to point out that most of the purchases had been approved in writing by prior Attorneys General pursuant to Government regulations.

The investigation did turn up some questionable perquisites on the part of a few FBI officials, including the former Director. One FBI official was asked to resign and was charged with a misdemeanor for using Bureau scrap material to build a bird house for his yard. Another was asked to resign, which he did, when it was found he used Government funds for FBI public relations activities when such funds were not authorized or appropriated for such purposes. Leaks to the press hinted that these expenditures were for lavish meals in exclusive Washington restaurants for the benefit of FBI officials. When the facts were in, the dinners turned out to be rather circumspect entertainment of foreign intelligence agency heads, paid for out of funds which had not been earmarked by Congress for such purposes. There was no corruption or diversion of funds for personal use as was intimated.

But the real target of the probe, started by Levi and continued with great enthusiasm by Attorney General Griffin Bell, was J. Edgar Hoover. It was alleged that Bureau personnel and materials were frequently used for work done at the Hoover residence. The allegation was half true—Bureau personnel did do maintainance and installation work at Hoover's home. In every instance, however, Hoover meticulously paid for the cost of materials.

In its final report to the public, the Justice Department left the impression that these services for Hoover were improper. Not once did the report mention that as head of America's counterespionage apparatus it would have been extremely unwise to have allowed non-Bureau workmen into his home who might have installed microphones for Soviet or Soviet bloc countries. Never did the report mention that Hoover had numerous threats against his life which necessitated unusual precautions. Never was it mentioned that Hoover paid for materials.

Hoover was neither the paragon that his admirers proclaimed nor the ogre that his detractors held up to scorn. He was a sincere human being somewhere between the two extremes but with real greatness. He demanded loyalty but gave it in equal measure. He was given neither to false modesty nor to overbearing conceit. When the press was full of stories that he was being pushed out of office, he could read with wry satisfaction the epigraph to a widely circulated story:

> Nixon: I wanted to see you to discuss with you the matter of retirement.
>
> Hoover: Why, that's ridiculous. You're still a young man.

As long as I knew him, J. Edgar Hoover kept a little plaque on his desk. It was headed "The Penalty of Leadership," and it read:

> In every field of human endeavor, he that is first must perpetually live in the white light of publicity. The reward is widespread recognition, the punishment, fierce denial and detraction. When a man's work becomes a target of the envious few . . . That which is good or great makes itself known, no matter how loud the clamor of denial. That which deserves to live, lives.

Charismatic, feisty, charming, petty, giant, grandiose, brilliant, egotistical, industrious, formidable, compassionate, domineering—all these adjectives were applied to Hoover and, to a degree, they all fitted him. He had both wide recognition and detraction—and he accepted this. He was a human being.

In a time when patriotism was unfashionable, it could be said of him that he loved and believed in America. His contribution to his country was the Federal Bureau of Investigation which he fashioned into a great organization. His mortal remains lie under a modest headstone barely visible in the neglected tangle of wild grape, weeds, and fallen branches which mark Congressional Cemetery in Southeast Washington. A much more fitting recognition is his name emblazoned over the entrance to the tremendous new FBI Headquarters Building. But the real monument to his genius and dedication is the Federal Bureau of Investigation which, beleaguered though it has been, will survive and be strong because the Nation desperately needs it.

CHAPTER SIXTEEN

The President is coming on the line . . .

—Charles Colson
Nixon Advisor

In J. Edgar Hoover's last days, pressure to force him out was building up. Fed by Bill Sullivan, detractors seized upon any episode, any controversial issue, which might put the Director in a bad light. And there were leaks from the White House that President Nixon was dissatisfied with a Bureau which refused to accept political dictation. These stories came from H.R. Haldeman, John Ehrlichman, and John Dean primarily. They were angry at Hoover's refusal to be a "team player" in the Dita Beard case and during the machinations over the Huston Plan. They hinted that Hoover was "too old," that he no longer "controlled" the FBI, and that morale was low.

The President, however, had ambivalent feelings when there were discussions about Hoover in the top White House echelons. He would have liked a Director who was in his pocket but at the same time he was aware that Hoover still had a very large following in, and strong support from, the Congress. He was ready to bide his time, hoping for Hoover's death or some disabling illness to solve his problem. While he waited, however, Nixon made no moves to find or prepare a successor. His choice would have been Jerry Wilson, but the former chief of the Washington Metropolitan Police Department had been badly tarnished by his handling of the May

Day demonstrations in 1971, when several thousand anti-war protesters were rounded up and herded into an improvised jail.*

White House aides preferred Joseph Woods, former Sheriff of Cook Country, Illinois but there was a disqualifier there too. He was the brother of Rose Mary Woods, Nixon's personal secretary, and it was feared that to appoint him would smack of nepotism, politics, or both. Attorney General Kleindienst came up with a compromise. Exactly 26 hours and ten minutes after he had announced Hoover's death, the President named a World War II submarine commander, lawyer, minor Connecticut politico, and Assistant Attorney General—L. Patrick Gray III—to be the Acting Director of the FBI.

At the Bureau, the feeling had been strong that Nixon would appoint someone from the ranks to succeed Hoover and I have already mentioned that the thought more than crossed my mind that I might receive the appointment. I was next in line, my FBI record was very good, and I felt and I was both liked and respected by the rank and file. Another logical candidate was John P. Mohr, Assistant to the Director in charge of all administrative operations. Before DeLoach had elbowed him out of the Number Three position, Mohr had served with distinction in this spot—and it had only been his hard-headed Dutchman manner which had earned him Hoover's displeasure. Mohr also had influential contacts outside the Bureau—something which I lacked.

But Richard Nixon wanted someone from the outside who would be his man, someone with no ties and no first loyalties to the FBI. In the spring of 1972, Gray was awaiting confirmation by the Senate for the position of Deputy Attorney General. In addition, he had been the Number One candidate for

*As a matter of record, Hoover was appalled by this. When Bill Sullivan urged that the Bureau retain the fingerprint cards of the 12,000 people arrested, he was opposed by Assistant Director Leonard M. Walters, who was in charge of the Identification Division. Sullivan argued that these prints would help identify future enemies of the United States. Foreseeing that the charges against most of the protesters would be dropped, Walters urged that the cards be returned to the police. Hoover agreed with Walters and the cards were returned.

an opening on the United States Court of Appeals in the southern district of New York.

Gray had been named Deputy Attorney General-Designate by Nixon in a move to consolidate the Presidential hold on the Justice Department. From the standpoint of White House insiders, he was the ideal candidate to take over the FBI and to end what they felt was the lack of responsiveness at the top of the Bureau pyramid. A great public relations campaign was mounted, however, to create the impression that the Gray appointment was non-partisan and non-political. It was presented as an interim appointment until the November election. As a White House spokesman put it, the President did not want the appointment to become "involved in partisan politics" as the campaign heated up. When questioned about the choice, Ron Ziegler, the President's press secretary, said, "I think you will find that Patrick Gray is not a political man."

Gray had no intimation that he was Nixon's choice when, on May 3, he received a call from Attorney General Kleindienst and was told to be at his office at 2:15 P.M. because "we're going to the White House." Gray thought that there had been a new development in the ITT matter but as he walked in the Attorney General's reception room, he was given the news by Ralph Erickson, the Justice Department's legal counsel. "I was stunned," Gray recalled. "I thought he was joking. I said, 'Come on, Erickson! Give me the straight scoop!' " It was not until he was in Nixon's presence that he really believed the news. "The President talked to me about the importance of the job and the fact that it had to be non-political," Gray said. "The President also told me that 'ours has not been a political relationship—ours is a professional relationship based on mutual respect.' "

What was his background?

Louis Patrick Gray III was born in St. Louis on July 18, 1916, and educated at Rice University in Houston. Appointed to the United States Naval Academy at Annapolis, he graduated as a commissioned line officer in the Navy. He served throughout World War II and the Korean war as a submarine commander and as commander of a submarine flotilla. While still in the service, he attended George Washington University School of

Law, receiving his degree in 1949. In June of 1960, he retired from the Navy (he had been serving as the assistant to the Joint Chiefs of Staff) to join the personal campaign staff of Richard Nixon whom he had known casually since 1947. After Nixon's defeat, Gray went into private law practice in New London, Connecticut. During the 1968 Presidential campaign, Gray again worked for Nixon. His reward was a job as executive secretary to Robert H. Finch, Nixon's first Secretary of Health, Education and Welfare. In 1970, he left government service to return to his law firm in Connecticut, and in December of that year was appointed Assistant Attorney General in charge of the Civil Division.

During the first week of his tenure as FBI Director, Gray continued to occupy his old space in the Justice Department, waiting for Helen Gandy to pack up Hoover's personal effects and memorabilia and to vacate the office in which Hoover had worked for so many years. During the time, Gray had many conferences with FBI officials but it was impossible to get his attention for more than a few minutes at a time. I probably had more talks with Gray than anyone else in the Bureau and he asked me to stay on to run the day-to-day operations. To provide transitional continuity, I agreed to this.

During one of our first talks, Gray discussed the possibility of using Military Air Command planes when he visited various Field Offices. Trained in Hoover's kind of budget management, I argued against the use of MAC because of the tremendous cost. But Gray insisted that the President did not want the Acting Director of the FBI to risk being hijacked and ending up in Cuba where he would be interrogated with sodium pentothal. I prepared a memorandum for him, emphasizing the costs, and I was convinced that when Gray saw the astronomical figures, he would change his mind. But Gray simply bypassed me and asked the Administrative Division to make the necessary arrangements. Before his short tenure was over, Gray was using MAC on a weekly basis, frequently starting out the week from New London, the nearest airport to his home in nearby Stonington. Gray visited every Field Office with the exception of Honolulu. Total costs of his use of the Military Air Command came to almost $200,000 during his term as Acting Director.

Gray made no secret of his intention to "woo the Field," as he put it. His set speech at every Field Office was calculated to ingratiate himself with Field personnel and he was successful because he told the Agents what they wanted to hear. Again and again, he promised to relax Hoover's rigid standards—which he did. But, as my friends in the Field reported to me, the effect was to drive a wedge between the Field personnel and Headquarters.

His first formal appearance took place on May 10, when he called all the SACs to Washington. The following day, the first regular meeting of the Executive Conference under Gray was held in the Director's conference room. This conference was more for publicity than for official business. Representatives of the media had been invited from all parts of the country to witness the event. After about fifty minutes with the press, Gray called the meeting to order. Some three minutes were spent in discussing whether the FBI should hire female agents but the question was tabled when Gray agreed to study additional data on the subject which he had not seen.

As the other officials were leaving, Gray asked me to remain behind. When we were alone, he said, "I want to hold a 'brain-storming' session with all the top officials. I think I can arrange to have it at Camp David if we can agree on a time when the President or his staff are not using it." I suggested instead that the FBI Academy at Quantico be used. The press, I pointed out, might attach some political significance to the use of Camp David. "I'll think about it," Gray said. I was soon to learn that when he said he would think about something it meant that he had already made up his mind and did not want to discuss it further.

"In the meantime," he continued, "I want you to arrange for each headquarters' Division to prepare a position paper outlining its operations, its problems, and its plans for the future. I also want some special 'white papers' prepared to assess the proper role for the FBI in the narcotics problem, in the establishment of an outside oversight group and the need for a new division on planning and evaluation."

Hurriedly, Gray went on, "I will be moving into this space tomorrow and it will take a little time for me to get settled and in the swing of things. You are the Number Two in command and will be my Chief of Operations—but, of course, I want to be consulted on major policy matters."

"Fine," I said, "but I think we should have frequent informal conferences, you and I."

"Yes," Gray agreed. "I will be available any time for consultation."

I returned to my office feeling greatly encouraged and convinced of Gray's sincerity but this was not to last for long. The next morning as Gray was moving into the Director's office, surrounded by reporters and photographers, the rest of us were reading the newspapers in shocked disbelief. Staring at us from the front page was Gray's announcement that the Bureau would remove all restrictions against the hiring of female Agents. Gray was quoted as saying that "this action has been unanimously approved by the Executive Conference." In fact, no vote had been taken, and if it had been placed before us, there would have been fifteen votes opposed, with Gray and possibly one other official voting for the hiring of female agents.

To me the action was a very serious tactical error. Not that Gray had made the decision on his own but that he had misrepresented the facts to the press. By the manner in which it was handled, Gray lost the confidence of the Executive Conference and his action raised serious doubts as to his honesty and good intentions. The professional staff was furious. Gray's deception was probably the deciding factor in what followed. Ten of the sixteen top FBI officials who had attended the Executive Conference meeting retired shortly thereafter. Various reasons were given, but I know that all ten were disenchanted with Gray because of his misrepresentation to the press. As of today, the other six have also retired, as have a very large number of the higher echelons in the Field. With very few exceptions, Hoover's staff has now long since departed.

Had I been wiser, I would have retired too. I was making pennies an hour since the retirement take-home income to which I would have been entitled almost equalled that which I was receiving. My salary had been frozen for several years because of the forced compression in the supergrade levels resulting from congressional reluctance to raise the ceiling on Government salaries. Hundreds of my subordinates were drawing as much salary as I. And bizarre as it seems, cost-of-living allowances for retired employees would have increased my retirement pay, had I left in 1972, so that my income would be greater today.

I certainly did not stay on out of any hope that I might become Director if Gray failed. I realized then that his failure might take the FBI down with him—as it nearly did. In any case, it was clear that the Nixon Administration would not appoint anyone from the ranks. But in my fifty-ninth year, I had completed thirty-seven years of Government service, thirty of them with the Bureau, and I felt that as the top-ranking career official, I was the logical one to provide continuity during the change of leadership, By remaining, I would have a chance to maintain the FBI that Hoover had created as intact as possible. Someone knowledgable had to train and guide the new Director and I saw this as my obligation.

When I decided to stay on, I had not the slightest inkling of all the problems which lay in store for me; nevertheless, I am glad that I did. I think I accomplished something in helping keep the FBI together—and I can hardly complain that I was ever bored.

When Pat Gray moved into the Director's office on May 12, he told a press conference that he was going to "open the window" on FBI operations. This was a complete reversal for him. During the Kleindienst confirmation hearings, Gray had privately railed against the "vultures" of the press and complained that reporters were unfairly and deliberately making news about which "the public doesn't give a damn." But he had learned how dangerous it was to take on the Fourth Estate and as a friend remarked, "The hearings were the biggest thing in Pat's life up to that time. He learned the significance of the media, and now he is playing them like a violin."

Gray's first order to me had been that the various Divisions prepare position papers and "white" papers for his study. As I began to dictate instructions, it became apparent that I had not absorbed enough of his thinking in our hurried conference to satisfy him. He was on his way home to Connecticut and was not available for more consultation. Fortunately, Carol Tschudy, my Administrative Assistant, understood my problem. She called my attention to a *New York Times* story which, to my surprise, set forth in great detail a description of what Gray expected in these papers. He called them his "avenues of inquiry" and they covered everything from FBI administrative operations to organized crime to intelligence investigations to drug abuse. In time, I became used to seeing in the newspapers what I considered internal FBI business.

I also learned that with Gray it was either feast or famine. He would either drop everything in my lap and take off or he would involve himself in matters in overwhelming detail, making notes in a very tight and precise handwriting. I would say his outstanding characteristics were complete loyalty to his superiors and a compulsive attention to small details.

Gray did not smoke or drink though he would occasionally accept a glass of wine. He appeared to be in excellent physical shape and had a vigorous workout every day. He always made a point of walking up the five flights from the basement garage to his office on the fifth floor. After twice having accompanied him up those stairs, I made it a point to use a different entrance to avoid the unaccustomed exercise. Gray was also a deeply religious man and attended 7:00 A.M. Mass every morning.

Gray brought with him to the FBI four staffers who had served with him in the Civil Division of the Justice Department. The top member of this personal staff was David D. Kinley, thirty years old, who had served with the Acting Director in other Government jobs. As far as I could tell, his main qualification was a family connection with *Parade*, the syndicated Sunday supplement. Perhaps it was a coincidence, but *Parade* published some very laudatory stories about Gray. I could work with Kinley. He was bright and alert, though there was never any doubt that his primary assignment was to advance Gray's interests, even if it had to be done at the expense of the Bureau.

The second member of Gray's staff was Mrs. Marjorie Neenan who had worked for him before. She, too, was completely loyal to Gray but she was easy to work with and always gracious. A third member was Daniel M. Armstrong III, who quickly became known as the "All-American boy." His experience with the United States Attorney's office in Brooklyn had convinced him that he was an expert in law enforcement and the FBI, which was a delusion. The fourth member was Miss Barbara L. Herwig. She was pleasant, though condescending, and a passionate advocate of Women's Liberation, which was to cause me problems when the first female Agents came aboard, to use Gray's expression.

Gray's personal staff, with the exception of Mrs. Neenan, shared his suspicion and distrust of the FBI career people who called them the "Mod Squad." It was hard to cope with their skepticism about the FBI but a pleasure to astound them, and Gray, with the kind of proficiency which had been taken for granted by Hoover. None of Gray's staff had Agent status; nor were they at all interested in attaining it. Gray did have this status and he was issued Agent's credentials and given FBI badge Number Two. Badge Number One had been Hoover's and was retired from use.

Pat Gray did not come to the FBI at an easy time for him or for the country. Three days after Gray had settled down in his new office, Arthur H. Bremer attempted to assassinate Governor George C. Wallace of Alabama, who was campaigning for the Presidential nomination. It was a Monday and Gray was on his way back from Stonington, so I took the first excited call from Attorney General Kleindienst who ordered a full FBI investigation. Not sure just what the FBI's jurisdiction was, I nevertheless told Kleindienst that we would move immediately. But Thomas H. Farrow, the Baltimore SAC, was already on his way to the scene of the shooting in Laurel, Maryland, with a group of Agents. He was contacted by radio and given the Attorney General's instructions that the FBI should take over the investigation. Kleindienst and I agreed that the FBI could act under the Civil Rights statutes and throughout the afternoon I called him at hourly intervals to keep him informed of developments.

At seven, I left the office knowing that everything possible was being done. Wallace was in the hospital and Bremer was in custody. But there was a message waiting for me when I arrived home that I was to call President Nixon. The operator asked me to hold and after a brief time, Charles Colson, a Presidential aide, came on the line, "Just a minute, Mr. Felt," he said. "The President is coming on the line." Fifteen seconds later I was talking to Nixon for the first time in my life.

"Hello," he said. "This is President Nixon. Please bring me up to date on the Wallace case."

"Mr. President, Governor Wallace is still undergoing surgery and his condition is listed as very critical. He is in the operating room at Holy Cross Hospital in Silver Spring. Three other persons, including a Secret Service Agent, were wounded in the shooting, but they are expected to recover. The would-be assassin, Bremer, is in Federal custody and has been taken to the Prince Georges County Hospital at Cheverly, Maryland."

Nixon interrupted. "What did they take Bremer to the hospital for?"

"Well, he was roughed up a bit by the people who captured and subdued him. Also, he was examined by a psychiatrist who says his initial impression is that Bremer is a mental case."

"How bad was Bremer hurt?" the President pressed.

"Not seriously," I answered. "He has a few bruises and contusions. That's all."

"Well, it's too bad they didn't really rough up the son of bitch!" Nixon said.

Not wanting to comment on the President's outburst, I went on. "The FBI has assumed full jurisdiction in the case, and the way it looks now, Bremer will probably be charged with violation of the Civil Rights statutes."

"Is that the best you can do? There ought to be a stronger charge."

"I agree and we are discussing it now with the attorneys in the Justice Department."

"Okay," he said. "I want you to give me reports on the case every thirty minutes."

I spent the next two hours alternately talking to the Bureau supervisors who were in constant touch with the Baltimore Office, and with the President. The President's demand that I call every thirty minutes meant that I no sooner got off the phone to the Bureau than it was time to call the President again. On my second call to the White House, Nixon said, "I want the FBI to take over responsibility for a twenty-four-hour guard and protection duty of Bremer. I don't want another Oswald case on my hands." I assured the President that this would be done and passed the word on to SAC Farrow in Baltimore who realized what problems this would make for him.

On my third call to the White House, Nixon did not come to the phone and I talked to Colson. I told him that the Secret Service, which had entered the investigation because it was not clear which agency had jurisdiction, had found some papers in Bremer's apartment in Milwaukee which contained writings, presumably Bremer's, indicating a radical bias. Colson relayed this to the President who ordered that these papers be impounded by the FBI at once. We did not discuss the formality of a search warrant.

At 9:00 P.M., I told the President that Wallace was still in surgery and paralyzed from the waist down. I added that Bremer's papers were being flown to Washington by the FBI. I explained that Bremer had refused to be interviewed until he could consult with an attorney. At 9:30 P.M., I talked to Colson. I had learned Governor Wallace would recover, but he would probably be paralyzed permanently.

At 9:50 P.M., Pat Gray called to say he had just returned to his apartment in Washington and had found out about the attempted assassination when he called Headquarters to check in. He said he would take over the responsibility of keeping the White House informed. The following day, Gray told me that he had called the White House at 10:00 and 10:30, and had spoken to Colson. Since there was little new to report, Colson had said that no further reports were necessary unless there were unexpected developments. Gray had also talked with Attorney General Kleindienst that evening. He suspected that both Kleindienst and Colson were annoyed because he had not been on the scene when a major case broke.

This displeasure should have slowed down Gray's travel away from Washington but it had not the slightest effect. He not only made the rounds of the Field Offices but he made a total of forty-one speeches to various groups in his almost one year in office. These speeches have been criticized because they had political overtones, but Gray denied this. It is interesting, however, that Gray did not use George William Gunn, a law enforcement-oriented Bureau writer. Instead, his speeches were written by Charles Lichtenstein, a political speechwriter for a number of Republican leaders, who was then employed at the Federal Power Commission.

While J. Edgar Hoover was alive, he insisted upon seeing all significant memoranda and other communications. As a result, the volume of material which we sent into the Director's office was enormous. I knew Gray could not handle this volume because of his inexperience. Also he made it very clear to me that he wished to delegate authority. Accordingly, I sent in to him about 10 percent of the material that came to me. But even this was too much. Gray had not been in the Director's office for more than a few days before he complained that too many matters were being sent to him for handling. He emphatically told me, "I'm expecting you to run the day-to-day operations of the FBI and until I become more familiar with procedures I will not be able to handle much paperwork." I was tempted to reply that it would help if he stayed in Washington more of the time, but I thought better of it.

After this, the only material I sent to Gray was on matters of major policy decisions or memoranda, such as the application for Attorney General approval for a wiretap, which required his personal signature. Some memoranda which I sent to him never came back and as the deadline for action approached, I frequently had to make the decision. After Gray left, in April of 1973, I found a number of memoranda for which we had been searching.

Gray thought he was working hard—and probably by most Government standards he was. When he centered his attention on something, he literally smothered it, and when he went home to Connecticut on weekends, he always took work along with him. That which did come back was usually covered with notations in his own precise handwriting—always in red ink.

To Gray's disappointment, the "brainstorming" session on the position papers which he had requested could not be held at Camp David, which had been scheduled for a White House function. So Gray, his personal staff, and the Executive Conference journeyed to Quantico. Each operating division submitted its papers and these were discussed in depth. Gray asked aggressive, but not always pertinent, questions. After the first day's session, we ate dinner together in a private dining room and I was surprised to see an open bar. Liquor had never before been permitted at the FBI Academy.

The discussions continued during the next day and Gray expressed himself as highly pleased by the presentations. It was very clear to us, however, that the primary value was not to develop new ideas but to brief him and his staff on FBI policies, procedures, and operations. It was at these sessions that Gray also told us that his staff people were not to "wear his stripes," but we were not long in learning how influential his staffers were. In fact, the Executive Conference was startled when, after discussing the carefully prepared papers, we found that there was to be no vote, as there had always been under Hoover. Policy decisions were made exclusively by Gray himself in consultation with his personal staff.

Gray made a number of immediate changes, many of them minor but designed to please the Field Agents. The first of these dealt with grooming standards. Though there had been no specific written guidelines during Hoover's regime, it was known that he expected all Agents to dress and groom themselves like the young businessmen in their area. Hoover frowned on long hair, mustaches, and beards. The only exceptions, and Hoover was never told about this, were in the cases in which FBI Agents needed beards and mustaches to be able to move among dissenters and radicals.

Gray also discontinued the recording of time in the office, known as TIO. Hoover had required a record of the time spent by each Agent in the office and the time spent actually investigating cases. The elimination of this rule by Gray probably did make life easier for the Agents and they appreciated it. Gray also relaxed the weight standards for Agents. Instead of requiring them to keep their weight at the "desirable" level set by insurance companies, they were now permitted to let it go up to the "maximum" level—in some cases a difference of fifteen to twenty pounds. Since he believed in physical fitness programs, Gray extended to Field Agents the privilege of working out, so long as they compensated for each hour in the gymnasium with one hour of overtime. Only Headquarters staff had been given this privilege in the past. But perhaps his most popular change was one which allowed Resident Agents to take their Bureau cars home with them at night. He argued that Agents would have a car available if they were called out at night—and it did save downtown storage charges.

An excellent program initiated by Gray had one Agent in each Field Office assigned the responsibility for coordinating all information on narcotics. Because of this new rule, the FBI was able to furnish information to drug authorities which resulted in breaking up numerous dope rings. He also formalized the practice of using FBI Agents as undercover men. This had been done previously but to a very limited extent, and without Hoover's knowledge. It had not been particularly successful, but the idea seemed to appeal to Gray.

I have pointed out Gray's compulsive habit of making detailed notes—whether of a telephone conversation, a personal interview, or a memorandum which he had reviewed. Once he had made a notation concerning policy, it was almost impossible to get him to change his mind—and this led to some unwise decisions. Frequently I could not understand his notations. "Someone is standing on the vents," he noted on one memorandum. Not even his personal staff could translate that for me. When I asked him what he meant, he smiled. "That's a submarine expression. When a sub is making a crash dive, all the air vents have to be quickly closed. To say that someone is standing on the vents simply means that someone is dragging his feet or obstructing progress." He would say he was holding "captain's mast" when he orally disciplined subordinates. When he said, "There's something hidden in the Claymore mines," he meant that there was a serious problem which was not readily apparent.

But to my mind one of Gray's major weaknesses in running the FBI was his continuing lack of availability over long periods of time. More often than not, he was out of town. And even when he was in Washington, he was often out of reach in the basement gymnasium, where he would not permit any interruptions, or locked up in long conferences with his staff. He met with the Executive Conference only at rare intervals. In the Justice Department he had been known as "Three-Day Gray," because of his extended weekends in Connecticut. He was very sensitive about this nickname, perhaps because it was so well deserved. One day, when I was in his office to discuss Watergate, Gray said, "There is another important matter. Yesterday I had a conversation with a Federal judge and he told me that one of my Assistant Directors is bad-mouthing me."

I almost choked when he complained, "This Assistant Director is calling me 'Four-Day Gray.' "

Controlling my impulse to laugh, I said, "Why don't you ask the judge to name names? Make him tell you who is supposed to have said this and where he got his information." Gray reddened; he must have realized that I knew his real nickname. "That's all for now, he said. Later the press began calling him "Two Day Gray"—and a look at his calendar substantiated the correction. (In fairness to Gray, I must repeat that he took bulging briefcases full of work to his home in Connecticut. He truly wanted to become an excellent Director of the FBI and he loved the assignment.)

There was another discouraging aspect of Gray's stewardship—probably it was unavoidable. Frustrated and angered by years of trying to impose their wishes on Hoover, Justice

Department career officials had a field day after his death. They were now able to control the FBI and a string of Justice Department requests of the Bureau were directed to Gray or to members of his personal staff. Almost without exception they were implemented without question.

Not all of Gray's changes were concerned with policy, procedures, or Justice Department interference. Among his first acts was to have a kitchen installed in an unused pantry-closet in his office. Squeezed into that small space were a new refrigerator and an apartment-size electric range. China, silverware, and cooking utensils were purchased, and a cook was hired at a salary of $10,000 a year. To stock the kitchen, every member of the Executive Conference was assessed $25, as a first installment for food. Gray also stocked a bar in the Director's office, something unheard of under Hoover. Dining was in the large conference room which Hoover had used for ceremonial purposes. Gray ordered a larger conference table, at a cost of $5,000, but when it arrived he would not accept it because it had a Formica top. He wanted the larger table so that he could invite more people to lunch. With fifteen members in the Executive Conference and four of his own staff, it was necessary to rotate luncheon invitations so as to accommodate visiting dignitaries. Gray invited Congressmen and Senators to these luncheons, and Assistant Directors were able to attend once a month. I fared a little better, attending about twice a month. One Assistant Director attended only one luncheon before a second $25 assessment was made and he later estimated that the average cost to him was $16.67 per luncheon.

The immediate and most noticeable effect of the kitchen and the gourmet meals—and they were that!—was the cooking smells which filled the public corridor. When Gray resigned and William Ruckelshaus took over, the kitchen was continued, as it was under Clarence Kelley, who made the cook his assistant.

But there was more on our minds during the Gray tenure than gourmet cooking. On September 8, 1972, Geoffrey Shepard, a staff assistant to John Ehrlichman in the White House, sent a memorandum to the Justice Department requesting information on criminal justice problems in fourteen designated states. It was made very clear that this material was needed for use in President Nixon's reelection campaign. The deadline set for the FBI to submit the material was already past when we received it. Kinley, Gray's personal staff man, received the request and passed it on to the proper Division. A teletype was sent to twenty-one Field Offices, quoting the exact language of the request and naming the White House as its source. Neither Gray nor I saw anything objectionable about furnishing criminal justice information to the President until the text of the teletype was leaked to *Time* magazine which blasted the Acting Director for politicizing the FBI. Gray hit the panic button and ordered a complete investigation of every clerk and every Agent who had handled the teletype to see if he could find out who had turned it over to *Time*. He was not so much concerned about the Bureau as about what the White House, almost paranoid about the press, would say to him.

At the time, we seemed to be continually at odds with the White House about almost everything. On September 22, for example, Gray called me. "Mark," he said, "I've just received a call from Lawrence Higby [Haldeman's aide]. I'm getting ready to leave for a speech in Detroit. Higby wants an FBI investigation of some sort of burglary out in Long Beach which involves medical information about the President. Will you call him and see what it's all about?"

When I called Higby, he was very excited about an incident which had occurred the day before. He told me that the office of the President's physician and medical consultant had been burglarized. "Thieves broke into the doctor's office late Wednesday night or early Thursday morning," he said excitedly. They were trying to photograph the President's medical records which were left scattered about the floor. The President wants the FBI to look into it."

"I'll check into it immediately and call you within the hour," I told Higby.

"Thanks. We want the FBI to go all out on it. Someone is trying to embarrass the President."

In very short order, the Los Angeles Office informed me that the matter was being routinely investigated by the Long Beach police who were convinced that it was the work of juveniles. The doctor's office had been burglarized several weeks before and a small amount of money had been taken. On both occasions, entry had been gained through a sliding door with a faulty catch and similar break-ins in the area were also being investigated. The President's file had been dropped on the floor but there was no indication that it had been rifled or photographed. This does seem unusual to an amateur, but it was checked thoroughly by experts.

When I relayed this to Higby, I added that there was no jurisdictional basis for the FBI to enter the case. Forcefully and aggressively, he demanded that the FBI "issue a press release about the case." I said, "Mr. Higby, there is no reason for the FBI to become involved in the case and, in any event, the FBI has no authority to issue a press release except when arrests are made by the FBI." Higby argued excitedly that there must be a press release. The only promise he got from me was that I would keep him informed. But Higby did not wait for me to call him. He called me—at least fifteen times during the next ten days. My answer was always, "No." I wondered why the White House was so interested in that press release. It was not until it became known that the "Plumbers" had broken into the office of Daniel Ellsberg's psychiatrist that I began to suspect that someone at the White House, knowing that the break-in by the "Plumbers" to photograph the psychiatric records of Daniel Ellsberg was bound to be discovered, wanted to be able to show that President Nixon had also been a victim of such tactics.

By the fall of 1972, disenchantment with Gray was becoming widespread at FBI Headquarters and the feeling was spreading to the Field. Field Agents had at first welcomed Gray but it had become clear that he was making the same set speech in every Field Office and was telling the Agents what they wanted to hear. There was resentment of Gray's airing of sensitive personnel matters in the press as part of his "open window" policy. Distrust of Gray's personal staff intensified when it became apparent that their primary aim was to advance Gray's interests, no matter what the cost to the Bureau.

Then, on November 20, 1972, Gray was hospitalized at Lawrence Memorial Hospital in New London for abdominal surgery and did not return to Washington until January 2nd, after a month of convalescing at home and at Key Biscayne, Florida. He had instructed me that during his absence I was to sign all reports and correspondence but because he had been away from Washington so frequently, his extended sick leave did not have a significant impact on the already hectic pace of my activities.

Shortly after he returned from sick leave, Gray confided to me, "You know, Mark, Dick Kleindienst told me that I might have to get rid of you. He says White House staff members are convinced that you are the FBI source of leaks to Woodward and Bernstein"—the *Washington Post* reporters who were writing up the Watergate story almost as fast as it was being investigated.

I said, "Pat, I haven't leaked anything to anybody. They are wrong!"

"I believe you," Gray answered, "but the White House doesn't. Kleindienst has told me on three or four occasions to get rid of you but I refused. He didn't say this came from higher up but I am convinced that it did."

This disclosure came as an unpleasant surprise. My contacts with Kleindienst had been frequent and friendly—there had never been the slightest indication that I was suspect. I could feel the anger rising in me but I was very appreciative of Gray's indication of support. Gray went on: "I told Kleindienst that you've worked with me in a very competent manner and I'm convinced that you are completely loyal. I told him I was not going to move you out. Kleindienst told me, 'Pat, I love you for that.' "

Startled as I was by this development, I did not want to be the one who prevented Gray from getting the permanent appointment as Director. "I certainly don't want it on my conscience that I stood in the way of your nomination. I have been thinking of retirement but I don't want it to appear that I am leaving under pressure. I am willing to accept a transfer to the west coast as Special Agent in Charge."

"No," said Gray, "I wouldn't do that to you. How many years have you served in the FBI?"

"Thirty-one years."

Half to himself, Gray said, "I wouldn't want to do this to anyone who has served his country and the FBI so ably and loyally."

I am grateful to Pat Gray for that!

Much later, I learned that the White House had frequently complained to Kleindienst that I was "Deep Throat," the mysterious source on whom Woodward and Bernstein relied in writing their sensational stories about Watergate. No one from the Nixon White House has ever told me why I was the principal suspect but their reasoning is obvious now. I was supposed to be jealous of Gray for having received the appointment as Acting Director instead of myself. They felt that my high position in the FBI gave me access to all the Watergate information and that I was releasing it to Woodward and Bernstein in an effort to discredit Gray so that he would be removed and I would have another chance at the job. Then there were those frequent instances when I had been much less than cooperative in responding to requests from the White House which I felt were improper. I suppose the White House staff had me tagged as an insubordinate.

It is true that I would like to have been appointed FBI Director on the death of Hoover. It is not true that I was jealous of Gray. Once the die was cast, I resolved, for the good of the FBI, to help Gray in every way that I could. It is true that I frequently said "no" to the White House staff members.

I never leaked information to Woodward and Bernstein or to anyone else!

CHAPTER SEVENTEEN

Senator Bayh is not going to believe it either.

—L. PATRICK GRAY III

During Patrick Gray's tenure as Acting Director of the FBI, there were frequent areas in which he and I had differences of opinion. Two were of particular significance. Looking back on it, I can't be sure that Gray ever really accepted the fact that J. Edgar Hoover did not have extensive personal files into which he crammed all kinds of material with which to blackmail Presidents, Attorneys General, and other Government officials. At least he stopped talking to me about it and I assumed he believed me. But Gray and I never agreed on his decision to recruit women Agents, or on his manner of arriving at that decision and of announcing it.

The "Secret Files"

David Wise, a severe critic of the FBI, wrote in his book, *The American Police State:* "The FBI maintains intelligence dossiers on hundreds of thousands of American citizens. Since 1939, the FBI has compiled more than 500,000 dossiers on Americans." He was referring to a portion of the general files—not Hoover's personal files—of which there are more than six and one half million at FBI headquarters.

These FBI files are not "dossiers"—a sinister word conjured up by those who are trying to create hysteria or sell copies of books. The files to which Wise refers actually do exist and properly so. They are maintained in the custody of the Files and Communications Division. A substantial portion relate to people who were investigated during World War II as possible Nazi or Japanese sympathizers. There are files on members of the Communist Party USA, the Ku Klux Klan, the Black September group of Arab terrorists, the Black Panthers, and the Weather Underground—all subversive or terrorist groups. There are files as well on many thousands of members of the crime syndicate, the so-called Mafia. Files are also kept on people involved in security investigations based on serious allegations, where the person under scrutiny was completely cleared of suspicion.

As to the files which Hoover kept in his office, how did they originate, how were they used, and what finally became of them? Other than Helen Gandy, Hoover's personal secretary, I know more about those files than anyone else in the Bureau because all those which did not fall into the category of his personal affairs were turned over to my custody.

During his forty-eight years as Director, Hoover carried on a tremendous personal correspondence with the high and mighty in government. He also had friends in all walks of life to whom he wrote: Walter Winchell, the columnist; Clint Murchison, the Texas oil millionaire; David Sarnoff, founder of RCA; Richard Cardinal Cushing of Boston; Sherman Billingsley and Bernard "Toots" Shor, New York restaurateurs; Jack Warner of Hollywood; Lela Rogers, mother of Ginger, and many others. He exchanged personal letters with incumbent Presidents and remained friends with Herbert Hoover, no kin.

Hoover's personal files also included letters, some rather obsequious, from various Bureau officials who were trying to extricate themselves from the Hoover doghouse or otherwise ingratiate themselves with him. No doubt, some of them contained bits and pieces of gossip involving the world's great which the official thought might interest or amuse Hoover. All of this correspondence was carefully kept out of the main

Bureau files and indices and maintained by Miss Gandy. As the years went by, the walls of her little office became lined with file cabinets. Forty-eight years is a long time and the paper accumulates. In 1971, Hoover instructed Miss Gandy to begin weeding out this correspondence but the work had barely begun by the time of his death.

From time to time, Hoover ordered that certain official FBI files be kept in Miss Gandy's office to prevent exposure to the eyes of rank-and-file personnel. For example, if the FBI had a file on an incumbent President, as it did in the case of President Nixon whose first application for a government job had been with the FBI, it would be kept in the Director's office. Extremely sensitive memoranda on Hoover's conversations with Presidents were occasionally retained by Miss Gandy and could be seen only with Hoover's express permission. As a result, there was a substantial volume of official FBI material in Miss Gandy's office, in addition to the personal papers, and this was designated the "Official and Confidential Files."

The day after Hoover's death, Associate Director Clyde Tolson instructed Miss Gandy to box all the *personal* correspondence and have it delivered to Hoover's home. Since he planned to retire, Tolson instructed that the Official and Confidential Files be sent to me for safekeeping and a final determination as to disposition.

This packaging process took one week and Acting Director Gray was completely aware of what was going on and offered no objections. During this period, Miss Gandy shipped thirty-four boxes of personal files to the Hoover house and also sent twelve boxes of Official and Confidential files to me, which Files I placed in combination-lock cabinets. Miss Gandy has testified before the House Committee on Government Operations that, at Tolson's direction, she destroyed all of Hoover's personal papers except those relating to his estate. Those she turned over to Tolson, who had been named Hoover's executor.

I made only a casual review of the material which Miss Gandy sent to me and my impression was that it was considerably less than startling. There were folders on President

Lyndon B. Johnson and President John F. Kennedy, both of which related solely to administrative procedures in conducting liaison between the White House and the FBI. In my opinion, all of it could have been immediately returned to the General Files, but I was resolved to hold the material intact and inviolate until Gray could review it for himself because he had made such an issue of the "Secret Files" only a few days before. I wanted him to know exactly what was in them.

I did return to the General Files the contents of three boxes which contained FBI monographs—booklets containing FBI research material concerning the Communist Party, the Mafia, the riots which erupted in the summer of 1967 and other similar material. Although confidential, these informative documents are available to any Agent for research purposes. Undoubtedly, Hoover kept a complete set in his office for ready reference. They could not be described as "Secret Files" by any stretch of the imagination and there was no point in holding them for Gray.

After three months of waiting for Gray to look at these files, I called in Cornelius Sullivan, an Inspector in the Domestic Intelligence Division, and instructed him to prepare a complete index and catalogue. It took him a week to complete this task and when he finished, he shared my impression that the files were old and of little current significance.

I sent a copy of the inventory to Gray but I don't know whether or not he read it; I never received any response. Despite my frequent suggestions, he never came to review these files and he was apparently satisfied that there were no "Secret Files" because he so stated to the media.

Unfortunately for the memory of Hoover, I was guilty of an oversight which later gave grounds to the critics who claimed that Hoover did, in fact, maintain "Secret Files" on prominent persons. This false impression came about in this way. During July, 1971, a very important memorandum which Hoover had dictated was found to be missing from the General Files. What made it particularly important was the fact that the person who was looking for it was none other than Hoover himself.

He talked angrily to me about this and after describing the

memo, which he had dictated following a conversation with President Nixon, he said, "Felt, I want you to personally check with all the top officials and find out who is holding this memorandum."

The first thing I did was to go to Mrs. Erma Metcalf, who took most of the Director's dictation, and request her to locate the original dictation in her stenographic notes. This she was able to do and she quickly typed for me a verbatim copy.

The memorandum related to domestic security matters so my next logical step was to interview William C. Sullivan. When I showed him a copy of the memorandum, he immediately recalled seeing it. He said, "I saw it less than a month ago. I am sure I sent it up for filing. The Files and Communications Division must have misfiled it."

"Bill," I said, "they have checked everywhere. Why don't you look through your papers and see if it has become mixed up with something else by mistake?"

Sullivan was very cooperative and within minutes, he found the original of the memorandum in a folder which he kept in a filing cabinet behind his desk. Taking it, I thanked him and went back to my office where I drafted an informal note to accompany it to the Director, telling him where I had found it.

Within a few minutes, I received a call from Hoover on the intercom. "Felt, what excuse did Sullivan have for keeping this memorandum in his personal custody?"

Not wanting to put Sullivan on the spot, I said, "He felt it was very sensitive and also that he might have to refer to it on very short notice."

Hoover stormed, "That's not a good reason. How many other Bureau files is he keeping in his office?"

"I don't know, sir. I believe . . ."

I didn't finish before Hoover went on. "Felt, I want you to conduct a survey to find out what other files Sullivan has and also check with all the other officials to see if they are holding anything."

I did not cause a physical inspection to be made of the offices of all top officials. I should have because I would have then discovered the so-called Kissinger Wiretap files which

Sullivan was holding and which he later smuggled out of the Bureau to Robert Mardian at the Justice Department. As it was, I merely submitted an instruction to all officials that each furnish me with a list of any files which he was holding in his office.

Sullivan's reply was the first to come back. He insisted that he had no additional Bureau files in his office. Assistant to the Director Mohr replied that he had six folders containing the results of a confidential personnel investigation involving a high Bureau official thirty years back. Assistant Director Thomas E. Bishop of the Crime Records Division replied that he had one file drawer of miscellaneous records from fifteen to twenty years old which had been accumulated in his Division during the tenure of Louis B. Nichols as Assistant Director in charge of that Division before he retired in 1957. All the other officials responded that they had not retained any Bureau files on a permanent basis.

I reported the results of my inquiries to the Director and my memorandum came back to me with a notation in Hoover's familiar blue ink, "I want Felt to take possession of these records and maintain them in his office."

Both Mohr and Bishop were glad to get rid of the musty files and when I gave them a quick examination I noted they were all very old. Without a detailed review, I put my new acquisitions in combination-lock file cabinets and promptly forgot about them.

Later, when all the "Official and Confidential" files were delivered to me by Miss Gandy, I put them in six new two-drawer combination-lock cabinets side by side with the files which I had obtained from Bishop and Mohr.

Because I paid little attention to any of these files—holding them temporarily until I could persuade the new Acting Director to look at them—I failed to explain the distinction between the files from Hoover's office and those which I had obtained from Bishop and Mohr to Neil Sullivan when he made his inventory. I didn't realize this when I looked at it and must accept full responsibility for the unfortunate results, when the Attorney General and congressional committees held up examples of the files which came from the Crime

Records Division as horrible examples of Hoover's "Secret Files." It is too bad that I was not consulted until after the damage was done.

The important point for me to make now is that the files which were found objectionable did not come from Hoover's office, and, furthermore, were never a part of General FBI Files.

But, in spite of this, all the furor never would have occurred had it not been for an incident in Elyria, Ohio, in October, 1972, caused by the extremely poor judgment of an FBI Agent stationed in Lorain County, who went beyond his instructions.

Since the early Fifties, the Crime Records Division of the FBI had made a practice of maintaining "Congressional Cards" on every Senator and Congressman. The purpose of the card was to set forth biographical data and any information from Bureau files or public records which would be of assistance to the Crime Records Division in maintaining congressional liaison. A brief record of all dealings with the particular Congressman or Senator was noted on the card. This was to make the FBI liaison more responsive and effective. Also noted on the card were any problems with a view to preventing similar situations from developing in the future.

The FBI has never investigated Members of Congress, congressional candidates, or governors unless there was an alleged violation of Federal law or the individual was being considered for a top-level Government appointment.

On January 13, 1972, as had been done every election year since the early Fifties, an informal note was sent to all Field Divisions by the Crime Records Division. It read as follows:

> RE COMING ELECTIONS
>
> Primaries will be held this year in each state to nominate candidates for Congress (House and Senate) and some Governors.* Pertinent background information and data from your files on major non-incumbent candidates

---

* Background data on Governors was also used to facilitate liaison.

> in your district should be forwarded informally by routing slip, not letter, to Crime Records as soon as they are nominated. But under *no* circumstances should you make outside inquiries such as checks of credit bureaus or newspaper morgues. Public source material readily available to you and data from your files will suffice. Continue to furnish pertinent data as it develops between the primary and general election. Also, be alert to any special elections to fill Congressional vacancies and submit pertinent data on the major candidates before the election dates. These matters must be handled with *extreme* discretion to avoid the implication that we are checking on candidates.

After the first inquiry in 1950, it was only necessary to develop the biographical data on congressional newcomers because cards would already have been filed on incumbents. As could be expected, for incuments with long tenure, additional cards would have to be stapled on as the list of contacts and correspondence grew longer.

The trouble began when the Resident Agent in Lorain County contacted a reporter friend on a newspaper at Elyria. Perhaps not such a good friend after all, the reporter wrote a story for his paper stating that the FBI was investigating a certain congressional candidate. And then the storm broke—wire services all over the country picked up the story and exacerbated the fears of FBI "secret dossiers" on Congressmen, Senators, and high officials.

Acting Director Gray did his best to explain, but no one paid any attention and on October 27 he issued a press release indicating that the program was being discontinued and the Congressional Cards were destroyed.

To the best of my knowledge, there was never any improper use of the information in Hoover's personal correspondence files or on any of the Congressional Cards kept by the Crime Records Division. Allegations of blackmail have been very few and none have ever been documented. On the contrary, Hoover went out of his way to protect the information in

Bureau files and in his personal files from being used improperly.

A short time after the Congressional Cards were discontinued, Gray called on the intercom and said, "Mark, can you come over for a minute?"

When we were alone, I asked him, "Okay, Pat, what's the story?"

He thought for a minute, and then said, "The Elyria story has really created problems. This morning Senator Birch Bayh contacted the Attorney General and asked him to discreetly find out what was in his FBI file. Kleindienst passed the request along to me and I want you to review the files, personally, and bring anything you find to me."

"Okay, I should be able to report back to you later today," I said.

Gray replied, "Thanks Mark. I'll greatly appreciate it. I want this kept just between us."

I thought for a minute, then I said, "There is no way to pull the files and not have a few clerks know but I am sure they won't think anything about it."

Gray waved me away, "That's all right. Just don't discuss it with anyone."

This project called first for an indices search to locate all references to Senator Bayh in various files. There were quite a few, and the stack of files brought in to me later took some time to review. All the material relating to Bayh was insignificant and most of it involved constituent or administrative matters. One file indicated that Bayh had been interviewed as a witness in a criminal case. There was absolutely nothing out of the ordinary.

I took the stack of files to Gray's office and put them on a corner of Gray's desk. "Pat," I said, "You're not going to believe this, but there is nothing here that isn't strictly routine."

I showed him the various reference pages, most of which were brief.

Gray looked up at me and smiled, "Senator Bayh is not going to believe it either."

At that time, I had not the slightest indication of why Senator Bayh would have such an interest in the FBI files. A book, *The Power Lovers,* by Myra MacPherson of the *Washington Post,* gave me a clue. Concerning Senator Bayh, she wrote, "He has, as they used to say in less liberated days, a 'Reputation.' Bayh scoffs, with the rejoinder, 'I get all the credit for all these beds I'm supposed to get in and out of and it's not so. The damn thing is so ridiculous.' "

The Bayh incident led me to the conclusion that *information which is not in the FBI files may have a more chilling effect than that which is*—particularly where a guilty conscience is involved.

It was not alone because of these incidents that Gray resolved to abolish the Crime Records Division although they were the primary reason. Another factor was that through the years, Hoover had been pleased with its operations and had been generous with promotions with the result that the number of Agent employees in that Division in Supergrade rank—from GS 16 through GS 18—was considerably above average. In fact, there were not enough Supergrade positions for all the Special Agents in Charge in the Field whom we all believed deserving of such recognition. Accordingly, one phase of Gray's plan was to do away with the Division involved, transferring to Field executive positions those Agent Supervisors who had Supergrade rank and absorbing the work in other Divisions and in his own office.

It was a plan which should have been phased in gradually. As it turned out, this abrupt upheaval created personal hardships which led to several retirements and one reduction in salary for an Agent whose family situation made a transfer unacceptable. On the other hand, some of those transferred moved on up the promotional ladder and were benefited by Gray's decision.

Women in the FBI

It all started in 1970, when a young woman in Denver, Mrs. Sandra Rothenberger Nemser, applied for a position as an FBI

Agent. When her application was refused, she filed suit against the Attorney General, the Director, and the Bureau, alleging that the refusal violated the Constitution and equal employment statutes. The Nemser suit was quickly followed by another action filed by Mrs. Cynthia Gitt Edgar, a staffer for Bella Abzug, the controversial former Congresswoman from New York. The American Civil Liberties Union supported the two suits.

At the FBI, there was almost unanimous opposition to permitting women to become Special Agents. The FBI is a quasi-military organization with combat-type operations taking place almost every day in fugitive apprehensions, raids, and other dangerous situations. A show of strength is often essential to ensure that an arrest is conducted without incident. Indeed because the FBI has so carefully stuck to this strategy great numbers of arrests are made with a minimum of risk.

The public does not realize how many thousands of dangerous arrests are made by the FBI each year. Ninety-seven percent of the fugitives apprehended are males. Because of this, we were convinced that allowing women to participate in arrests would increase the risk for everyone in the action. Another compelling argument was that sooner or later most women Agents would marry and want to have children. Normally, this would mean that they would leave the FBI to devote themselves to child raising. The time and money spent on training—and it is substantial—would therefore be wasted.*

In the Nemser and Edgar instances, moreover, we were convinced that the individuals did not really want an FBI career but were merely intent on making a case for Women's Liberation.

Dwight Dalbey, Assistant Director in the Office of Legal Counsel, prepared the Bureau's position paper. All FBI offi-

* As our culture changes, my arguments will lose validity. Chances are that women will evolve to become as strong as men because of more vigorous childhood games, participation in sports and, for some, employment at manual labor. We are also approaching the time when more women will prefer a career to child raising.

cials were opposed to hiring female Agents, with one exception. John Mohr argued that we should become sexually integrated—not because he believed it proper but because he was sure we could not defend our case successfully given the tenor of the times. "If we can't win," he said, "let's give in gracefully."

It was up to the Civil Division of the Justice Department, which Gray then headed, to defend the Bureau in the court actions, and he was anything but sympathetic to the Bureau's position. He argued that the law suit should not be contested and that the FBI should begin accepting female applicants for the position of Agent. He would not budge from this position, not even listening to our arguments until Dalbey threatened to hire an outside lawyer.

Dalbey's next step was to contact a cross-section of Field Agents, ranging from SACs to new Agents. They were asked to give careful consideration to the question in the light of their own experiences and to document their responses with specific examples. Opposition to female Agents was unanimous, with case after case cited to demonstrate the inherent dangers. Then, in the midst of the controversy, Hoover died and Gray became Acting Director.

At the first regular Executive Conference meeting under Gray, we spent all of three minutes discussing the question.

"Who wants to open the discussion?" Gray asked. I pointed out that Dalbey was our coordinator in the matter and suggested that the meeting be turned over to him. Gray agreed.

"Mr. Gray," Dalbey said, "with one exception we are all strongly opposed to the hiring of female Agents. Mr. Mohr is in favor." He smiled. "You and I have had some heated discussions on this subject, and I know you agree with Mr. Mohr. Since we last talked, however, an extensive survey has been made in the Field and you should know of the results. SACs, Supervisors, and Agents are unanimously opposed, and they strongly document their positions. You have not seen any of this new information and it is too long to read here. I suggest you read it first and then we can vote on the question."

Gray hesitated for a moment and then nodded agreement. As I pointed out in a previous chapter, Gray had already made up his mind. Had he admitted that, he might have saved the day, but he had already told the media that the decision to hire female Agents had been unanimously approved by the Executive Conference.

To add insult to injury, the very same day, David Kinley, Gray's non-FBI Administrative Assistant, brought me the official communication to the Field Offices announcing the decision. It was obvious that Kinley had been working on it for some time.

After reading it, I said, "Dave, you haven't changed the minimum height requirement."

"That's right," he replied. "The Boss wants exactly the same standards for females as for males."

"But, Dave, a minimum height requirement of five feet seven inches limits the field to tall women. You're discriminating against average women." When, after a thirty-minute argument, he would not change his ground, I called Gray. Before I could speak my piece, he cut me off.

"The women must measure up exactly as the men. There will be no exceptions," he said.

"This is discriminatory. You are only opening the door part way. We should be consistent."

"Mark, I don't want any more argument about it. My mind is made up. Don't push me too far." *

My suspicion that their interest was just a matter of principle was confirmed when Nemser and Edgar immediately dropped their suits and never applied for FBI employment. The number of women applicants, moreover, was only a trickle. Two were selected for a training class which began in July of 1972—Susan Lynn Riley, formerly with the Marine Corps, and Joanne E. Pierce, a former nun. Since the new FBI Academy at Quantico had been designed to handle a few

* Director Clarence Kelley subsequently eliminated all height requirements. These are the reasons the FBI now has some very tall women and some very short men.

women police trainees, there was no problem. What developed, however, was not unexpected: the women could not pass the physical tests.

These tests were not unusual, but three turned out to be very difficult for women. Every trainee was expected to do fifteen push-ups, three pull-ups, and run two miles in sixteen and a half minutes—in addition to other tests. A pull-up is similar to a chin-up, except that it is done with the palms facing forward. It is difficult and was designed to simulate climbing a high wall or fence, where the palms must face the wall. The test was included in our training based on actual pursuit situations in which Agents had trouble climbing high fences.

About three weeks before the class was to graduate, Assistant Director Thomas J. Jenkins of the Training Division brought me some disturbing news. Riley and Pierce could not pass these three tests, though they had made conscientious efforts. There was, he assured me, no way we could expect them to succeed by graduation time.

Never before had a trainee been graduated without qualifying in every way. All had to pass the physical tests, the academic tests, and the firearms tests. And Gray had said that there could be no exceptions. I could see the news stories in the media about the male chauvinists who had rigged the tests to disqualify two women. So we rigged it the other way—in favor of the two women trainees—by revising the standards. Each physical test, effective immediately, was rated on a point basis—so many points for each test, with a total of eighty-five points required for graduation. Under the new system, a trainee could completely fail two tests and still have enough points to graduate. Pierce and Riley passed the two-mile run, reportedly with some help from their male classmates and I did not ask any questions. They were still unable to do the push-ups and the pull-ups but they had the qualifying points to graduate.

I could have put this monkey on Gray's back. After all, it was his idea. But Jenkins and I never told him what we had done. Jenkins subsequently took his problem to medical experts at the Naval Hospital in Bethesda. They pointed out that these tests were discriminatory against women for physiological reasons. We accepted their suggestion that women be allowed to do push-ups with their knees on the floor instead of the normal fashion of supporting the body with the toes. They were also permitted to do the pull-ups with their feet on the ground and the bar at chin level. They could then lean backward to arm's length and pull back to a horizontal position.

There were also "coeducational" problems. Two trainees, a man and a woman, went on a trip together—the male Agent was married—and both were dropped from the rolls. The woman trainee appealed to Barbara Herwig, Gray's Women's Lib representative on his personal staff, who saw in the expulsion a male chauvinist plot. She appealed to Gray who sustained the action that had been taken. Herwig, however, did not intercede for the male participant in the escapade.

At no time was there any rush of female applicants. The total number of women Agents on FBI rolls has fluctuated between thirty and one hundred-fifty. They are capable and competent and do a good job, but in tough or dangerous situations they are not above using womanly guiles to leave it to the men.

CHAPTER EIGHTEEN

People on your staff are trying to mortally wound you.

—GRAY TO PRESIDENT NIXON

For all of the publicity and the investigations by both the Ervin Senate Committee and the Special Watergate Prosecutor, many aspects of the Watergate affair remain an enigma. Did the Democratic National Committee actually have advance warning of the break-in, as some have alleged? Did columnist Jack Anderson really know in advance? What was the real purpose behind the break-in? Did the CIA have a role in the affair? Why did not President Nixon destroy the incriminating tapes? I don't know the answers to these questions and we may never find out.

There is one further question and this concerns me directly as the second-ranking FBI official at the time of Watergate. Why did FBI detractors labor so hard to give the public the impression that we dragged our feet in the investigation? As the Nixon tapes amply proved, the President, who was kept fully informed of FBI activities by Acting Director Gray and the Justice Department, laid it on the line when he complained that the FBI was "out of control" because it was pushing too vigorously to determine the facts of the break-in.

The FBI's task was difficult and had many frustrations. The Acting Director, a political appointee, was caught between his duties as FBI Chief and his ties to the Nixon Administration.

More to the point we were trying to elicit information from

a White House whose staff, both high and low, was either evasive or downright obstructive. One Agent in the Washington Field Office, who was assigned to the case, said to me, "Trying to interview these people is like trying to get information from the Black Panther Party." It reminded me of my days in the Kansas City Office when members of the Mafia simply refused to talk. As the then Assistant Attorney General Henry E. Peterson of the Criminal Division has said, "Nobody sounded innocent"—and many were not. From the very beginning it was obvious to the Bureau that a cover-up was in progress but this made us more determined than ever to get under it.

The FBI first learned of the Watergate break-in during the early hours of Saturday, June 17, 1972. The first report came from the Washington police. Five men had been apprehended in the Watergate Office Building. This information was relayed to Robert G. Kunkel, SAC of the Washington Field Office, at his home, and he instructed an Agent to get to the scene as quickly as possible. Within minutes, a second call from the police was relayed to Kunkel. An "explosive device" had been found in the offices of the Democratic National Committee in Watergate. Kunkel immediately dispatched FBI bomb specialists to the building. He had barely put down the receiver when he received a third call—this one directly from Chief of Police Jerry V. Wilson who told him that one of the "burglars" had been identified as James W. McCord, Jr., a former employee of the Central Intelligence Agency.

Kunkel quickly dressed and dashed to the Field Office. Agents had already examined the "explosive device" and reported to him that it was a microphone and radio transmitter hidden in a smoke detector case on the wall of a conference room. Kunkel then ordered an all-out investigation for possible violation of the Interception of Communications statute—a primary investigative jurisdiction of the FBI.

The dummy smoke detector did indeed look like an explosive device. It contained several batteries wired together and a battery operated wristwatch, both basic components of a bomb. The microphone and radio transmitter were obviously for bugging purposes but the wristwatch was puzzling. Kunkel deduced that the wristwatch was there to give a continuous signal to permit the monitor to get an accurate fix on the radio frequency.

Because of the unusual circumstances, the Night Supervisor in the General Investigative Division decided to notify me at home, which he did at 7:00 A.M. When he briefed me on the steps being taken by Kunkel, I approved and asked that he be instructed to press the investigation energetically as a major case. At 8:30, I was in my office calling the Night Supervisor for an additional briefing.

"This is getting rather complicated," he said. "I'd better come over to your office."

A few minutes later he was telling me, "Here is what we know so far. At approximately 2:30 this morning, a security guard at the Watergate complex noticed a partially open basement stairwell door which had tapes placed across the spring bolt to prevent it from locking. He removed the tape but when he saw the same door taped again about forty minutes later, he telephoned the police at once and they were on the scene within minutes. The police surprised and arrested five individuals at Democratic headquarters and they were identified as James Walter McCord, Jr, Bernard L. Barker, Frank Anthony Fiorini, Virgilio R. Gonzales, and Eugenio Martinez y Creaga. They had in their possession burglary tools and eavesdropping and photographic equipment."

"What in the world were they doing?"

"Several ceiling panels had been removed as well as an air vent cover. They had been taking apart the telephone equipment. All of them were wearing surgical-type plastic gloves. It looks like they were getting ready to install more eavesdropping equipment or to repair or put new batteries in equipment already there."

"Where are they now?" I asked. "What did the police do with them?"

"They're all in jail. Bond has been set at fifty thousand dollars for all but McCord and his bond is thirty thousand. They're charged with burglary."

"Have they said what they were doing?"

"They haven't said one word. They didn't even call an attorney but one showed up anyway. It's very mysterious."

I thought for a minute. "Tell Kunkel we've got to go all out on this. We'll cooperate with the Washington police but we will take charge. This thing has all kinds of political ramifications and the press is going to have a field day."

I thought of other aspects of the case that would have to be covered. Gray was out of town, as usual, and he would have to be briefed as soon as I had a more complete picture.

"There's one other thing," the Night Supervisor said. "The arrested men had twenty-four hundred dollars in their possession, including thirteen new one-hundred-dollar bills." It would be some time before the significance of those one-hundred-dollar bills would be known to the Bureau but they proved to be one of the links between the "burglars" and the Committee to Re-Elect the President (CREP) At the time it made no sense that men who were committing a burglary would carry around such a sum of money. In fact, none of it made any sense. Obviously, the police had broken up some kind of political espionage operation. But the utter stupidity of it all left me completely baffled. What could anyone find at the Democratic National Committee which would be worth the risks?

At 10:00 A.M., I called Kunkel for a further briefing.

"Mark," he said, "there's a lot more to this than meets the eye. Shortly after these men were arrested and taken to the Second District Station, a Washington attorney named Michael Douglas Caddy appeared at the station and said he was representing the five subjects. Because they had not made any phone calls, Caddy was asked how he became aware of the arrests. He wouldn't tell the police a thing and, when pressed for an explanation, he left saying he would contact the U.S. Attorney."

"Bob," I asked, "how many Agents do you have working on the case?"

"Eighteen," he said after a little mental arithmetic.

"Are you sure that's enough?"

"That's enough for now but this thing is going to expand all over the place in a day or two."

I agreed with him thoroughly and asked him to keep me briefed and to let me know if he ran into any problems. I also told him that I would have to call Gray in Los Angeles but because of his inexperience and his aggressive nature, I knew he would ask many questions. It was not the same as it had been with Hoover who was sharp, brief, and to the point.

"We have a three-hour time advantage," I told Kunkel, "so I'll wait until one o'clock to call Gray. That's ten o'clock Los Angeles time. I want to brief him as completely as possible."

"We should have a lot more information by that time," he said. "We're getting search warrants to go into the rooms which the subjects occupied at the Watergate Hotel."

The search of the subjects' rooms turned up an additional $3,500 in crisp new one-hundred-dollar bills of the same series as those found at the time of the arrests. Also, an envelope containing a personal check made out by one E. Howard Hunt, Jr., was found and he was quickly identified as a CIA employee from November, 1949, until April, 1970. From FBI files we learned that a full-field investigation had been conducted on Hunt in July of 1971, when he was being considered for a staff position at the White House. A query was made and Alexander P. Butterfield told FBI Agents that Hunt had been used by the White House on "highly sensitive matters" but that he was no longer employed there.

When I called Gray, he had already left his hotel and was en route to Santa Ana, California, where he was to deliver a speech at Pepperdine College, so my message had to be relayed through the Senior Resident Agent at Santa Ana. Gray called back immediately after his speech and we discussed the case at some length. He seemed as surprised as I was and we jointly wondered who would try such a stupid escapade. He instructed that the investigation be pressed vigorously and that he be briefed daily.

I kept Gray posted at Palm Springs on Sunday, at San Francisco on Monday and at Sacramento on Tuesday. He returned to his office at 7:35 A.M. on Wednesday, June 21, and waiting on his desk was a detailed summary of the investigation to date which I was sure he would want to send to the Attorney General. For reasons which he did not explain, he ruled against passing it on. This seems very strange now, because much later I learned that throughout the investigation, he was sharing all the Bureau's knowledge with the White House Staff.

From the start of the Watergate investigation, bits and pieces of information began leaking to the press. The White House, for reasons which we now know, raised the roof with Gray, accusing the FBI of being responsible and ordering him to put a stop to it. It may be significant that among these leaks was one story that Gray planned to call off the FBI investigation and that he was not going to permit his Agents to subpoena the record of Presidential aide Charles Colson's telephone toll calls. Since, as we later learned, this leak came from the White House, it is reasonable to believe that John Ehrlichman, Bob Haldeman, or John Dean felt they had neutralized the FBI.

On Saturday, June 24, Gray called in SAC Kunkel and twenty-six Agents from the Washington Field Office who were working on the case. He accused them of "suffering from flapjaw," and as he later put it, "I literally put my track shoes in their backs" giving them "a strong verbal direction that we were going to press the investigation to the hilt." The Agents considered this accusation a serious reflection on their integrity but when Kunkel attempted to speak out in defense of his men, he was brusquely silenced by the Acting Director.

The leaks continued, however, and the *Washington Post's* Woodward and Bernstein team was soon giving their readers details of the investigation, sometimes within hours after the Bureau had learned of them. The White House was furious, and Ehrlichman called Gray on the carpet and told him, in no uncertain terms, that the leaks must stop. Gray reacted by sending an inspection team to the Washington Field Office to question all the Agents working on the case. When that did not stop the leaks, he ordered Assistant Director Charles W. Bates to personally grill the men under oath.

The effect of all this action was to further antagonize the

Agents, but it did nothing to stop the leaks. Numerous times when Gray was out of the city, John Dean called me, demanding that other steps be taken to silence the leakers. I refused to take such action and frequently I was able to point out to him that some of the leaks could not possibly have come from the Bureau, since they included information to which we were not privy. This did not mollify Mr. Dean.

It was this sequence of events which led both the White House Staff and top Justice Department officials to the conclusion that I was "Deep Throat." Haldeman so stated in a television interview but later he has written that he believes the culprit, if that is the right word, to be John Dean's assistant, Fred Fielding. Haldeman points out that any information which passed through the hands of Fielding found its way to *The Washington Post.* Haldeman also wrote that after they cut Fielding off from the information, the leaks became less accurate and consisted more of conjecture than of fact. I have no information, one way or the other, as to the truth of this contention and it obviously did not stop the White House from continuing to bestow the title upon me.

I did talk to Bob Woodward on one occasion during the Watergate investigation. He requested an interview, which I gave him, but to make sure that what I said would not be misquoted, I asked my assistant, Inspector Wason G. Campbell, to be present. Woodward, however, was not looking for information. He simply wanted to check out the information he and Bernstein had collected and he asked me to tell him which was accurate and which was not. I declined to cooperate with him in this manner and that was that.

While all this was going on, the FBI investigation was proceeding in spite of the cover-up. And, as we progressed, Howard Hunt's involvement became increasingly apparent. He was placed at the scene and eventually admitted that it was he who had called Douglas Caddy, the lawyer who had appeared at the police station unbidden to bail out the "burglars." This of course, explained how Caddy had known of the arrest. We also discovered that White House records listed Presidential counsel Colson as Hunt's "supervisor" beginning in June of 1971 and running to March of 1972—at least four months after Hunt began to recruit secret operatives who were later implicated in the Watergate break-in. Colson's private secretary had initialed Hunt's pay vouchers and his private phone line to the White House was billed to the home address of Catherine Chenow, secretary to the "Plumbers" unit. A White House internal memo dated March 30, 1972 was found which described Hunt as "very effective for us" and requested that he be shifted to the Committee for the Reelection of the President.

Pieces of the puzzle began to fit together when we discovered that G. Gordon Liddy had accompanied Hunt on several trips to recruit employees for "security work" with the Republican Party. Telephone numbers in the possession of some of the arrested men turned out to be those of Liddy at CREP. A cashier's check covering a number of campaign contributions had been given to Liddy at CREP and deposited to the account of Bernard Barker at the Republic National Bank in Miami.

Alfred Baldwin III, a former FBI Agent, admitted that he had been working for James McCord and that he was assigned to monitor the microphones planted in Democratic headquarters from Room 419 in the Howard Johnson Motel, directly across the street from Watergate. Baldwin told us that while he was occupying this room, Liddy had counted out some $18,000 in crisp new one-hundred-dollar bills in the presence of Hunt and had given the money to McCord. Liddy was also known to have shredded large numbers of documents at the offices of CREP. (On July 28, Liddy was fired from CREP, ostensibly for refusing to talk to the FBI.) Baldwin also made it clear that the Democratic National Committee headquarters had been bugged for some time. Transcripts of the overheard conversations which had been made by Baldwin had been given to McCord who seemed to be in charge of the monitoring operation.

The FBI struck pay dirt when its digging turned up Michael Richardson, a Miami photographer. Richardson told the Agents who interviewed him that a week before the break-in a man he tentatively identified as Bernard Barker from photographs he was shown had come to his store in a Cuban neighborhood. The man had two rolls of exposed thirty-five millimeter film which he wanted developed immediately and printed in eight-by-ten enlargements. There were thirty-eight negatives in all. Richardson said that they were photographs of documents, most of which had an emblem and "Chairman, Democratic National Committee" printed on them. The documents were photographed against a background of shag carpets. Hands in clear-type gloves held down the corners of each document.*

The delaying and obstructing tactics of officials at the White House and at CREP, to which Gray had acceded, led to an airtel dispatched by SAC Kunkel to the Acting Director. (An airtel is a message prepared in the form of a teletype message but sent by mail. It is designed to get the same attention as an urgent teletype, but at a fraction of the cost.) Dated late in June, the airtel bluntly highlighted the difficulties encountered in dealing with the White House and asked that the Bureau take a tougher stand.

Kunkel pointed out that Dean's insistence on sitting in on all FBI interviews with White House staffers had a chilling effect. This procedure had been approved by Gray at Dean's request. Kunkel further complained that Dean had kept the contents of Hunt's White House safe in his possession for five days before turning them over to the FBI. Agents, moreover, had encountered resistance from Dean in their efforts to obtain records of Colson's toll calls. Kunkel referred to FBI efforts to locate Catherine Chenow, the "Plumbers" secretary, and Dean's contention that she was on a European vacation and that he did not know how to get in touch with her. (In his book on Watergate, Dean would admit that he had known where Ms. Chenow was in England and that he had sent Fielding, his assistant, to bring her back so that she could be

* This, like the tell-tale tapes on the Watergate doors which alerted a security guard, made little sense. Why should the film have been taken to a commercial photography shop for developing, risking discovery of the Watergate operation, when secure photo labs were available? As evidence of this kind accumulated, some suspected that the "burglars" wanted to get caught.

coached before the FBI interviewed her.) I am convinced this airtel was the reason why Gray later transferred Kunkel to St. Louis—a demotion.

As the coordinator of the cover-up, Dean was very anxious to know of the progress of the FBI investigation. As we learned much later, Dean arranged to meet with Gray in the Acting Director's efficiency apartment in Washington. Not feeling secure even there, they conducted their business in a nearby park. As a result of this secret meeting, which Gray did not report to the FBI professional staff or to his personal assistants, Gray ordered the preparation of a summary of all developments to that time. This summary, dated July 21, was directed to the Attorney General and quickly forwarded to Dean.

Dean then asked Gray for the "raw files" on the case, together with copies of teletypes setting forth leads and results of interviews. In this way, he hoped to keep abreast of the Bureau as it followed those leads. Gray obliged by asking Kunkel for copies of these documents, explaining that he wanted to be more thoroughly familiar with the case's day-to-day progress. Dean himself came to Gray's office to collect the first package of this sensitive material. He continued to request more material and Gray obliged him by turning over to Fielding a second package of reports and teletypes on October 2, 1972. This conspiracy was first disclosed by Gray at his disastrous confirmation hearings. FBI Agents conducted twenty-six interviews with White House staff and sixty with individuals at CREP—and Dean received copies of the interview reports of most of these.

Agents were reluctantly forced to conduct their interviews with employees of CREP in the presence of a committee attorney. In this instance, permission for the attorney's presence was granted by Assistant United States Attorney Earl J. Silbert, who was handling the Watergate case. CREP's reason for demanding an attorney be present was the fact that the DNC was suing CREP for damages, which made a committee attorney's presence necessary. But several CREP employees contacted us and asked that they be interviewed again without the knowledge of committee officials. The presence of a

CREP lawyer during the original interview, they said, had prevented them from being completely candid. They also said that all committee employees subpoenaed to testify by the Watergate grand jury were later debriefed by CREP attorneys about what they had testified.

According to one of the employees who came to us, Hugh Sloan, Jr., who supervised committee finances, had kept a briefcase full of money in his safe. From February to April of 1972, our informant told us, Sloan had disbursed large sums to various committee officials for unknown purposes—$50,000 to Jeb Stuart Magruder, $100,000 to Herbert L. Porter, and $89,000 to Gordon Liddy. Another employee on reinterview told us that some committee officials were drawing red herrings across the FBI's trail to keep us from getting at the truth. Reports on these second interviews, however, were among those which Gray provided to John Dean. He alerted CREP officials who challenged these employees. This certainly discouraged others from coming to the Bureau with important information.

The first concrete indication I had of Gray's role in holding back information came when we began to trace the source of the money that had been in the possession of the Watergate "burglars." Agents discovered that Bernard Barker had deposited four checks totalling $89,000 in his Miami account. The checks were drawn on the Banco Internacional of Mexico City by Manuel Ogarrio, an attorney. The next step, obviously, was to interview Ogarrio. But Gray flatly ordered me to call this proposed interview off because it "might upset" a CIA operation in Mexico. I did not know at the time that less than a week after the break-in, President Nixon had called H. R. Haldeman to the Oval Office for a report on the case. Haldeman had concluded his remarks by saying that "the FBI is out of control."

The two had then discussed the possibility of directing General Vernon A. Walters, the new Deputy Director of the CIA, to tell Gray to "stay the hell out of this . . . we don't want you to go any further into it." Haldeman then asked, "And you seem to think the right thing to do is to get [the FBI] to stop?"

"Right! Fine!" the President said.

"They say the only way to do that is from White House instructions." Haldeman said. A little later he spelled it out even more clearly. "And the proposal would be that Ehrlichman and I call them in and say, ah . . ." Nixon picked it up with, "All right, fine. How do you call him in . . . I mean just . . . Well, we protected Helms from one hell of a lot of things" (precisely what those things were neither Nixon nor Helms has ever explained).

Less than two hours later, Haldeman, Helms and Walters were meeting with Ehrlichman in his office at the White House. When Walters returned to CIA, he wrote a memorandum recording what he was told.

> The bugging affair at the Democratic National Committee headquarters at the Watergate Apartments had made a lot of noise and the Democrats are trying to maximize it. . . . The investigation was leading to a lot of important people and this could get worse . . . Haldeman asked what the connection with the Agency was, and Director Helms replied that there was none. Haldeman said the whole affair was getting embarrassing and it was the President's wish that Walters call on Acting Director Gray and suggest to him that since the five suspects had been arrested, this should be sufficient, and that it was not advantageous to have the inquiry pushed, especially in Mexico.

Walters wrote that Haldeman told him to go to Gray and to tell him "that I had talked to the White House and suggest that the investigation not be pushed further." Haldeman assured Walters that Gray would be receptive because "he was looking for guidance in the matter." These instructions were given to Walters, according to his memo, despite Helms's repeated assertions that the FBI investigation would not expose any covert CIA programs. The record shows that Walters *did* see Gray that very same day to pass along the instructions which he had received from Haldeman. According to Walters, Gray replied that "his problem was how to low-key the matter now that it was launched . . . Gray then said this was a most awkward matter to come up during an election year and he would see what he could do."

Three days later, on June 26, Walters was again summoned to the White House where John Dean told him, "The investigation of the Watergate bugging case is extremely awkward and there are a lot of leads to important people." On the twenty-eighth, Dean said to Walters, "The problem is how to stop the FBI investigation beyond the five suspects." And on that same day, Helms phoned Gray requesting that the FBI not interview Karl Wagner and John Caswell, two CIA case officers, because they were engaged in highly sensitive assignments. Gray passed this down to me as an order. I was able to stop the interview of Wagner but Caswell had already been questioned. Both were thought to have information concerning E. Howard Hunt.

The CIA was less than cooperative in other ways, with inquiries from FBI Agents running into a stone wall or, worse still, encountering outright deception. For example, we asked the CIA about a man named Pennington, who had once been James McCord's supervisor. CIA gave us a summary on a former employee named Cecil H. Pennington who had no connection with McCord. It was more than a year before we learned that the man we wanted was Lee Pennington, who had been closely associated with McCord, both personally and professionally. William E. Colby, Helms's replacement as CIA Director, brushed this fact aside airily by saying that "we were trying to keep publicity away from the CIA."

By July 5, the delays and obstructions to the FBI investigation had gotten to the point where Kunkel, Bates, and I requested an appointment with Gray to discuss the problems. Kunkel restated the points he had made in his airtel and we all argued strenuously against the restrictions which had been imposed on us, particularly the stop on an inquiry into the Mexico City operation.

"Look," I told Gray, "the reputation of the FBI is at stake. As Acting Director, this is even more important to you than to us. In the future, you are going to have to convince skeptical U.S. Senators that we did a good job on this case. We can't delay the Ogarrio interview any longer! I hate to make this sound like an ultimatum, but unless we get a request in writing from Director Helms to forgo the Ogarrio interview, we're going ahead anyway!"

Gray hesitated and then looked at Bates and Kunkel. The expressions on their faces told him that he was facing near mutiny. He drew a long breath and said, "I'll call Helms today."

"That's not all," I went on. "We must do something about the complete lack of cooperation from John Dean and the Committee to Reelect the President. It's obvious they're holding back—delaying and leading us astray in every way they can. We expect this sort of thing when we are investigating organized crime, but we can't sit still and accept it from the White House and CREP."

"Mr. Gray," Kunkel broke in, "the obstructions we are encountering do a grave disservice to the President. I think you should call and tell him what the problems are."

"Bob is absolutely right," I said. "The whole thing is going to explode right in the President's face." Gray demurred. He thought it would be better to call Clark MacGregor, the new head of CREP, who was with Nixon in San Clemente. When we left Gray, however, I told Kunkel, "Get a teletype ready for Mexico City telling them to go ahead with the interview. If we haven't heard anything by the close of business today, send it."

Gray bowed to our ultimatum. He immediately called General Walters who noted in a memorandum, "He [Gray] said that the pressures on him to continue the investigation were great. Unless he had documents from me to the effect that their investigation was endagering the national security, he would have to go ahead with the investigation of the money transaction." Describing a meeting with Gray on July 6, Walters wrote, "I had a long association with the President and was as desirous as anyone of protecting him. I did not believe that a letter from the Agency asking the FBI to lay off this investigation on spurious grounds ... would serve the President."

Gray called me on the intercom that same day to tell me that there would be no letter from CIA and to proceed with the interview of Ogarrio. I did not tell him that instructions to that effect had been sent out the previous evening. Gray also called Clark MacGregor to inform him of the conference with his mutinous aides. As a result of that conversation, President Nixon called Gray. I have no source for what was said except what Gray said during his confirmation hearings. According to that testimony, he said, "Mr. President, Dick Walters and I feel that people on your staff are trying to mortally wound you by using the CIA and the FBI and by confusing the question of CIA interest in, or not in, people the FBI wishes to interview. I have just talked to Clark MacGregor and asked him to speak to you about this."

There was a slight pause and the President is supposed to have said, "Pat, you just continue to conduct your aggressive and thorough investigation."

The FBI worked very closely with the U.S. Attorney's office and with the Justice Department lawyers who were handling the case before it was handed to the Special Prosecutor. They were furnished the results of FBI investigations on a daily basis. When it became apparent that many of the suspects and witnesses were reluctant to discuss the case with us, let alone to tell the truth, the names were turned over to Earl Silbert who had them called before the Federal Grand Jury where they could be placed under oath and where the inducement to tell the truth was more compelling. It was the evidence which we collected which led to the successful prosecution of the five original suspects, plus Hunt and Liddy.

It was at this point that Gray again called Bates, Kunkel and me into his office. The ostensible purpose of the meeting was to bring Gray up to date on events, but when we took our places in his private office, the first thing Gray did was hold up a note pad on which he had drawn seven squares arranged in a circle, with a line connecting each square. There were no names on the note pad but we knew that Gray was referring to the five original Watergate burglars, McCord, Barker, Fiorini, Gonzales, and Martinez, plus E. Howard Hunt and Gordon Liddy.

"Can the investigation be confined to these seven subjects?" he asked.

"We do not have all the evidence yet," I told Gray, "but I am convinced we will be going much higher than these seven. These men are the pawns. We want the ones who moved the pawns." Both Bates and Kunkel agreed with me. The investigation still had a long way to go. Gray never raised the point again. He had run up a trial balloon and it had been shot down.

In fact, no one could have stopped the driving force of the investigation without an explosion in the Bureau—not even J. Edgar Hoover. For me, as well as for all the Agents who were involved, it had become a question of our integrity. We were under attack unfairly for dragging our feet and as professional law enforcement officers we were determined to go on. That we were doing a good job, moreover, cannot be denied. When Assistant Attorney General Petersen testified before the Senate Select Watergate Committee, he was able to say, "The investigation was 90 percent completed at the time the Special Prosecutor was appointed." In fact, the Special Prosecutor delayed the day of indictment for the higher-ups because he and his staff had to familiarize themselves with the intricacies of the case before proceeding.

Attacks against the FBI did not stop—and one charge hurled at us was that we failed to investigate the so-called dirty tricks of Donald L. Segretti and others who were working undercover for CREP. The simple fact is that the Justic Department told us it would not be necessary to investigate these aspects of the case. Ordinarily, the Special Agent in Charge is authorized to use his own initiative in the investigation of criminal cases. But Justice Department authorization is required in cases dealing with the Civil Rights statutes and others including the Election Law statute. In the Watergate case, substantial information about the dirty tricks was furnished to the Justice Department and, in each instance, we were told that no further investigation was necessary. After the Special Prosecutor took over, the FBI was requested to probe into this area—and it did so very effectively.

While running the FBI for our traveling Director, I had frequent contacts with John Wesley Dean, the President's Legal Counsel. I have already related our problems with Dean over leaks to the press. Another had to do with the contents of E. Howard Hunt's safe in the White House where Dean turned over some, but not all, of this material to the FBI. Of course, "Deep Throat" leaked details to *The Washington Post* which carried the story. Dean called me to object to a reference in the article which disclosed that one of the items in the safe was a hand gun. This was embarrassing to Dean and the Presidential staff because it raised questions as to the efficiency of a White House security system under which Hunt had been able to smuggle a weapon past the guards. When Dean called me to ask that the FBI issue a press release denying that a gun was involved, I said, "John, that's a ridiculous request. We are not going to do it. The answer is, No!" Dean put down the phone without comment and later in the day the Information Officer at the Justice Department issued an obfuscating statement, presumably at Dean's request.

The safe also contained four items which Dean did not turn over to the FBI. There were two folders which Dean and Ehrlichman turned over to Gray secretly with instructions that they must "Never see the light of day." (More about these folders later on.) There were also two "Hermes" notebooks which Dean later shredded—one containing a list of names and the other with notes made by Hunt.

Watergate was a trying time for the FBI and a difficult period for me. Given my position as Acting Associate Director and Gray's extended absences from Washington, I assume full responsibility for the conduct of the Watergate investigation. In spite of the roadblocks, the FBI did an excellent job, as the record will attest. During the first eighty-four days of the investigation, more than 1,500 people were interviewed, 1,900 leads were handled, 120 subpoenas were served, 130 investigative reports totaling more than 3,500 pages were submitted by 330 Agents in 51 Field Offices who worked more than 14,000 man hours. The prosecution was based upon information developed by the Bureau.

The FBI apologizes to no one for this achievement.

CHAPTER NINETEEN

Mark, you argue too much.

—RICHARD KLEINDIENST

When I became a Special Agent in the FBI, I had expected to track down criminals, to investigate subversives, and to enforce those laws which fall within the jurisdiction of the Bureau. As I rose in the pyramid, I realized that there were other duties, some exciting and some onerous. But until November of 1972, I never suspected that I would have to deal with a latter-day Indian uprising. I may be many things but General Custer I am not. Nor did I think that I would be a participant in the second Battle of Wounded Knee.

This historic battleground had been the site of one of the last confrontations between the U.S. Army and embattled American Indians clinging to tribal lands being taken over by the white man. Historians still disagree as to whether the first Wounded Knee was a battle or a massacre. It took place in 1890 when the Seventh Cavalry, General George Custer's old unit, encountered some 350 Sioux Indians and killed most of them. The FBI's involvement at Wounded Knee did not begin until eighty-two years later.

In the fall of 1972, the American Indian Movement (AIM) organized a Trail of Broken Treaties caravan which crossed the country from the west coast to Washington, D.C., to publicize injustices being done to Indians. AIM was composed principally of Indian militants who had been joined by sympathizers from other activist groups. When AIM failed to receive the impossible concessions it demanded from the Federal Government, a number of its more lawless members occupied the Bureau of Indian Affairs building on Constitution Avenue on November 2, 1972. All BIA employees were allowed to leave peacefully but no one was allowed to reenter the building and what came to be called the "Sack of the BIA" continued for a week.

Members of the Washington police and FBI agents stood by, on orders from the White House that there was to be no interference with AIM members. On November 8, the White House gave in and agreed that if the occupation were ended there would be no arrests. Taking advantage of this amnesty, AIM members left the BIA building, many of them loaded down with loot. While police and the FBI watched in frustration, office equipment and many boxes of BIA files were piled into a caravan of vehicles which took off in all directions.

It was only then that the FBI was ordered to take action. The Justice Department ordered FBI Agents to recover the stolen property and to gather evidence to be used in the prosecution of those responsible for the thefts. Fortunately, police and FBI Agents had taken the license numbers of the cars and the descriptions of many of the thieves. But recovery of this government property took much valuable time and eventually led to a head-to-head clash with columnist Jack Anderson and his assistant, Les Whitten.

When authorities reentered the BIA building, they found a complete shambles. The files which had not been stolen were scattered throughout the rooms and corridors. Corners were piled high with human excrement. Total damage was estimated at millions of dollars—and this did not include the priceless and irreplaceable records of the Indian Bureau.

It was clear to law enforcement officials the weakness displayed by a presumably strong President would only lead to further trouble and that was exactly what happened. The "Sack of the BIA" taught AIM that the media could be manipulated and exploited by the use of violent tactics. Later in November, two of the most aggressive AIM leaders—Dennis Banks, a Chippewa Indian, and Russell Means, an Oglala

Sioux, arrived at the Pine Ridge Indian Reservation in South Dakota, near the site of Wounded Knee. They threatened to seize the Bureau of Indian Affairs building on the reservation and to oust the elected tribal officials whom they accused of being too subservient to the Federal Government.

The Tribal Council, under the leadership of President Richard Wilson, an Oglala Sioux, wanted no part of AIM and it responded by passing a resolution banning Banks and Means from the reservation. Undaunted, the agitators went elsewhere and there were less publicized incidents in Iowa and North Dakota. In February, there was a clash between AIM and the local police at Custer, South Dakota, after a young Indian, Wesley Bad Heart Bull, died of stab wounds inflicted by a white man. AIM reacted by destroying several police cars and setting fire to the County Courthouse and the local Chamber of Commerce.

All this while the FBI was conducting an extensive search to locate the BIA office equipment and files stolen after the "Sack of the BIA." Recovery of the office equipment was relatively easy but finding the files proved to be more difficult.

John G. Arellano worked as an informant for the Washington police. Posing as an Apache Indian, he ingratiated himself with a group of AIM members who were thought to be trafficking in the stolen files. Leaders of this group were Henry L. Adams, an Assinboine Sioux, and Anita Collins, origin unknown, who had assumed the Indian name of Puma Jackson.

On January 24, 1973, Arellano informed his superiors that Adams and Collins were conferring with Jack Anderson, seeking to sell the documents stolen from the BIA. Anderson has vehemently denied this; yet, in a December 11, 1972, column, he had reported that his assistant, Les Whitten, had seen thousands of the documents taken from the Bureau of Indian Affairs. On January 30, Arellano reported that Adams had just received several boxes of BIA files and was holding them in his Northwest Washington apartment. He further reported that Adams and Collins were driving to North Carolina to pick up several additional boxes of files.

This information, relayed to the FBI, presented a tactical

problem. We could move in to recover the files immediately available or wait a few days and also pick up those coming up from North Carolina. After consultations between the FBI, the United States Attorney, and the Justice Department, it was decided that Agents should place Adams's apartment under twenty-four-hour surveillance until Adams had returned from North Carolina. The Justice Department ordered us to arrest anyone trying to remove files from the apartment.

The surveillance did not last long. At 9:00 A.M. the following day, a station wagon pulled up in front of the Adams apartment and a man entered the building. Within a few minutes, he and Hank Adams attempted to leave the building, each carrying a heavy box. They were immediately arrested, and the boxes were found to contain some of the missing files. A third carton of files was recovered in the lobby of the building.

The man who had arrived in the station wagon haughtily described himself as Leslie H. Whitten, Jr., of Jack Anderson's staff. He expected to be released on the spot and became quite angry when the Agents were unimpressed. The three boxes were confiscated and Adams and Whitten were taken to the FBI Field Office for photographing and fingerprinting—then to the United States Commissioner for arraignment. They were released without bond. Later in the day, Anita Collins was also arrested. She too was released without bond.

The next day, Special Agent Dennis Hyten, who had coordinated the case, received a wrathful phone call from Jack Anderson who berated him for what had happened and threatened, "Hyten, I'll get your job." Too startled to reply, Hyten listened as Anderson slammed down the receiver. John J. McDermott, who had replaced Bob Kunkel as SAC in Washington, realized that Anderson's call was a possible obstruction of justice, so he had Hyten call Anderson back, with another Agent listening in on an extension, to see if the threat would be repeated. Anderson admitted that he had made the threatening call and again said that he would get Hyten's job.

Apparently intimidated by Anderson, the Justice Department made it clear that it wanted no confrontation with him.

Whitten insisted that he had no intention of buying the files, looking at them, or even showing them to his boss—and the Grand Jury accepted his lame story that he was present merely to provide Adams transportation to return the stolen files to the BIA. Adams, of course, told the same story—and when no effort was made by the Justice Department to get an indictment, the matter was dropped.

Instead of letting it go, however, Anderson used the incident to accuse the FBI of wrongdoing. And he manipulated the situation beautifully. It provided him with column fodder which he exploited to the fullest for several months, wrapping himself in a cloak of martyrdom by claiming that the White House was using the FBI to harass him. The record showed that there was no connection between the White House and the arrest of Les Whitten. But even as Anderson played his "injured innocence" role to the hilt, trouble continued.

The Indian leaders of AIM had moved the center of their agitation from Custer, where the burned-out buildings no longer attracted media attention, to Rapid City, South Dakota. Soon the threats of violence to this quiet community became so great, and of such concern to FBI headquarters, that I ordered extra Agents sent there to observe and to be available to investigate Federal violations.

During the night of February 9, more than sixty Indians ran amok through the streets of Rapid City, breaking windows and destroying other property. Indians from other states, as well as other sympathizers, began to arrive in response to AIM's request for assistance. I ordered more Agents into the area, increasing our staff to thirty for I knew from informants and from our own observation that AIM was planning a new confrontation which would rival the "Sack of BIA," and I wanted the FBI to be ready. But I had no way of anticipating the incredible mismanagement soon to be demonstrated by the White House and the Justice Department.

As February passed, it began to appear that trouble could be averted. Several hundred men from the South Dakota National Guard had moved in and their presence had a stabilizing effect. Also, the attention of AIM members was occupied by impeachment proceedings against one of their enemies, Oglala Sioux Tribal President Wilson, whom they accused of mismanagement of Indian Tribal affairs. As the quiet continued, the National Guard was sent home. United States Deputy Marshals on the scene were also returned to their home posts and everyone began to breathe more easily.

On February 24, the impeachment proceedings against Wilson collapsed as he was retained in office by a vote of fourteen to four in the Tribal Council. Dissatisfied AIM members could not accept this and they gathered to discuss further action. We began to hear rumors of a planned imminent takeover of the BIA building on the Pine Ridge Indian Reservation, the second largest reservation in the United States, about twice the size of Delaware. Available Federal personnel, including FBI Agents, concentrated there. Whether it was coincidence or a ruse we will never know but the target was not Pine Ridge. It was Wounded Knee.

Hardly a likely setting for an armed clash between militant Indians and the Federal Government, Wounded Knee was a tiny community, the home of seventeen families, primarily Oglala Sioux. The town consisted of a church, a trading post, and a few dwellings, spread across three square miles. At the point where the two principal roads converged were the church and the trading post. What interested AIM, however, was the historic and symbolic significance of the old Indian battleground.

During the afternoon and evening of February 27, more than 200 members and supporters of AIM gathered at Calico Hall, near Pine Ridge. Many were carrying rifles, pistols, knives, and clubs. Late in the evening they left Calico Hall, saying they were bound for Porcupine. Their real destination was Wounded Knee, where they were to remain for seventy-one days. Witnesses later said that they converged on the town brandishing weapons, shooting in the air, and knocking out street lights. Throughout the night, there was systematic looting of the trading post, whose shelves were stripped bare. Eleven white residents were held as hostages. Many of them were elderly, mostly members of the Gildersleeve family which owned the trading post.

Early in the morning of February 28, Attorney General Kleindienst dutifully called the White House for instructions. As in November, the White House established a policy of avoiding interference or making any show of force. In establishing this policy, no one at the FBI was consulted—indeed, Acting Director Gray was on Capitol Hill for the first day of his confirmation hearings which were to occupy his time and his thoughts for the next forty days.

"Containment" was Kleindienst's policy—the establishment of roadblocks on five access roads into Wounded Knee to prevent anyone from entering or leaving the little town—an exercise in utter futility as we would soon learn. Kleindienst called me but only to let me know of the plans which had already been made by people who had no idea of the terrain. And he casually informed me that FBI Agents would be used to assist in manning the roadblocks.

I exploded, "General, your plan isn't going to work at all. Anyone wanting to leave or get in will simply bypass the roadblocks. Do you realize that the perimeter you are trying to hold will be more than fifteen miles? It's rolling country and your containment line will leak like a sieve." Kleindienst paused and I could hear his hand being put over the mouthpiece of the phone. After a wait, he came back on the line and said, "I know that, Mark, but it's the best we can do. It would take a regiment to make a firm containment."

"General," I answered," the FBI Agents we have in South Dakota are there for investigative functions, not guard duty."

Kleindienst became impatient. "More U. S. Marshals are being brought in but we still won't have enough to man the roadblocks. We have no choice but to use the Agents. I'm not asking you, I'm telling you!"

"What you are proposing is a siege. Why not use the South Dakota National Guard as was done in Rapid City?"

"Mark, we already thought of that but the Governor of South Dakota will not deploy the National Guard on an Indian reservation where the U.S. government has exclusive juridiction. I'm sure he's glad to be rid of the problem."

Still trying to avoid the improper use of FBI Agents in an

operation of this kind, I persisted. "The only Federal outfit which can muster the manpower to put a cordon around Wounded Knee is the Army. Why not let the military handle it?"

"Mark, I don't want to argue anymore. The White House wants to low-key this incident and there's no way we are going to use the Army. This is it. I am instructing you to assist in manning the roadblocks."

Had J. Edgar Hoover been alive, there would have been no problem. He would simply have refused to let Agents be used in this manner and that would have been that! But I did not have Hoover's muscle or authority, nor did Gray. I gave up. All I could do was to make it very clear that the Agents would be under the supervision of SAC Joseph Trimbach who was on the scene—and that we were not lending personnel to the U. S. Marshal or to the Justice Department. Kleindienst agreed to this but he insisted that Trimbach coordinate his activities with Ralph Erickson, his special assistant, and with Wayne Colburn, Director of the U. S. Marshals Service.

"All right, Dick," I said, "but I certainly hope the Government is prepared to have more backbone than it did at the 'Sack of the BIA.' That was a fiasco and if the Government doesn't show more firmness now, this thing could go on for weeks."

"Mark, I hope you're wrong. But the White House policy is to go to any lengths to avoid force. We figure if we can bottle up the Indians for a while, they'll just leave."

That is how the FBI became involved at Wounded Knee.

From the first day, there was little doubt that the AIM "occupation troops" had no intention of leaving Wounded Knee. Rifle shots were fired at the roadblocks, low-flying observation planes were shot at and the occupiers began digging foxholes and trenches. A statement was issued by Russell Means from Wounded Knee presenting AIM's demands for an immediate Congressional investigation into Indian treaties and conditions on Sioux reservations. Reporters were told that the hostages would not be harmed unless Federal authorities came too close. And thus began one of the most badly bungled Government operations that I have ever witnessed.

On Thursday, March 1, Erickson, Kleindienst's assistant, arrived at Wounded Knee to coordinate law enforcement efforts and to begin negotiations with the Indians. On the same day, Senators George McGovern and James Abourezk, both of South Dakota, also arrived at Wounded Knee. In a meeting with the occupiers, they promised that hearings would be convened by the Senate to hear their grievances. The Senators then departed, grandly assuring the press that their objectives had been accomplished.

On March 1, I received another call from Kleindienst. "Mark," he asked, "what is the FBI policy regarding the use of firearms?"

I explained that Agents were not to use firearms except in self-defense or to protect an innocent third party. Kleindienst then asked, "If an Agent does have justification to shoot, does he shoot to wound or to kill?"

"An Agent would only use his firearm under very restrictive conditions and then he would shoot to kill."

"Mark, we are going to use a different policy at Wounded Knee. Instruct the Agents that they are never to use firearms unless they are first fired upon and then they should shoot to wound, not to kill."

"Dick," I stormed, "that's ridiculous! Your new policy is far less restrictive than FBI policy. We shoot only under the most compelling circumstances. It takes far more justification to kill than to wound. Wounded Knee and the roadblocks are over one mile apart and under FBI policy, there would be no return fire from the roadblocks even if fired upon—"

"But—" Kleindienst started to interrupt.

"Now, listen, Dick. This is very important. Your policy is just going to encourage the exchange of gunfire. If you aren't going to move in, why not just tell everybody to stay under cover. No one is going to get hurt that way. Most of the shooting so far has been at night and the Agents have not been returning that fire."

"Mark, you argue too much!"

"I wouldn't be a good subordinate if I didn't point out the flaws in your policy. What makes you think it's possible to shoot to wound, especially when you are shooting at distances of over fifteen hundred yards? For God's sake! How would you know whether you are shooting at a man, woman, or child? Let's keep the more restrictive FBI policy."

"Mark, I don't want to hear any more arguments. You have your instructions. See that they're put into effect today!" He was already hanging up the phone, so he probably didn't hear me say, "That's absurd."

And absurd it was but that was the policy followed during the siege. Every night there was firing back and forth between the two sides. On occasion, there were fire fights during which thousands of rounds were exchanged though no one had the slightest idea at whom he was shooting. For the AIM members, it was a kind of game, and frequently they seemed to be deliberately trying to draw return fire. It was a miracle that the casualty list remained as small as it did. When it was over, two AIM members had been killed and seven wounded. A U. S. Marshal was shot through the spine and paralyzed from the waist down. One FBI Agent was badly wounded in the arm. It was hard to resist calling Kleindienst and telling him, "I told you so."

During the seventy-one days of the siege, the failure of the Government to respond decisively was compounded by a lack of clarity and uniformity in its negotiating position with the Indians. Erickson confused the issue by a "walk-through" offer which would have allowed anyone who wanted to leave Wounded Knee to do so without being arrested. When this had no results, he urged the occupiers "to send the women and children . . . out of Wounded Knee before darkness falls tomorrow." The media and AIM took this to be an ultimatum and the occupiers issued a nationwide call to militants for assistance in the second Battle of Wounded Knee. The other Indians on the reservation responded by threatening to assemble a large force to evict the AIM occupiers if the Government did not act and the tension increased.

Agents and Marshals, limited solely to returning fire, anxiously awaited some affirmative plan by Government officials to end the stalemate. None was forthcoming. Later, some of the AIM leaders told us that the most effective step by the Government would have been to remove all Federal forces at the outset because that was what had brought in the media and given AIM the publicity it wanted. AIM leader Vernon Bellecourt said that if the Government had withdrawn, the occupiers "would look foolish occupying something no one cares about."

During the early stages of the siege, a press poll of citizens across the country showed that 51 percent of those questioned accepted AIM's position and only 21 percent sympathized with the Government. Wounded Knee was a political forum—a guerrilla theater. No danger of a Federal attack existed and the nation's attention was focused on the drama. Congress had promised to listen and the Government's lack of position gave AIM much to gain and little to lose.

At first, it was planned to keep food and supplies from entering Wounded Knee in the hope that this would force the occupiers to capitulate. But the Indians could come and go almost at will through the thinly guarded perimeter in the rolling hills. Sympathizers flew planes into the area and the press could come and go. An order by a Federal judge to allow reasonable supplies through the roadblocks was hardly necessary—and to provide meat for their nightly barbecues, the Indians slaughtered the cattle on farms within the perimeter.

The Community Relations Service (CRS), then a branch of the Justice Department, had been set up to act as an arbitration service and a calming influence in racial situations. Now its representatives were sent to Wounded Knee. But unfortunately, that calming influence was interpreted as support by the militant Indians. And support it was, in a very tangible way. Cars used by the CRS entered the perimeter with full tanks of gasoline and left with them empty. Our suspicions of the role the CRS was playing were heightened when some of the court-approved supplies included a gross of sanitary napkins which, along with gasoline, are one of the key components of Molotov cocktails.

As days turned into weeks and weeks into months with no action by the Government, the local Indians, some of whose homes had been destroyed and whose cattle had been slaughtered, became increasingly resentful. To prevent gasoline and other incendiary supplies from reaching the AIM occupiers, the local Indians set up their own roadblocks about one mile farther back on the road to Pine Ridge. Members of the CRS team were stopped and their cars searched—and careful checks of gasoline gauges, were made on the way in and out.

The situation came to a head on April 23, almost two months after the siege began. Resentful of the Oglala Sioux roadblocks, CRS complained to the Chief U.S. Marshal who, with two of his deputies, proceeded to one of the Indian roadblocks. According to a senior Justice Department official present, the argument with the Oglala Indians became so "belligerent and rough that we decided to file assault charges against them." Eight of the reservation Indians were arrested and taken to Rapid City for arraignment.

When Tribal President Wilson announced that he was organizing 500 reservation Indians to reestablish the roadblock, the Justice Department passed the buck and made a counterannouncement that the FBI would prevent this. SAC Richard G. Held of the Chicago office, who had been rotated to Wounded Knee as the senior FBI official on the scene, called me to report on the situation.

He said, "Mark, the Marshals caused this ruckus and now they are trying to put the monkey on our back. The Justice Department didn't consult with me about the statement that the FBI would prevent reservation Indians from setting up their roadblock again. As a matter of fact, we couldn't stop them anyway. We don't have enough Agents."

I did not bother to consult with Kleindienst or Gray. "Dick," (Richard Held) I said, "we've been pushed around long enough. Unless you hear to the contrary from me or from Gray, take no action involving physical force to prevent these people from setting up another roadblock. We both know the FBI has no responsibility for this sort of thing. Disregard what they say."

Held said, "I'm glad to hear you say that, Mark, because tempers out here are getting pretty frayed."

Held called me again to say that negotiations between Deputy Assistant Attorney General Richard Hellstern and the

Indians from Pine Ridge had broken down. Tribal President Wilson had set out from Pine Ridge with some 500 of his followers, including women and children, to reestablish the roadblock. Chief Marshal Colburn had also proceeded to the area where he had positioned his men to stop Wilson and his supporters.

"Your instructions are not changed," I told Held. "FBI Agents are not to take part or to use force to prevent the Indians from setting up their roadblock again."

But the White House, which had been so tender-hearted about using any force against the lawbreakers at Wounded Knee, had no compunctions about using it against the reservation Indians who were the victims of the occupation. Within twenty minutes my orders had been countermanded. Hellstern had called Kleindienst who had read the riot act to Gray. Held was instructed to tell the Indians that they could have a "small" roadblock, just so long as they did not interfere with the Community Relations Service operations. Gray instructed Held to go to the site to inform Wilson of the White House decision and to do his best to prevent violence.

Dick Held was the only person who could have handled this assignment. Some years before, he had been made an honorary member of the Sioux Nation in a ceremony at which wrists were cut and blood was mingled. Six feet five inches tall, he was given the Indian name of Tall Elk. Following Gray's instructions, Held immediately flew to the scene on a Government-chartered helicopter. He found Wilson's supporters already advancing on the U.S. Marshals' line, women and children before them. The Marshals were standing with their rifles at the ready position. Had Held not arrived on time, there could have been a brutal carnage, courtesy of the Justice Department—all of it recorded by the TV cameramen who had been alerted and were present.

(Later in the day, the White House went back on its word to permit the "small" roadblock but by that time tempers had cooled and bloodshed was prevented.)

The occupation of Wounded Knee was finally ended when, on May 7, an agreement was reached for the evacuation of the town on the following day at 7 A.M. On the night of May 7, a number of persons were arrested attempting to sneak out but many others were able to slip past the roadblocks. On the morning of May 8, guns and ammunition were sent out and 129 persons, mostly Indians, came out. Fifteen arrests were made but only thirty-five weapons were confiscated. The remainder had been secretly removed during the previous nights while Kleindienst and the White House were scratching their heads.

United States Marshals then entered the little town without incident, disarming anti-personnel mines and collecting Molotov cocktails. Not much was left of Wounded Knee. The trading post had been burned to the ground and several homes were burned-out shells. Garbage covered the area and there was a terrible stench from the remains of slaughtered cattle. The original residents moved back to sift the rubble in search of their belongings. They had been the real losers in a series of events that could have been prevented had the Government moved swiftly and decisively.

Why did the AIM Indians give up? Time was a factor. But other factors were even more important. Public opinion had shifted away from the militant AIM occupiers and they were no longer viewed as innocent civil rights demonstrators under siege by a heartless Government. Even Senator McGovern changed his mind and called for the forcible ouster of the occupiers. "We cannot have one law for a handful of publicity-seeking militants and another for the ordinary citizen," he said.

Lack of food was another contributory factor. By the end of April, the occupiers were down to a daily diet of oatmeal for breakfast and boiled beef for dinner. And the single electric transformer serving Wounded Knee had been knocked out by a stray bullet, cutting off electric power. Hot plates used to cook food were useless. The water supply was low since the town's pumps were electrically operated. There was no radio or television to help the AIM members pass the time. And sanitation was almost non-existent, so that the occupiers were increasingly suffering from viral infections.

Of all the AIM members and sympathizers arrested in connection with the siege, only a handful were convicted of violating Federal laws on a Government Indian reservation. The two leaders, Dennis Banks and Russell Means, were not in Wounded Knee at the time of the evacuation but they were charged with assaulting Federal officers, burglary, and larceny. Their trial lasted for more than eight months—radical lawyers William Kunstler and Mark Lane appearing as the principal defense attorneys.

The trial ended suddenly on September 16, 1974, when one of the jurors suffered a stroke. The Government, for reasons best known to it, refused to continue with eleven jurors, and United States District Judge Fred J. Nichols dismissed the case, alleging Government misconduct, illegal involvement of the military, and failure to produce material on discovery.

The alleged government misconduct? The Bison State Telephone Company, at the direction of the U.S. Marhsal, had installed three telephones on one party line leading from Pine Ridge to Wounded Knee. Two of the phones were installed inside the trading post at Wounded Knee and a third, on the same line but with a different number, connected with the principal government roadblock. The purpose of the phone line was to allow AIM members to communicate with the outside world as well as with FBI Agents at the roadblock. Agents testified that they listened in on some of the conversations between AIM members and their sympathizers. There was no testimony that any evidence had been gathered in this fashion. (The phone bill run up by AIM was $1,400. The Government paid it.) This was the alleged Government misconduct.

Illegal involvement of the military was because Agents and Marshals used equipment borrowed from the military. And Army officers had been present at the scene to assess the situation in case military intervention had proved necessary.

Failure to produce material in discovery proceedings resulted from admitted delays due to the difficulty in supplying the multitudinous documents demanded by the defense.

Banks was convicted of only one crime connected with his AIM activities. It was not his first brush with the law, nor his last. He had served in the Air Force during the Korean War but after his discharge he had drifted into freight hopping, drinking, and petty thievery which landed him in prison. In July of 1974, a South Dakota court convicted him of riot and assault for his part in an AIM riot during which two buildings were burned down. Banks then skipped town, forfeiting $10,000 bail, $9,000 of which had been put up by United Methodist Church agencies.

He was arrested by FBI Agents in January, 1975, at the home of a Costa Mesa college professor in northern California. By that time he was also wanted in Oregon, where authorities alleged that he was one of the men in a camper who had fired at a State Trooper. Two men had fled after the shooting. They were identified as Banks and Leonard Pelletier who was wanted for the murder of two FBI Agents on the Pine Ridge reservation on June 26, 1974. The two FBI Agents, Jack R. Coler and Ronald Williams, had been ambushed while searching for a Federal fugitive on the reservation. Pettetier was later tried and found guilty of these murders in a Fargo, North Dakota, Federal court.

One of the legacies of Wounded Knee to the Pine Ridge reservation was to give it the highest murder rate in the country—twenty-three killings in 1974, many of them attributable to fights between AIM members and reservation Indians. But there was a second legacy that was entirely within the FBI. Gray's popularity with the rank-and-file, which had declined considerably in the wake of the Watergate investigation, plummeted during Wounded Knee when Agents blamed him for failure to protect the Bureau's interests and Agents' wives blamed him for unnecessarily exposing their husbands to the hazardous and bitter-cold conditions of the Pine Ridge winter. One Agent, SAC Herbert Hoxie, was at the Command Post and exposed to the weather so long that he contracted pneumonia and almost died.

CHAPTER TWENTY

Let him twist slowly, slowly in the wind.

—JOHN EHRLICHMAN

The record amply demonstrates that President Nixon made Pat Gray the Acting Director of the FBI because he wanted a politician in J. Edgar Hoover's position who would convert the Bureau into an adjunct of the White House machine. Before becoming President, Mr. Nixon had applauded Hoover's independence from political direction, but once in the Oval Office he saw the possibilities of making the FBI a White House police force. What Nixon did not foresee was that the Bureau's professional staff would fight this tooth and nail. What Gray never understood was that his impact on the FBI would be minimal if he spent so much of his time away from actively directing Bureau activities while he traveled the land making speeches.

His long illness and his longer convalescence after abdominal surgery, together with his lack of experience with FBI operations, all combined to make him an ineffective leader. And no sooner did he return from one speech making tour, than he would be off again, beating the drums more for the Nixon Administration than for the FBI. But for all of this, he was never really trusted by the White House which felt that he was not adequately handling the job to which he had been appointed.

As the days after Nixon's second inauguration passed, Gray

became less and less confident that he would be given the permanent appointment as FBI Director. One by one, others named to varying federal jobs on a temporary basis were given permanent status by the President but there was no word about Gray. Suspecting that he was being shunted aside, he confided to me that he was seriously considering dropping his Government career and returning to the practice of law in New London.

Finally, on February 15, 1973, the White House seemed ready to drop the second shoe. Gray received a phone call summoning him to the White House the following morning. When he returned, he described to me his lukewarm reception by a blank-faced John Ehrlichman and his brief meeting with the President. During his fifteen minutes with Ehrlichman, he was grilled on his ability to handle the post of FBI Director and questioned about his health. Nixon was no more sympathetic.

"Pat," he said, "you're not ruthless enough in getting polygraphs to stop those leaks. Get tougher." Gray promised that he would but he left the White House not knowing whether he would get the appointment. On Friday, February 17, however, Ron Ziegler, Nixon's press secretary, announced that Gray had been named the permanent head of the FBI. Noting that Gray would be the first FBI Director to require Senate confirmation, Ziegler added that he was "confident" that there would be no difficulties. This was gainsaid by the Senate Democratic whip, Robert C. Bryd, who let it be known that he would oppose Senate confirmation because Gray was "a bone of contention and a source of division" within the Bureau.

This should have been a warning to Gray. But instead of turning for assistance to seasoned veterans in the Justice Department who were wise to the ways of Capitol Hill, he relied on the amateurs of his personal staff for the preparation he badly needed. It was not a good time for any FBI Director to face the Senate. Political bombs were bursting in Washington. *Time* had just disclosed that the FBI had been wiretapping White House personnel and certain members of the press at the request of Presidential aides, and Wounded Knee was making unpleasant headlines. Nevertheless, Gray was supremely confident that he could handle the Senate Judiciary Committee.

Things started off well when Gray was presented to the Committee by Connecticut's two Senators, Democrat Abraham Ribicoff and Republican Lowell Weicker. Gray read a statement outlining in glowing terms his "accomplishments" during his ten months as Acting Director. And then, in his inexperience, he took a step which almost guaranteed his downfall. He offered to make the entire Watergate file available to any Senator who wished to see it. The files, he added, would be available to Senators alone and not to staff. Attorney General Kleindienst was aghast, and the White House, which knew what those files contained, was furious. Even the Senators were startled.

"Do you mean the entire file–lock, stock, and barrel?" an incredulous Senator Byrd asked.

"Yes, sir," Gray answered. "We are proud of that investigation."

His opening statement completed, Gray was pressed by Senator Sam J. Ervin, Jr. for an explanation of a speech he had delivered the previous August before the City Club of Cleveland. Erwin along with others felt the speech had been political. Gray insisted that the invitation had come directly from the City Club, but he was later forced to admit that it had been set up by the White House. Senator Ervin then asked about the "Congressional Cards" which the FBI kept on Senators and Congressmen. Gray answered that the practice had been discontinued by him. What, the Senator asked, about the incident in September, 1972, when the FBI had been used to collate criminal justice information for the political use of the White House? Gray answered that he had been out of town at the time but that he had admonished those responsible for acceding to the White House request. This answer came as a surprise to us at the Bureau for it was the first time that anyone in the FBI learned that he had been "admonished."

Ervin next referred to newspaper reports that Donald Segretti, the inept dirty tricks expert, had been shown transcripts of two interrogations of himself that had been conducted by the FBI. Gray opened a Pandora's box with his reply. He described how, at John Dean's request, he had ordered the preparation of a detailed summary of the investigation. Since it was his duty to keep the Attorney General fully informed, he had had the summary sent to the Justice Department, knowing full well that it would be sent to the White House. So far so good. But like many inexperienced witnesses, Gray could not let it go at that. He had to elaborate.

"Later," he told the committee, "Mr. Dean asked to review the interview reports of the Federal Bureau of Investigation, and I submitted these to him." This was like saying that he had admitted the fox into the henhouse. "What is being driven at is this. The allegation [that FBI interview reports were shown to Segretti] is really directed toward Mr. Dean having any of those reports and showing it to Mr. Segretti [at the Republican Convention] in Miami. I can tell you this. When the newspaper report hit, I called John Dean and asked him if he had done this and he said, 'I did not. I didn't even have those documents with me.' " But the cat was out of the bag that Gray had allowed FBI reports to be shown to a man under FBI investigation.

The only consolation for those of us following the hearings was in Sam Ervin's concluding remarks after the first round of questions: "Mr. J. Edgar Hoover never had a more ardent admirer in the United States Senate than myself, and there is nobody in the United States who has more respected, throughout the years, the work of the FBI. As a practicing attorney and a judge, I had many contacts with FBI Agents. I have been impressed by the highest standards of conduct and the high character which they possess."

But from then on it was all downhill for Pat Gray. In the days of the hearings which followed, Gray hedged and attempted to evade the pointed questions of Democratic members. Senator John V. Tunney returned to the allegation that Segretti had been shown his own file and questioned the propriety of making Watergate investigative files available to the White House. Then he moved to the general question of FBI files.

"Do you know how many names you have in the files that you have secret dossiers on?" he asked. Gray objected to the term "dossier" and Tunney asked him, "Do you know how many people in the country have files?" It was perfectly clear that Tunney was talking about investigative files but Gray went into a long discussion of fingerprint records and so on for the next twenty-five pages of the record. Tunney was finally able to ask: "Did you personally give or authorize the giving of the Dita Beard memorandum to the ITT corporation?"

"No, I did not."

"Do you have any idea how the Dita Beard memorandum ended up in the hands of the ITT corporation?"

Reversing his field, Gray admitted that John Dean had requested access to the memorandum so that it could be turned over to ITT.

"And it was made available?"

"It was made available to him by me."

But it was Senator Edward M. Kennedy of Massachusetts who really drew blood. "This week's *Time* magazine contains information on alleged wiretaps on newsmen—according to the article—requested by the White House, authorized by the Justice Department, installed by the FBI. How do you respond to these charges?"

Gray squirmed. "I would have to say, first, that with regard to the general matter of wiretaps—"

Kennedy interrupted. "No, just on these charges. How do you respond specifically?"

"How do I respond to these charges? When I saw this particular article and checked the records and indices of the Federal Bureau of Investigation, and I am also told that the Department of Justice checked the records of the Internal Revenue Division . . . there is no record of any such business here of bugging news reporters and White House people."

Gray had expected this question and he had thought out an answer that was technically true but completely misleading. There was no official record of the so-called Kissinger wiretaps in the FBI because Assistant Director Sullivan had personally sequestered the wiretaps in his own files, along with the records, logs, and letters of authorization from Attorney General John Mitchell. Sullivan had then secretly turned them over to Assistant Attorney General Mardian who later delivered them to the White House. Therefore, there was nothing in FBI files to indicate the existence of the Kissinger wiretaps. But Gray had unofficial knowledge of their existence, though he had absolutely nothing to do with them. Had he admitted this, he would have been home free. But as President Nixon's man in the Bureau, and out of political loyalty, he resorted to a circumlocution which led him deeper and deeper into trouble as Senator Kennedy pressed relentlessly for unequivocal answers.

Gray was not prepared for this kind of cross-examination, in effect a psychological assault, and matters became worse when Kennedy directed his fire at the FBI's handling of the Watergate investigation. Perhaps, had he been at his desk more often, Pat Gray might have been able to avoid the pitfalls and also to defend the Bureau adequately. With only a smattering of knowledge, however, he blundered—and it did not take Kennedy very long to expand the scope of his questioning and drag Herbert W. Kalmbach, Nixon's personal attorney, and Dwight Chapin, the White House appointments secretary, into the picture in a way that damaged Gray. In fact, Gray was compelled to answer some of Kennedy's questions about Chapin and Kalmbach in a written statement.

It read, in part, as follows:

> After checking the records, I have found that Mr. Kalmbach was interviewed on September 4, 1972, in Los Angeles. This interview was conducted at the request of Assistant U.S. Attorney Silbert, who directed the Grand Jury inquiry. Mr. Silbert wanted us to find, from Mr. Kalmbach, details concerning payments of money to Segretti such as how much was paid, where the money came from, and whether reports were made by Segretti. Mr. Kalmbach said that in either August or September, 1971, he was contacted by Mr. Dwight Chapin and was

> informed that Captain Donald Henry Segretti was about to get out of the military service and that he may be of service to the Republican Party. Mr. Chapin asked Kalmbach to contact Segretti in this regard, but Mr. Kalmbach said he was not exactly sure what service Chapin had in mind other than he believed he would be of service to the Republican Party. He said he did not press Chapin in this regard. He did contact Segretti and agreed that Segretti would be paid $16,000 per year plus expenses and he paid Segretti somewhere between $30,000 and $40,000 between September 1, 1971 and March 15, 1972. . . . He said he had no knowledge of what Segretti was doing to justify these expenses or to earn his salary. He said the money he used to pay Segretti came out of campaign funds. . . .

In the give and take of questioning, Gray might have been able to gloss over many of the details but his written statement had invidious overtones which infuriated an already angry White House. Every hour he spent on the stand, therefore, saw his White House support erode further. His offer to open the FBI's Watergate files to the Senators, moreover, put him in a damned-if-you-do-damned-if-you-don't situation when the American Civil Liberties Union submitted a letter to Chairman Eastland which strenuously raised the question of violation of privacy. Said the ACLU:

> . . . These files contain information about individuals which should not be disclosed without careful consideration of their rights. . . . We, therefore, request that you take steps to insure that safeguards along the lines we have suggested be established to protect individuals who may be mentioned in any FBI documents prior to transmittal to Congress of any additional FBI information. . . .

This left Gray under hidden but real attack by the White House for having offered the files in the first place, under pressure from the members of the Committee to allow staff members to see them, and under criticism from the ACLU for being ready to violate the privacy of individuals under investigation. With Gray subjected to this cross-fire, the Senators haggled for hours. But there was no respite for the Acting Director when the Senators shifted to other subjects, some already covered but now rehashed with some vehemence.

Why had Gray acceded to John Dean's demand that he be present when the FBI was conducting its interviews? Why had Gray not acted when he learned that Dean had taken possession of the contents of E. Howard Hunt's safe at the White House? Why was Dean allowed to retain some of the contents of that safe? How was it that he had no knowledge of the Kissinger wiretaps?

And then Gray made his most serious mistake. While another witness was testifying, Gray called John Ehrlichman about a terrible secret in his closet known only to himself, Ehrlichman, and John Dean. As he was subsequently to admit to Senator Lowell Weicker of Connecticut, Gray had destroyed two folders of material which Dean had removed from the White House safe of E. Howard Hunt. The material had been withheld by Dean from FBI Agents.

Gray was naively unaware that the call was being recorded and even had he known, who could have guessed that it would subsequently be made public during the Watergate Hearings which were to follow? The call was a major indiscretion, first because it delivered Gray into Ehrlichman's hands and second because it hinted at matters which would eventually kill any chance of Gray's confirmation. Gray's first comment was: "The thing I want to talk to you about is, I am being pushed awfully hard in certain areas and I'm not giving an inch. And you know those areas and I think you have got to tell John Wesley . . . [Dean] to stand very tight in the saddle and to be very careful about what he says and to be absolutely certain that he knows in his own mind that he delivered everything he had to the FBI and doesn't make any distinction between," Gray paused, "but that he delivered everything to the FBI."

Ehrlichman replied in a cavalier tone, "Right."

Gray went on, "And that he delivered it to those Agents—"

"All right."

Gray was obsequious, "You know I've got a couple of areas up there that I'm hitting hard and I'm just taking the attack."

Ehrlichman: "Okay."

"I wanted you to know that."

Ehrlichman, ironically: "Good. Keep up the good work, my boy. Let me know if I can help."

Gray: "All right. He [Dean] can help by doing that."

Ehrlichman: "Good, I'll do it."

The "it" was to ask Dean to lie for Gray if anything came up about the documents from the Hunt safe which Gray had destroyed. Immediately after talking to Gray, Ehrlichman called Dean and said cheerily. "Hi. Just had a call from your favorite witness."

Dean: "Which is?"

Ehrlichman: "Patrick J. Gray."

Dean: "Oh, really?"

Ehrlichman: "And he said to make sure that old John W. Dean stays very, very firm and steady in his story that he delivered every document to the FBI and that he does not start making distinctions between Agents and Directors."

Dean: "He's a little worried, isn't he?"

Ehrlichman: "Well, he just does not want there to be any questions. He says he's hanging very firm and there's a lot of probing around."

Dean, in a disgusted tone: "Yeah, he's really hanging tough. You ought to read the transcript. He makes me gag."

Ehrlichman: "Really?"

Dean: "Oh, it's awful, John."

Ehrlichman: "Why did he call me? To cover his tracks?"

Dean: "Yeah, sure. I laid this on him yesterday."

Ehrlichman: "Oh, I see. Okay, John."

Dean: "Laid it on him, too. You know, to confuse the issue, so I don't have any idea what he said up there today."

Ehrlichman: "I see. It was a funny phone call. Said he is going to object to the jurisdiction of the group to get into the substance and that their only jurisdiction was to—to procedural efforts and competence and he says the ACLU put in a letter to the same effect."

Dean: "Yeah. Wally picked up an interesting one on the

grapevine today that the strategy now is to proceed in this one as it did in Kleindienst."

Ehrlichman: "Down to the point of calling you?"

Dean: "Down to the point of calling me!"

Ehrlichman, laughing: "Let him hang there. Well, I think we ought to let him hang there. Let him twist, slowly, slowly in the wind."

Dean: "That's right, and I was with the Boss this morning and that is exactly where he was coming out. He said, 'I'm not sure Gray is smart enough to run the Bureau the way he is handling himself.' "

Ehrlichman, laughing: "Well, okay. You're on the top of it. Good."

While Gray slowly twisted in the wind, the Senate Judiciary Committee called a series of anti-FBI, anti-Gray witnesses. Among them was Joseph Rauh, Jr., national vice chairman of Americans for Democratic Action, who surprisingly had some good words to say about the FBI, even as he cut up Gray.

"Let me hasten to make an important point concerning the use of FBI files by Mr. Hoover," he testified. "As far as I know, from thirty years or more of FBI watching, Mr. Hoover never used the FBI files for partisan political purposes. There is a real distinction between the use of the files to discredit one's critics—unfair and even dangerous as I believe that practice to be—and the use of FBI files in the partisan political arena. For the first time, that cloud of political partisanship hangs over he FBI. . . . What is at stake in Mr. Gray's nomination is at the least the integrity of the FBI and at the most the integrity of our political system. . . ."

Under other circumstances, it would have been high comedy when the columnist Jack Anderson appeared as a watchdog of FBI integrity—and then quoted from FBI summaries, classified of course, which had been sent to the White House in the past for the information of Presidents. "No serious person ever accused Hoover of running a political police force," Anderson said—and no one laughed when he added, "not even me." Anderson also accused Gray of lying about the arrest of his assistant Les Whitten of purloined Bureau of

Indian Affairs files fame. And to no one's surprise, Whitten paraded his injured innocence before the Committee.

There was a series of other witnesses, some testifying against Gray and others simply venting their spleen on the FBI. But while their testimony was droning on in a Senate hearing room, the White House and the Justice Department were moving to put Gray in a completely untenable position. When the Committee convened again to continue Gray's testimony, he was forced to inform the chairman and the ranking minority member that something new had been added. On orders from Attorney General Kleindienst, Gray withdrew his offer to allow the Senators to review the FBI's Watergate files. Only the chairman, the ranking minority member, and their counsel were to have access. This alone might not have caused too much of a furor. Senators were too busy to sift through FBI files. But Kleindienst had also instructed Gray that he was to limit his answers to procedural matters and to decline to answer anything which related to substance—in other words to keep his mouth shut about Watergate.

The first question when the Committee was called to order elicited a reply from Gray, "Mr. Chairman, I will have to respectfully decline and request that the answer be obtained by you, sir, or by the ranking minority member, or the chief counsel to the Committee, or the minority counsel, because that is a matter of substance and I am not permitted to discuss that. Furthermore, there is a source of information involved, an FBI source of information in connection with that."

What the White House had done, in effect, was to make Gray appear to be a part of the general cover-up and in comments to the media, Senator Tunney suggested that the Nixon Administration "has decided to throw Mr. Gray to the wolves." Senator Birch Bayh, the Indiana Democrat, put it even more bluntly. "With friends like Mr. Gray has down at the White House," he said, "he doesn't need any enemies." To compound Gray's troubles, President Nixon refused to allow John Dean to testify, on the grounds of executive privilege.

But it was on Thursday, March 22, the last day of the hearings, that Senator Robert Byrd administered the *coup de grace.* Of a tired and discouraged Pat Gray, he asked: "The next day [June 28, 1972] Mr. Dean called you at 10:45 A.M. regarding leaks concerning material delivered to the FBI. What particular leak and what specific material did he have in mind?" (Senator Byrd was probing into Dean's actions concerning the contents of E. Howard Hunt's safe.)

"He was calling me then about those rumors that were continuing, as he put it, to the effect that the FBI was dragging its feet in the investigation and that a gun had been found in Mr. Hunt's effects. That was the subject of the call . . . as best as I can recollect it, sir."

"On that same afternoon, at 4:35, you called him. You state that you have no recollection of the substance of that call. Could it have been with respect to Mr. Hunt's properties?" Byrd asked.

Gray was exhausted. "No, I do not think it was . . . but I just don't know."

Then Byrd sprang the trap. "Going back to Mr. Dean. When he indicated that he would have to check and see if Mr. Hunt had an office in the Old Executive Office Building, he lied to Agents, didn't he?"

A hush settled over the hearing room. Dean *had* lied, in an attempt to steer suspicion away from the White House over its connection with the Watergate burglary. Hesitating for a moment, Gray spoke very slowly. "I would say, looking back on it now"—he paused and took a deep breath—"and exhaustively analyzing the minute details of this investigation, I would have to conclude that probably is correct. Yes, sir."

Gray knew, the Committee knew, and the audience knew, that in admitting that Dean had lied, the Director-designate had cut himself off from whatever remained of White House support. And in admitting that he had known that Dean had lied but had done nothing about it, he had destroyed his credibility and his image of integrity.

From that point on, Gray refused to talk to reporters and withdrew into himself. On April 5, he requested President Nixon to withdraw his nomination to the post of FBI Director. By then there was not the slightest chance that he could be confirmed by either the Judiciary Committee or the Senate.

President Nixon's comment in acceding to Gray's request was typical. "In fairness to Mr. Gray," he said, and the phrase elicited ironic smiles in Washington, "and out of my overriding concern for the effective conduct of the vitally important business of the FBI, I have regretfully agreed to withdraw Mr. Gray's nomination."

Having allowed Pat Gray to twist in the wind, the President had finally cut him down.

CHAPTER TWENTY-ONE

B—but he's the President.

—William Ruckelshaus

As he entered his office on the morning of April 25, 1973, Senator Lowell P. Weicker, the Connecticut Republican, was stopped by his secretary. Acting Director Gray of the FBI, then sitting out his days until President Nixon appointed a successor, had called urgently three times, Weicker was told. Somewhat surprised—the Senator and Gray came from the same state but they were hardly close friends—he returned the call immediately.

When Gray came on the line, he said, "Senator, it is very urgent and very important that I see you right away. Can you come down to my office?"

Twenty minutes later, Weicker was in the Acting Director's office. For a while, Gray talked despondently about his problems with the White House and the difficulties of the confirmation hearings. Then he exploded a bomb. On June 28, 1972, just eleven days after the Watergate break-in, Gray said, he had been summoned to the White House for a conference with John Ehrlichman. When he arrived, he was surprised to find John Dean there. Ehrlichman had come directly to the point.

"Pat," he said, "John has some files he wants to turn over to you."

Dean had then handed Gray two folders. He explained that

they had come out of Howard Hunt's office safe in the Executive Office Building—the office he (Dean) had denied knowing about. Dean said the rest of the material from the safe was being turned over to FBI Agents who had requested it. Dean added that the folders had nothing to do with Watergate and contained "highly sensitive, classified national security material with political overtones.

"They shouldn't see the light of day and they must never become part of the FBI's own files because they are political dynamite," Dean had told Gray. Then he left the office.

Ehrlichman had been more explicit. Gray told Weiker that Erlichman had ordered him to "deep six" the documents. [Ehrlichman later denied the statement.] Gray then told Weicker that he had kept the documents in his office for two weeks and then taken them to his home in Connecticut. He solemnly assured the Senator that he had retained them until December, then had burned them in his fireplace. He denied having read the documents—something which Weicker found hard to believe.

The facts would come out much later, on August 3, 1973, when Gray testified before the Senate Watergate Committee. In his testimony he admitted that he had looked at the documents before burning them and that they had appeared to be top-secret State Department papers. "I read the first cable," he told the Watergate Committee. "I do not recall the exact language but the text of the cable implicated officials of the Kennedy Administration in the assassination of President Ngo Dhin Diem of South Vietnam. I had no reason then to doubt the authenticity of the 'cable' and was shaken by what I read.

"I thumbed through the other 'cables' in this file. They appeared to be duplicates of the first 'cable.' I merely thumbed through the second of the two files and noted that it contained onionskin copies of correspondence. I did not absorb the subject matter of the correspondence and do not today, of my own knowledge, know what it was." * Neither

* E. Howard Hunt later admitted that some of the material, including the 'cablegram,' was forged by him for possible political use if Edward M. Kennedy had become the Democratic Presidential candidate.

the Committee nor the public could quite believe that Gray had burned the contents of the folders without having carefully read them.

But on that April day of 1973, Senator Weicker, without any knowledge of what the two folders contained, realized the seriousness of Gray's confession. Already angered by White House tactics in the Watergate case, he knew that he now possessed a lethal weapon. "Don't do anything about it right now," he told Gray. "Let me think it over and decide what you should do." Naive as usual, Gray agreed.

It did not, however, take Weicker very long to come to a decision. The following day, without consulting Gray, he gave the story to a reporter friend on *The New York Daily News* and it broke dramatically in that paper. The wire services immediately picked up the account of Gray's malfeasance and the media across the country gave it tremendous coverage. Weicker made no secret of the fact that he was the source of the story but insisted that he had released it to "protect" Gray.

The furor at FBI Headquarters and in every FBI Field Office was such that Gray could no longer remain in office. On April 27, two days after his "confidential" discussion with Weicker, the Acting Director resigned and the news was flashed to President Nixon as he was returning from Key Biscayne on Air Force One. Hours later, Nixon publicly accepted the resignation. The terse announcement made no mention of a successor.

I talked with Gray shortly after that and we discussed what the President might do. "I recommended that you be designated Director," Gray told me, "but I don't know whether those White House people will pay any attention to what I say." I gathered that his recommendation had been made either to John Ehrlichman or John Dean—which was just about the worst thing that could have been done to advance my candidacy. In my dealings with the White House *troika*, I had always put the interests of the FBI first and had never been forgiven for it.

Certainly I would have wanted the appointment. But uppermost in my thoughts was the state of mind at the FBI. Tension was mounting among a staff already in a state of shock over the disclosure that Gray had destroyed Watergate evidence. Could we keep the Bureau on course? The FBI had always been a closely knit and dedicated organization. Now it was confronted by another major change and the possibility that a new outsider would be brought in. I kept thinking, "If only the President sees the light and appoints a new Director from the ranks this time."

Several of the top officials were well-qualified. My own chances should have been good since I was next in line as Associate Director and had been running the Bureau while Gray was learning the ropes and delivering speeches. When one of the wire services reported that I was to be named Director, I thought the problem had been solved—and my secretary spent a busy half-hour assembling photos and biographical data.

Then, as suddenly as it had started, the rumor subsided. I was left again to sit at my desk wondering—but not for long. At 2:50 P.M., the President announced, without consultation with anyone at the Bureau, that he was appointing William B. Ruckelshaus to succeed Pat Gray. Cut off from the White House, we got the news from the wire services. Now that I have carefully reviewed the White House tapes, I know that there was never a possibility that Nixon would appoint anyone from the professional staff to head the FBI. He believed that the Bureau was "out of control" and that it had pushed the Watergate investigation too hard. He was still looking for someone who was politically malleable to direct what had once been the "world's greatest law enforcement agency."

Nixon's feelings about me are clearly revealed in an Oval Office discussion with John Dean on February 28, 1972. Dean was briefing the President on a story which had appeared in *Time,* disclosing for the first time the existence of the Kissinger wiretaps.

"The other person who knows and is aware of it is Mark Felt," Dean said, "and we have talked about Mark Felt before."

"Let's face it," Nixon answered. "Suppose Felt comes out now and unwraps. What does it do to him?"

"He can't do it," Dean said.

"How about his career?" Nixon asked. "Who is going to hire him? Let's face it—the guy who goes out—he couldn't do it unless he had a guarantee from somebody like *Time* magazine who would say, 'Look, we will give you a job for life.' Then what do they do? He would get a job at *Life,* and everyone would treat him like a pariah. He is in a very dangerous situation. These guys, you know—the informers. Look what it did to Chambers.* They finished him."

This was not the only Oval Office conversation about me and the tenor of all of them was that I would not cooperate with White House schemes. I never quite made the "enemies' list" but I think I came pretty close to it. Whatever Nixon, Dean, and Ehrlichman may have thought about me, I was and am proud of my FBI record and of the fact that I am the only insider ever to have climbed to the top of the FBI pyramid, if only for two hours and fifty minutes.

By law, the Associate Director takes charge of the FBI during any period when it is without a designated Director. From a practical standpoint, I made good use of those nearly three hours. This was time enough to make some new rules and to abolish some of the burdensome and unnecessary administrative procedures imposed by Gray.

The most onerous of these rules grew out of the White House phobia about leaks—ironically since the leaks were for the most part coming out of the White House. This phobia caused even the most trusted people to be viewed with suspicion. Gray's response was to direct that an "accountability log" accompany each sensitive document as it made its way up and down the various levels of authority until it reached the action point where after it would be filed along with the log. This sounded like a good security system but it proved absolutely unworkable in the FBI.

I tried to talk Gray out of implementing this plan but

---

* Whittaker Chambers, a *Time* senior editor, had been forced to resign after testifying that Alger Hiss was a Soviet espionage agent. In times of trouble for himself, Nixon frequently drove out secretly to the Chambers farm in Maryland to seek his advice and always professed a deep friendship and loyalty to Chambers.

without success. He just could not understand that the tremendous volume of sensitive documents circulating at FBI Headquarters made the plan a bottleneck. Many secretaries, clerks, and messengers handled documents in addition to Supervisors and other officials—and as a result each log would soon look like a nominating petition. Gray remained adamant but he never knew that we applied his rule only at Headquarters and not in the Field. When I rescinded the plan, there was a great sigh of relief. Looking back, it is too bad that I did not take greater advantage of my tenure as Acting Director. Ruckelshaus did not come aboard for some days, so I had plenty of time.

When we learned (again through the press) that Ruckelshaus had announced that he was coming to the FBI only until a permanent Director was chosen, there was consternation in the Bureau. It meant going through all the headaches and controversies of breaking in a temporary caretaker. And that was all Ruckelshaus's proved to be—security guard sent to see that the FBI did nothing which would displease Mr. Nixon.

Two days after his appointment, Ruckelshaus arrived at the FBI building in his own limousine, surrounded by the inevitable entourage—a personal staff to protect him from the FBI "enemy" that he had been told about by the White House and the Justice Department. His first instructions to me were to "set up a conference of all Agents as soon as it can be arranged." I had momentary visions of all 8,500 FBI Agents pouring in from all over the country but I said nothing. Instead I ordered the Special Agents in Charge of the fifty-nine Field Offices to report to Washington for a meeting with their new boss. This meeting was held on May 2, ironically the anniversary of J. Edgar Hoover's death. For the second time in twelve months, we had to begin the education process.

Whereas I had resolved all my doubts in favor of Gray and had greeted him with some enthusiasm, I am afraid that this was not true on that blue Monday when Ruckelshaus arrived. We gave Gray full support and as much cooperation as he would allow. We covered his mistakes. When he did not deal fairly with us, we told ourselves that he was acting under pressure from the White House or the Attorney General. If we argued vehemently with him, we nevertheless implemented his instructions to the best of our abilities. But as Ruckelshaus and his entourage marched into the Director's office, I had a feeling of unease—a sense that things were wrong and that I should do something about it. Here was a man who would be in charge of an investigative jurisdiction covering more than a hundred laws, many requiring different approaches and different procedures. Gray, at least, had come from the Justice Department. Ruckelshaus was fresh out of the Environmental Protection Agency. I felt like an endangered species myself.

After ten months of attempting to educate Pat Gray, we were starting all over again. And then we would have to restart with the permanent Director. "My God," my assistant, Wason Campbell said, "we'll have to go through this twice more." This was the consensus throughout Headquarters and it contributed to a reception that was, to understate it, cool. This is not to say that there was any thought of insubordination or of allowing the FBI to drift off course. It was more a sense of despair.

Perhaps we should have been sorry for Ruckelshaus who realized our attitude from the very beginning. In fact, the very first document he saw when he took over was a telegram to the President. It had been written and sent to Mr. Nixon after the new Acting Director made his statement that he was only going to be a caretaker. He mentioned three months.

THE HONORABLE RICHARD M. NIXON
PRESIDENT OF THE UNITED STATES
THE WHITE HOUSE
WASHINGTON, D. C.

MISTER PRESIDENT. THIS MESSAGE, BY UNANIMOUS ADOPTION, IS FROM THE ACTING ASSOCIATE DIRECTOR, ALL ASSISTANT DIRECTORS AND ALL SPECIAL AGENTS IN CHARGE OF FBI FIELD OFFICES THROUGHOUT THE UNITED STATES. THE HALLMARKS OF FIDELITY, BRAVERY AND INTEGRITY AND OF DEDICATION TO CONSTITUTIONAL PRINCIPLES OF EQUAL JUSTICE AND PRESERVATION OF THE RIGHTS OF ALL CITIZENS

HAVE MADE THE FBI A REVERED INSTITUTION IN OUR NATIONAL LIFE. J. EDGAR HOOVER'S PRECEPTS OF CAREFUL SELECTION OF AGENT PERSONNEL AMONG HIGHLY QUALIFIED CANDIDATES, RIGOROUS TRAINING, FIRM DISCIPLINE, AND PROMOTION SOLELY ON MERIT HAVE DEVELOPED WITHIN THE FBI LAW ENFORCEMENT LEADERS OF PROFESSIONAL STATURE RESPECTED WORLD-WIDE. IN THE SEARCH FOR A NOMINEE FOR THE FBI DIRECTORSHIP, WE URGE CONSIDERATION OF THE HIGHLY QUALIFIED PROFESSIONALS WITH IMPECCABLE CREDENTIALS OF INTEGRITY WITHIN THE ORGANIZATION ITSELF. WE DO NOT SUGGEST THERE ARE NOT MANY OTHER HIGHLY QUALIFIED LEADERS OF PROVEN INTEGRITY, BUT AT THIS CRITICAL TIME IT IS ESSENTIAL THAT THE FBI NOT FLOUNDER OR LOSE DIRECTION IN ITS SERVICE TO THE NATION BECAUSE OF LACK OF LAW ENFORCEMENT EXPERTISE OR OF OTHER QUALITIES ESSENTIAL TO THE FBI DIRECTORSHIP. NONE OF US SEEK PERSONAL GAIN. THERE IS A VAST RESERVOIR OF QUALIFIED EXECUTIVES WITHIN THE FBI'S OFFICIALDOM FROM WHICH A NOMINEE COULD BE SELECTED. WE ARE MOVED TO ADDRESS YOU THUSLY, BECAUSE OF OUR DEVOTION TO OUR SWORN DUTY TO THE PEOPLE OF THE NATION, BECAUSE OF OUR LOVE FOR THIS GREAT INSTITUTION, AND BECAUSE WE HAVE SEEN NO INDICATION OF CONSIDERATION OF FBI OFFICIALS, AMONG WHOM THERE IS AN INHERENT NONPARTISANSHIP AND A DEEP REVERENCE TO THE CALL OF DUTY TO ALL THE PEOPLE OF OUR NATION.

RESPECTFULLY

ALL FBI OFFICIALS

I quote this in its entirety because it is unique. It was the unanimous declaration of fifteen top FBI officials at Headquarters and all the Field executives, written by Assistant Director Leonard M. Walters of the Inspection Division and cleared by me. When I handed this document to Ruckelshaus, he read it slowly without saying a word. Then he looked at me over his glasses.

"Has this been sent?" he asked.

"Yes."

"Have copies been released to the press?"

Again my answer was in the affirmative.

Ruckelshaus rose to this feet and without a word put the telegram down in front of me, then walked out of the room. He never made further reference to the telegram and for that matter neither did the President. We never received an answer, formal or informal, from the White House.

It has been alleged that the telegram was an attempt on my part to unseat Ruckelshaus and to promote my own candidacy for the Directorship. But there was no need to unseat someone who presumably would barely warm the Director's chair. And by this time I knew that as long as John Dean and John Ehrlichman were in the White House, I would have less chance to receive the appointment than the man in the moon. The telegram was an attempt to serve notice on the President that the FBI could not survive another outsider and perhaps it ultimately tilted the decision in favor of Clarence M. Kelley who was acceptable to the insiders because of his prior service in the FBI before he became Kansas City's chief of police. (Kelley had also been active in the Society of Former FBI Agents.)

The attitude toward Ruckelhaus was not improved when his wife Jill, on the collegiate lecture circuit, was quoted as saying that her husband was going to the FBI "with a clean broom." An inflamed FBI saw this as a slap in the face and an attack on our integrity. When I heard of this comment, I called Ruckelshaus and told him that I had to see him right away. "Come on over," he told me. As I entered the inner sanctum I was jarred by the sight of Ruckelshaus lolling in an easy chair with his feet on what I still felt was J. Edgar Hoover's desk. Ruckelshaus let me stand there for a few minutes while he finished reading a paper he had in his hand. Finally he said, "What can I do for you?"

"Mr. Ruckelshaus, your wife is being quoted as saying that you were 'going to the FBI with a clean broom.' This is having a devastating effect on employee morale, which is already bad enough."

"She was misquoted," he said. "She didn't say that. Nothing like that at all. Nothing at all."

"Mr. Ruckelshaus, if that's the case, you should make some

sort of statement to the personnel to counteract the extremely adverse effect."

Dismissing me with a wave of his hand, he answered, "I'll think it over." He never made any denial and he never brought it up again with me.

My relationship with Ruckelshaus was stormy at times. He had come to the FBI determined to protect the President at any cost, whereas I became more wary and disillusioned with every passing day. My objective was to protect the Bureau. But even more than Pat Gray, Ruckelshaus divorced himself from day-to-day operations. He would only review mail and material relating to Watergate and the Ellsberg case. He had no interest in anything else.

On the third day of his tenure, all the SACs reported for the conference which Ruckelshaus had ordered. I introduced him to the group and he spoke briefly. He said that he could understand the traumatic effect of the revelations about Gray's destruction of documents and his sudden resignation. He appealed to the Agents in Charge for their cooperation. In all, he spoke for about ten minutes, then abruptly turned the meeting over to me, and left the room. There had been no applause. There had been no questions, and for that matter no time for them. It was in and out, and I thought of the staggering expense of bringing fifty-nine SACs from all over the country, including Alaska and Hawaii, for this brush-off. To salvage some of the taxpayers' money, I turned the meeting into an all-day work conference. Only once before in my experience had there been a conference of all the SACs at one time—the meeting called by Gray ten months earlier.

News of this meeting leaked to the press, of course, and there were stories that we had spent the day making disparaging remarks about Ruckelshaus and suggesting ways to get rid of him. It may be a blow to his pride but there was no mention of him whatsoever.

My next chilling incident with the new Acting Director came about as a result of the Ellsberg case. We already knew that John Ehrlichman had met secretly with Federal Judge Matt Byrne who was presiding over the Ellsberg trial in Los Angeles—a meeting at which Ehrlichman had improperly discussed the possibility of Byrne's appointment as permanent

FBI Director. We realized that public notice of the meeting could well compromise the trial and lead to the reversal of a conviction by the Court of Appeals. Then, during the closing days of the trial, *The Washington Post* alleged that wiretaps had been placed on Ellsberg's phone by the White House "Plumbers." This led Judge Byrne to demand proof from the Government that the evidence against Ellsberg had not been tainted.

Ruckelshaus immediately ordered an investigation. The wiretaps mentioned in the *Post* piece obviously referred to the Kissinger wiretaps which had been placed at the White House's behest. But even though it was certain that Ruckelshaus had been briefed on the subject—after all, the Attorney General and the Justice Department were well aware of the situation and edgy about it—we duly reported the facts to the Acting Director. He was told how the tapes had been made and why, that Bill Sullivan had squirreled them away in his office, and how they had ended up at the White House via Assistant Attorney General Mardian. There had, moreover, never been a tap on Ellsberg's phone.

We further reported that Ellsberg, as a house guest of Morton Halperin who was suspected of being one of those who were leaking National Security Council secrets to the press, had used the phone. Several of his conversations had therefore been overheard but they in no way related to the *Pentagon Papers* theft and publication, for which Ellsberg was being tried. Our reports to Ruckelshaus were delivered to him on an hourly basis and we felt that he should have immediately relayed them to the Attorney General and to Judge Byrne as an indication of the Bureau's responsiveness and good faith—and more important, to lay to rest any suspicion that the data were not prejudicial to Ellsberg.

Instead, for reasons none of us could fathom, Ruckelshaus let the reports accumulate on his desk. Finally, after five days, he sent the following memorandum to the Justice Department and to Judge Byrne:

> Shortly after assuming office as Acting Director of the FBI, my attention was called to the newspaper allegation that FBI personnel had been tapping unidentified news-

> men. I was also informed that a search of FBI records had not disclosed the existence of such wiretaps. Nevertheless, on May 4, 1973, I initiated an investigation to interview present and retired FBI personnel for the purpose of determing, if possible, whether there had been such taps. . . .

This completely misleading statement convinced the FBI that its worst suspicions about Ruckelshaus had been well founded. The memorandum implied that the FBI had withheld information when, in fact, the exact opposite was true. The "clean broom," moreover, was clearly attempting to unload blame for the wiretaps on the FBI and to provide a cover for the activities of important Presidential aides who were being increasingly embarrassed by the Ellsberg trial—a shabby political maneuver. A "clean broom" was indeed needed, but to start sweeping at the very top.

The roughest sessions I had with Ruckelshaus were over White House instructions to produce specifics on FBI wiretaps made during previous Administrations. First we were asked to furnish a list of the number of wiretaps placed every year beginning with 1941. I explained to Ruckelshaus that no such statistics had ever been kept. Records *were* kept of each person overheard on wiretaps but no distinction was made whether or not the individual was a "tappee" or an uninvolved party. The records, called the Electronic Surveillance Index, consisted of index cards which merely contained a name and file number. The Index was maintained to provide the Justice Department with ready reference as to whether a particular person had been overheard on a tap when such information was needed for prosecution purposes. Names of potential defendants in criminal cases were routinely checked against this Index.

What the White House wanted, for strictly political purposes, was a review of thousands of files to determine whether the Index Record referred to a person on whom a wiretap had been placed or to the many people who might have called him. Over my strenuous objections, however, the information was compiled—and sent to the White House—and the following day Senate Republican Leader Hugh Scott of Pennsylvania released it to the media. Ruckelshaus told me that Nixon had personally handled the transmittal of this information to Senator Scott.

The second White House request for additional wiretap information brought about an even more violent disagreement with Ruckelshaus. This time the White House wanted the names of all persons who had been wiretapped between 1960 and 1968—the Kennedy-Johnson years. I told Ruckelshaus, "Look, they have no legitimate use for this information. You know what they'll do with it. Remember what happened the last time. They're desperately trying to show that previous Administrations tapped reporters and Government officials. Then they'll release it to the news media—and the FBI will look bad. It's like a small child saying, 'He did it first.' We shouldn't be a party to this kind of political shenanigan."

When Ruckelshaus still insisted that we comply, I said, "We have purposely avoided putting all this information into one file for security reasons. For the FBI to consolidate this is bad enough but to provide a duplicate file multiplies the risks."

Ruckelshaus gave me a long look, took a deep breath, and slowly let it out. "B—but he's the President."

"For God's sake! President or not, just tell him no!"

I turned on my heel and walked out, hoping that I had convinced him. I had—but only until my retirement a short time later. Then Ruckelshaus ordered the list prepared and sent to the White House. It was politics all the way.

My decision to retire undoubtedly pleased the Acting Director. He regarded me as a thorn in his side because I frequently disagreed with what he wanted to do. After I had left, he proudly boasted to reporters that he had forced me and several old "Hooverites" out of the Bureau. It was true that we were forced out—but only in the sense that we retired because we could not accept the politicization of the Bureau and because we did not trust him. But we left of our own free will. Perhaps he realized how we felt when, after the "Saturday Night Massacre" in which President Nixon fired the Special Prosecutor in the Watergate case, he himself was "forced" to resign. William Ruckelshaus finally stood up to the President but it would be interesting to know what his thoughts were at the time.

I had remained in the FBI, as I have already recounted, at considerable personal sacrifice and with the feeling that I would be needed to keep on course the organization to which I had devoted most of my adult life. My inclination had been to resign when Nixon appointed Ruckelshaus—and my experiences with him had convinced me that I could do little more to protect the FBI. Now, having made the decision to retire, my primary concern was to see that my successor would be able to run the Bureau, which is essentially what I had been doing.

I talked to Ruckelhaus about this, putting it as diplomatically as I could.

"It is very important for you to select a replacement for me," I told him. "When Gray was here, he abolished two key positions—Assistant to the Director-Administrative and Assistant to the Director-Investigative. This means that the Associate Director has been functioning as Chief of Staff to coordinate and direct the day-to-day operations of thirteen divisions."

"But I don't want to make such a key decision when I am not permanent," he said, evading the issue. "This decision should be left to the Director who is appointed by the President and confirmed by the Senate."

"That will take weeks," I said. "How are you going to direct and control the operations of the FBI in the meantime?"

"I'll think about it," he said, which meant that he intended to do nothing. I would have stayed on longer, through a transition period, but he did not ask me to do so. The White House was too anxious to get me out.

When it became clear that Ruckelshaus was not going to take any action on what I regarded as a vital recommendation, I instructed all the top FBI officials to submit their recommendations for a new Associate Director directly to Ruckelshaus rather than to me. This they did and four strong candidates emerged as logical replacements. I was encouraged and reassured but Ruckelshaus paid not the slightest attention to the need for an Associate Director.

Meanwhile, the White House selection process for a new Director was under way. The list had been narrowed down to three contenders: Clarence M. Kelley, Assistant Attorney General Henry Peterson, and William C. Sullivan. U. S. District Judge Matthew Byrne of Los Angeles, a highly qualified candidate, had fallen by the wayside when news of his conference with John Ehrlichman about the job during the Ellsberg trial leaked to the press and smacked of "arm twisting."

Kelley and Sullivan were the only serious candidates. Henry Peterson was on the list as an attempt to show the country that other men of some stature were being considered. Kelley had served as an adviser and consultant on security during the Republican National Convention in Miami and was highly regarded by law enforcement experts. Sullivan was the man the White House really wanted. He had shown himself to be a pliant tool of the Nixon staff and his thinking about the threat from the "New Left" matched that of President Nixon.

Ruckelshaus continued to assure me that President Nixon was giving thought to appointing a career FBI man to the job. To give credence to this, he selected two of the names which had been suggested to him for the position of Associate Director and sent both men to the White House to be interviewed as candidates. They were interviewed by Alexander Haig and other Presidential aides. The interviews were perfunctory and designed solely to give the impression that insiders were being considered. It was window dressing and nothing more.

Clarence Kelley eventually received the appointment—and we felt that if the new Director had to come from the outside, he was a good choice. Insiders would accept him because he was respected and, having served many years in the Bureau, he would be no amateur. But the front-runner, until the very last minute, was William C. Sullivan. When Ruckelshaus told me that it would be Kelley, he added, "But Sullivan came *that* close to being appointed." He held up his hand, the thumb and forefinger about a sixteenth of an inch apart.

CHAPTER TWENTY-TWO

You are lying to protect Gray. . . .

—JAY HOROWITZ
OFFICE OF THE SPECIAL WATERGATE PROSECUTOR

My indictment on April 10, 1978, was only the most recent of my problems with the Federal Government since my retirement. I was not being allowed to become a private citizen.

During the last six months of 1973, Watergate and all its ramifications filled the newspapers and overflowed the television tubes. Among those being accused of improper activities was L. Patrick Gray III. On Monday, February 25, 1974, I responded to a pre-emptory summons by Jay Horowitz of the Office of the Special Prosecutor investigating Watergate. With him in his office was Francis Martin, a young aide. Both lawyers were evasive when I tried to find out what they wanted of me. When I pressed for an answer, Horowitz said, "You realize that you might have violated the law." I realized no such thing and told Horowitz so but he would not explain.

The questioning, both in his office and later before the Watergate Grand Jury, was a game of cat-and-mouse. I was asked about many matters, some of which seemed hardly germane to Watergate but the questions always returned to the so-called Kissinger Wiretaps of White House personnel and news reporters who were suspected of involvement in the leaking of secret and sensitive information to the media. This was approached from every possible angle, in the hope, I suppose, that I could be tripped up or made to contradict myself. I told the truth so there was no way that my story would change.

What finally became clear was that the matter at issue was a statement made by Gray in 1973 during his Senate confirmation hearings that there was no record of those wiretaps, made in 1969-71, in FBI files, a statement which was strictly and narrowly true.

My knowledge of the matter was limited to what I had learned as a result of an inquiry which I had conducted at the time of the retirement of Assistant to the Director William C. Sullivan. From this I knew that the wiretaps had been conducted and that Sullivan kept all the records in his office. I also knew that when Sullivan had been forced out of the FBI by Hoover in September, 1971, for insubordination, he gave the wiretap files to Assistant Attorney General Robert Mardian who took them to the White House where they ended up in the safe of John Ehrlichman, President Nixon's adviser for domestic affairs. Horowitz hoped to prove that Gray committed perjury when he denied to the Senate Judiciary Committee that FBI files contained any record of the Kissinger Wiretaps. My only recollection was that I had discussed the Sullivan affair with Gray, including details of the case of the purloined files.

Finally, Horowitz put before me a very faint, almost unreadable document, which appeared to be a photocopy of a carbon copy of a memorandum dated February 26, 1973, two days before Gray began his testimony before the Committee. There were no initials on the document, neither mine nor those of anyone else, though there would have been had it been an official FBI memorandum. I was barely able to make out that the document briefly described each of the Kissinger Wiretaps. It also listed a wiretap on a Navy Yeoman, which had also been placed at the request of the White House. This Yeoman, an aide to the Navy representative on the National Security Council, had been suspected of leaking sensitive information to columnist Jack Anderson.

When I told Horowitz I could not recall having seen the memorandum before, he made no attempt to conceal his anger. Very sharply, he informed me that the memorandum had been prepared in the Domestic Intelligence Division of the Bureau and that Miller had testified he personally brought it to my office on February 26. I had no reason to doubt Miller's word and I told Horowitz so. The content and the timing of the memorandum, however, made sense because on February 26 *Time* magazine made the first public disclosure of the wiretaps. It would have been standard operating procedure for the FBI to give the Director a detailed memorandum on what a news story was all about.

Horowitz, however, would not be denied. Nor would he accept my explanation that I had seen hundreds of documents every day, not a few of which concerned wiretaps. Because of the volume, I had to read hurriedly and could not possibly recall everything I had seen. An exasperated Horowitz would not accept this explanation and tried in every possible way to force me to "admit" that I remembered having personally given the document to Gray. He wanted me to testify that I personally carried the memorandum to Gray—which was ridiculous because if I could not remember it how could I possibly testify that I carried it to Gray? Horowitz argued that I should remember the matter because it was unusual. I countered by pointing out that I saw unusual documents every day. (I later recalled that February 26 was the day when the Indian uprising at Wounded Knee was exploding and undoubtedly I could have recalled little else that happened that day.)

Without testimony from me that I recalled the memorandum and, even better, that I personally carried it to Gray, the possibility of a perjury case against Gray was extremely remote.

Horowitz was furious. "You are lying!" he shouted.

"And you are trying to force me to commit perjury so that you can convict Gray of the same offense," I replied.

All of this was rehashed before the grand jurors, and with each repetition, Horowitz became more accusatory and more hostile, communicating his antagonism to the Grand Jury; and by their attitudes and questions, it was obvious that the grand jurors believed Horowitz and not me.

There were two days of this adversary dueling. Then, declaring a recess, Horowitz asked me to accompany him to an adjoining office.

"You are lying to protect Gray," he said. "Why do you do this after the terrible damage he did to the FBI?"

"I have no reason to protect Gray," I answered, "and certainly not to the extent of putting myself in the middle. Look! I could save myself all this trouble by testifying the way you want me to but I don't remember and I won't do it!"

Very coldly, as if he had not heard me, Horowitz continued, "It is perjury to testify that you don't remember something when you really do. You leave me no choice but to have you indicted for perjury."

I refused to be intimidated and insisted, "I'll take a lie detector test!"

Horowitz said scornfully, "What good would that do with an FBI Agent conducting the test?"

"The FBI does not use the polygraph anymore. You can get your operator."

Horowitz rose to his feet. "I have no confidence in the polygraph, no matter who administers the test." When I insisted that I be given the test, he paid no attention.

Back in the Grand Jury room, he once more asked me the key questions and once more my answers were displeasing to him. Finally he jumped to his feet and told me that I was excused. Escorting me to the door, his parting words were, "You will hear from me later."

With this unpleasant thought in mind, I left the dark corridors of the United States Courthouse and walked into the spring sunlight. What a relief it was!

An interesting coincidence is that Horowitz's aide, Francis Martin, was subsequently transferred to the Civil Rights Division of the Justice Department where he assumed a leadership role in my indictment for allegedly violating the civil rights of members and supporters of the Weather Underground.

The days of harassment were not over. Four months later, the Special Prosecutor's Office was again on my back. Early in June, I received a call from the FBI—a request to interview me about leaks of FBI information to *The New York Times*. On

June 13, 1974, Special Agents Angelo Lano and George Midler appeared at my front door. I had never met Lano but I knew that he had coordinated the Watergate investigation in the Washington Field Office. I knew that he was still working on additional investigation which was requested by the Office of the Special Prosecutor.

Lano promptly informed me that the interview would not be conducted in my house but at a nearby Holiday Inn. This could only mean one thing—the interview would be secretly recorded. I started to object to having to leave my home but held back because I knew it was to my ultimate advantage to have an exact record of what was said. As a former Associate Director, I would have expected to be questioned in Director Kelley's office, as a matter of courtesy, but perhaps the Special Prosecutor thought I would be more vulnerable in strange surroundings.

Before I sat down in the motel room, Lano was advising me of my Constitutional Rights. He put a form under my nose on which my signature would acknowledge this formality and was indignant when I signed without reading it. Restraining my anger, I informed him that I had gone through this procedure with more subjects than he would ever know—and thus we were off to an unpleasant start.

I asked Lano if the investigation he was conducting was an internal FBI matter or the business of the Special Prosecutor.

"Strictly internal for the Inspection Division," he said, but when the specifics of the questioning came up, there was no doubt in my mind that he was working for the Special Prosecutor in a further attempt to prove that I had lied to the Grand Jury.

Donald Segretti, who had been interviewed by the FBI concerning some of the alleged dirty tricks of the 1972 campaign, told the Agents that he had been contacted by John Crewdson, a Washington correspondent for *The New York Times*. Crewdson, he said, had shown him a number of FBI documents and he was able to describe them in sufficient detail so that the Agents could identify several of them. One was very significant—a copy of the February 26 memorandum which Horowitz had tried so desperately to have me recall. I told Lano and Midler what I had said to Horowitz and to the grand jurors—that I had no independent recollection of having seen the memorandum prior to my first interview in the office of the Special Prosecutor.

My only contact with Crewdson had been a long distance telephone call from him, just prior to my retirement in June of 1973, during which he questioned me about the Kissinger Wiretaps. William Ruckelshaus had issued a five-page public statement about the Kissinger Wiretaps on May 14, 1973, and I did not tell Crewdson anything which was not already public knowledge. This hardly made me a prime suspect, but, of course, I did not know that the White House and top Justice Department officials were convinced I was the mysterious "Deep Throat." Though I had disclosed nothing to Crewdson, the rumors had already resulted in my being "convicted" in the eyes of the Special Prosecutor.

I never gave any FBI documents to John Crewdson, or to anyone else outside the FBI, and to this day, I have never met Crewdson—something I repeated to Lano and Midler for three hours. But the intent of Lano's questioning was clear. He was not interested in plugging leaks but in getting some sort of an admission from me that I did, in fact, have recollection of the February 26 memorandum prior to the time it was shown to me by Horowitz. I could then be indicted for perjury or forced to testify against Gray. Many hours of FBI investigative time were thus wasted and I realized how desperately the Special Prosecutor wanted "bodies" to haul into Federal Court.

The incident was ended, I thought. Then, in mid-November, 1974, *The Los Angeles Times* and *The Washington Post* carried front page stories about the leaks to Crewdson and the "investigation" of W. Mark Felt. An anonymous source was quoted as saying that Crewdson had been seen entering my office with an empty briefcase which was "bulging" when he left, unobserved by the three secretaries in the outer office. This story obviously was leaked from either the office of the Special Prosecutor or the FBI.

Concerning the news story, I can only repeat that I have never met Crewdson and that I never gave him, or anybody else, FBI documents.

The balance of 1974 passed quietly enough. But the critics of the Bureau were not to be deterred and in 1975 I was interviewed on five separate occasions by the staff of the Senate Select Committee on Intelligence Operations—an exercise in futility and frustration since most of what I said was ignored and the rest taken out of context.

Twice FBI Agents, investigating alleged corruption and abuse of power by high Bureau officials, called on me. I answered their questions patiently, admitting that I had attended several dinners at a Washington restaurant, paid for by FBI funds and held in honor of the heads of England's MI-5, Israeli Intelligence, and the Special Branch of the Canadian Royal Mounted Police. I also "confessed" that the Exhibits Section of the FBI had done some picture framing for me—photos of Hoover, the Attorney General, and so on, which had hung in my office on the fifth floor of the Justice Department Building.

On November 18, I was interviewed by staff members of the House Committee on Government Operations as to the disposition of the Official and Confidential files which Hoover had maintained in his office. In December, I appeared to testify before the whole Committee, chaired by none other than Congresswoman Bella Abzug. Her primary objective appeared to be to dominate the scene, and she was much less interested in any possible irregularities of file management than in what juicy gossip I might have seen in FBI files—the "goodies" as she called it.

On February 1, 1976, I testified before an executive session of the Senate Select Committee on Intelligence Operations where I made absolutely no impression whatever. I was convinced that the minds of members and staff were already made up and they did not want to be confused with the facts.

CHAPTER TWENTY-THREE

> A strict observance of the written law is doubtless *one* of the highest duties of a good citizen, but it is not the *highest*. The laws of necessity, of self preservation, of saving our country when it is in danger, are of higher obligation. To lose our country by a scrupulous adherence to the written law, would be to lose law itself, with life, liberty, and property and all those who are enjoying them with us; thus sacrificing the end to the means.
>
> —THOMAS JEFFERSON, 1818

While the pendulum of public opinion has begun to swing back toward the right of the political spectrum, there are still those who regard the actions of the Weather Underground Organization (WUO) as "political activism," and because its members are United States citizens, aggressive FBI action to stop bombings, terrorism and even murder is somehow improper. At least that is what Attorney General Griffin Bell believed, because it was he who authorized the indictments of L. Patrick Gray III, Edward S. Miller, and me for allegedly violating the civil rights of members and supporters of the WUO whose apartments were entered surreptitiously in last-ditch efforts to obtain intelligence concerning the activities of fugitive WUO bombers.

It is time to review the record of terrorism in the United States. Just what was the situation in the late Sixties and early

Seventies? There were dissidents who talked of kidnapping Dr. Henry Kissinger and visiting heads of state. There were plans to paralyze the nation's Capitol by widespread sabotage. Policemen were being ambushed and murdered. Heroin and LSD were being pandered to our young people. Hundreds of bombs were exploding all over the country. These terrorists openly bragged of their Communist beliefs, their ties to unfriendly foreign countries, and of their intentions to bring down our government by force and violence.

Some terrorist groups were small, but they were growing. Some represented hostile foreign governments directly and most were getting support, financial and otherwise, from these very same governments, whose interests were being well served by the disruptions and sabotage which the radicals were able to bring about. To say that I was concerned about the activities of terrorists would be putting it very mildly indeed. And whether formally declared by Congress or not, the United States was at war with North Vietnam.

By far the most threatening of these groups was the Weather Underground Organization which maintained direct ties to foreign governments and organizations, some of which are still decidedly less than friendly to the United States. Originally the WUO members called themselves Weathermen, from a leftist folksong carrying the lines, "You don't need a weatherman to know which way the wind blows." When many of the members became fugitives and went into hiding, the name was changed to Weather Underground Organization. Those members who were not fugitives remained in place as the aboveground support apparatus of the fugitives, but all referred to themselves as members of the Weather Underground.

Confirmed records show that between 1968 and 1974 members of the WUO made hundreds of visits to Russia, the People's Republic of China, Cuba, Cambodia, North Vietnam, Algeria, to Lebanon for meetings with the Palestinian Liberation Organization, and Libya, which has been notorious for giving sanctuary and financial support to terrorists. These are only the known foreign contacts and it is estimated that WUO members made thousands of clandestine contacts overseas which were never detected by our intelligence agencies. It was reported by a reliable high-level source that one of the trips to Algeria was financed by the PLO.

There were also credible reports that the WUO was active in smuggling hard drugs into the United States as a means of financing its operations. This illegal traffic reportedly operated out of the Green Mountain commune at Richmond, Vermont, less than one mile from the Canadian border, easily penetrated by both drugs and fugitives. There were alleged contacts with the Mafia in Boston and Providence as well as with the notorious drug dealer of the "French Connection."

Communique #4 of the Weather Underground Organization, dated September 15, 1970, claimed the "honor and pleasure" of arranging the escape of Dr. Timothy Leary from the California State Prison facility at San Luis Obispo. In his book, *Confessions of a Hope Fiend,* Dr. Leary gave full credit for his escape to the WUO and intimated that the money used to spirit him out of prison, and from the United States to Algeria, came from dope peddlers.

Communique #4 went on to proclaim:

> With the NLF (The Vietnamese National Liberation Front, commonly referred to as the Viet Cong) and the North Vietnamese, the Democratic Front for the Liberation of Palestine and Al Fatah, with Rap Brown and Angela Davis, with all black and brown revolutionaries, the Soledad Brothers and all prisoners of war in Amerikan concentration camps, we know that peace is only possible with the destruction of U. S. Imperialism.

The most frequent foreign travel of WUO leaders was to Cuba, where hundreds of visits have been confirmed between 1968 and 1974. These young radicals idolized Fidel Castro, who frequently paid their travel expenses. In Cuba, all their expenses were paid while they received Communist indoctrination and training in guerrilla warfare from the Directorate General of Intelligence (DGI), the Cuban intelligence apparatus under the complete domination of the Soviet KGB. Some of the radical young Americans were recruited for espionage and intelligence-gathering missions for the Cubans. Some were trained as "sleepers" to be called upon by the DGI for espionage operations in the United States far in the future.

More often than not, these visits to Cuba were followed by serious disruptions in the United States. Mark Rudinsky, alias Mark Rudd, one of the top WUO leaders, went to Cuba for indoctrination and training during the winter of 1968 and returned in the spring of that year to organize and lead radical students in the takeover of Columbia University, where his followers seized the principal buildings, took the Senior Dean hostage, vandalized classrooms and closed down the University for thirty days.

Enthused by the unprecedented publicity, Rudd went to Chicago, where he helped organize and lead the violent antiwar demonstrations there during the National Convention of the Democratic Party in the summer of 1968.

One year later, a delegation which included Bernardine Dohrn and Kathy Boudin, two of the most influential WUO leaders, was invited to Cuba as guests of Fidel Castro for a meeting with representatives of North Vietnam and the Viet Cong. The Vietnamese Communists were deeply concerned over the lull in antiwar activity in the United States and the purpose of the meeting was to prod the American radicals into more vigorous opposition to American involvement in Vietnam. The Communists demanded "action" instead of "talk," and their objective was to strengthen their bargaining position at peace negotiations.

Glad to oblige the Communists, Dohrn and Boudin returned to the United States and promptly organized the WUO "Days of Rage" to protest the trial of the eight radical leaders who led the disruption of the Democratic National Convention the previous year. Helmeted WUO members attacked the police following a rally at Chicago's Lincoln Park.

While it may not have been so intended by the radicals, this stepped-up opposition to the Vietnam war actually delayed the final peace agreement because it promoted North Vietnamese intransigence at the negotiating table. This delay cost many additional lives of American servicemen and probably contributed to the final collapse of South Vietnam and the pathetic refugee situation which confronts the world today.

Bernardine Dohrn was the most dangerous member of the Weather Underground Organization, and her career of violence would fill a book by itself. Her sadistic nature is well illustrated by a remark attributed to her in the January 10, 1969, issue of *The Guardian,* a self-described radical newspaper published in New York. The article described Dohrn's reaction on first learning of the gruesome murders carried out by the drug-crazed Charles Manson clan in Los Angeles and quoted her as saying, "Dig it. First they killed those pigs, then they ate dinner in the same room with them. They even shoved a fork into a victim's stomach! Wild!" She was referring to Sharon Tate, who was several months pregnant at the time she was murdered.

Naomi Jaffe, a radical with similar feelings about the rest of the "pigs," visited North Vietnam in the spring of 1968. On her return to the United States she bragged that while in North Vietnam she shot down an American fighter plane with an antiaircraft gun. Jaffe implied this was part of a training program, and upon returning to the United States she wore on a chain around her neck what she claimed was a small piece of fuselage from the plane she had shot down.

In the spring of 1969, another WUO member, Linda Evans, visited North Vietnam. On her return she described an antiaircraft gun used by Viet Cong female soldiers and was reported to have said that she cradled the gun in her arms and wished for an American plane to fly over.

There were reports of wounded American prisoners of war being "brutalized" by the fanatical young radicals from the United States.

These were the people with whom the FBI had to deal. These were the problems which confronted me as an Associate Director of the FBI. The line between domestic terrorism and foreign subversion was being drawn razor-thin and in some cases, particularly as it related to the WUO, it did not exist at all.

None of this was new to the FBI. In the years before World War II, it had received specific directives from President Franklin D. Roosevelt to be responsible for the internal security of the United States. Early targets included the Nazi-financed German-American Bund, the Soviet-directed

Communist Party USA, and the "native" Fascist groups. The FBI had done its job with notable success, receiving the Nation's plaudits for its work. To those who could measure the peril, the situation, in some ways, was far more dangerous in the late Sixties than it had been in the late Thirties. In both periods, the FBI operated on the theory that it is better to anticipate violence, to prevent it wherever possible, and to contain it no matter what the source.

Thus, the FBI moved with equal vigor to thwart terrorism and lawlessness on the part of a broad range of militant organizations: the Minutemen, Ku Klux Klan, Black Liberation Army, and the Jewish Defense League, an organization of violence-prone young people ready to take the law into their own hands in actions which they mistakenly believed would help the State of Israel. Having learned who the members were, FBI Agents interviewed them in the presence of their parents and confronted them with the Bureau's knowledge of their terrorist plans. Some of the more recalcitrant members were taken before Federal Grand Juries by attorneys of the Department of Justice. The Department was fully aware of what was going on in all these cases.

The FBI, therefore, was breaking no new ground when it turned its attention to the WUO and to allied organizations which drew inspiration from it. Since it split off from the Students for a Democratic Society (SDS), aggressive enough but still not sufficiently violent for the "crazies," the WUO had embarked on a course of terrorist activism unprecedented even for those stormy days. The catalogue is long and grim. By this time the WUO had acquired a national reputation for violence impressive enough to invite comparison with the PLO, the Red Brigade of Italy, and the IRA. They had claimed credit for, or were convincingly identified with, many separate bomb plants and bomb explosions across the nation. Among the most daring they took credit for were these:

Already mentioned were the rioting in Chicago during the Democratic National Convention in 1968 and the "Days of Rage" rioting of 1969.

On October 9, 1969, the WUO's "Woman's Militia" charged police lines in an effort to destroy a military induction center.

The same day, another group assaulted police lines in the Chicago business district. Twenty-four policemen and scores of "demonstrators" were injured.

On November 8, 1969, a police headquarters in Cambridge, Massachusetts, was subjected to sniper fire by the WUO. Subsequently, twenty-three WUO members were arrested and their leader was charged with assault to commit murder. They were later released by the trial judge on a technicality.

On December 6, 1969, several Chicago police cars were bombed. The WUO claimed credit.

On March 6, 1970, thirty-four sticks of dynamite were exploded in the 13th Police District Station House of the Detroit Police Department, killing one officer and injuring a number of others. The WUO did not claim credit for this atrocity but evidence exists that it was the work of the WUO.

On March 6, 1970, a WUO bomb factory in New York's Greenwich Village—a luxury townhouse—was demolished when antipersonnel bombs consisting of nails tied to sticks of dynamite exploded prematurely. Three of the WUO were killed.

On April 20, 1970, the Illinois Crime Investigating Commission issued a report in which the WUO was described as "an immediate and long-range threat" to the security of the United States and as having "risen beyond revolution to the level of anarchy." The Commission reported that, in just one Chicago bank, the Underground had funds running into a six-figure amount.

On May 10, 1970, the National Guard Association Building in Washington, D. C., was bombed. Four years later the WUO took credit.

On May 22, 1970, the WUO formally "declared war" on the United States and warned that "We will attack a symbol of institution of Ameri*k*an injustice." (This deliberate misspelling was to cast a Fascist slant on the American system.)

On June 9, 1970, a bomb exploded in New York City police headquarters, injuring three people. One day later, the WUO took credit for this crime and stated that it had planted the bomb because "The pigs in this country are our enemies." The WUO, the statement continued, was "adopting the classic guerrilla strategy of the Viet Cong and the urban guerrilla strategy of the Tupamaros."

On July 28, the WUO issued a warning to the Attorney General of the United States: "Don't look for us, dog; we'll find you first."

A series of bombings of university buildings, churches, and public buildings followed, culminating in an explosion in the Senate wing of the Capitol Building in Washington, D. C., on March 1, 1971.

In May 1972 a bomb exploded at the Pentagon. The WUO boasted that this bombing and that in the Capitol Building had been its work. According to the General Services Administration, it was the sixty-third bomb attack on a Federal building since January 1970.

Who is to say that it was not the responsibility of the FBI to track down these criminals? Eighteen leaders of the WUO had been charged with a number of the crimes detailed above and the FBI had to find them. It wasn't easy. We were dealing with sophisticated revolutionaries—some trained in Cuba and trading expertise and support with other terrorist groups. Their underground network was extremely effective but, even so, some of the fugitives were forced to leave the country.

Ordinarily, the FBI can rely on good citizens to cooperate in helping to track down criminals. This was not so in the case of the WUO fugitives who were protected and supported by a cadre of hard-core sympathizers, many of whom were members of the aboveground WUO apparatus. At every point we were blocked by the hostility of those who might have given us leads as to the whereabouts of the badly wanted fugitives. Doors were slammed in Agents' faces. Parents said they would not cooperate even if they knew where their fugitive children were. It was considered chic to thwart the FBI by giving aid and comfort to the revolutionaries at war with the United States. These supporters did not seem to mind the Cuban and Soviet connections of the WUO. That the fugitives were admitted bombers who boasted of their Marxist-Leninist ideologies did not deter their friends.

Confronted with this difficult situation, the Agents were further frustrated by tight Bureau restrictions which had been imposed by Hoover in 1966 on some of the most effective techniques for penetrating clandestine conspiracies between persons in this country and foreign governments which had been standard operating procedures in previous years. In addition to making drastic reductions in the number of wiretaps and microphone installations, Hoover flatly prohibited the use of "Black Bag Jobs," mail covers, and mail openings. (Black Bag Jobs have been more recently referred to as Surreptitious Entries. The name originated many years ago because the lock-picking and related equipment needed for a surreptitious entry were usually contained in a small black bag. A surreptitious entry is the warrantless entry into premises without the permission or knowledge of the person occupying the space.)

Attorney General Griffin Bell seemed to harbor the misconception that I invented the technique of surreptitious entry. Nothing could be more far-fetched. It had been a standard, although infrequently used, procedure for as many years as I can recall. It was known to Presidents, Attorneys General, and to any Government official with enough brains to figure out where a Communist Party membership list or confidential data about the Mafia from "Anonymous Sources" really came from. Certain Agents were trained in lock-picking techniques.

The Department of Justice and the FBI have always distinguished between investigations designed to gather intelligence and those for the purpose of gathering evidence to be used in court against a person charged with a crime. As I understood it, intelligence gathering is not intended to result in criminal charges and is therefore not limited by Fourth Amendment prohibition against "unreasonable searches and seizures." For this reason a different set of rules has always been applied. Further, as I understood it, the traditional warrant procedures available in routine criminal cases need not be followed in situations where the intelligence gathering relates to agents of foreign powers. This is especially true when, as was the case with the WUO, the very information upon which an application for a warrant would be based was too sensitive to present to a magistrate.

We know now that in the Weather Underground Organization cases, as the pressures mounted from both inside and outside the Bureau for intelligence concerning these dangerous fugitives, some of the techniques which Hoover had banned were revived. At the time, I was still in the Inspection Division and had no knowledge of this change in direction.

The record is very clear, however, that in the late summer of 1970 Hoover discussed the problems of terrorism in the United States with a gravely concerned President Nixon who wanted aggressive action taken. William C. Sullivan, who was in charge of all investigative operations in 1970 and 1971, publicly stated in 1976 that Hoover told him in the fall of 1970 to use any means necessary to locate and apprehend these dangerous fugitives. Sullivan said he assumed these instructions were relayed from the White House and he passed them on to Agents in the Field Offices where the search for the bombers centered.

Hoover is dead. Sullivan was killed in a hunting accident in 1977. There were no witnesses to the conversation between these two men, so we will never know for sure just how far the instructions went. The important fact is that Agents subordinate to Sullivan were clearly convinced that they were acting properly on the highest authority.

As far as I was concerned, the restrictions were not lifted until Hoover died in May 1972, and L. Patrick Gray III was appointed Acting Director. The White House was clearly the moving force behind the infamous "Huston Plan," the rise and fall of which I was clearly aware at the time. Early in his tenure, Gray had a series of conferences with FBI staff and with representatives of the Intelligence Community with regard to the resumption of FBI surreptitious entries primarily in the foreign intelligence field. There was no doubt in my mind but that Gray had been instructed by either the White House or the Attorney General to implement portions of the Huston Plan, and I was not the least surprised when he gave orders to survey the feasibility of reinstituting FBI participation in this activity.

On September 5, 1972, an event occurred which shook the world and brought the problem of terrorism into even sharper focus. A group of Palestinian terrorists, calling themselves the

"Black September Organization," broke into the compound of the Israeli athletes participating in the Summer Olympic Games being held in Munich. It was a vicious attack. Two members of the Israeli group who resisted were immediately shot and killed and the rest were held as hostages. Twenty-three long hours of negotiation ensued and it was finally agreed that the terrorists and hostages would be escorted to the Munich airport where a plane would be provided to fly them to an undisclosed destination. At the airport, a shoot-out developed during which nine additional members of the Israeli Olympic squad, five of the terrorists, and one German policeman were killed. Altogether, seventeen persons were killed. The world was horrified!

Shortly afterwards, the [redacted] * FBI Office requested Headquarters permission to make a surreptitious entry into the offices of a suspected Palestinian terrorist group to learn of any terrorist plans for the United States and to identify any possible terrorists who were residing here. The request was approved by a Unit Chief in the Domestic Intelligence Division, still in shock, no doubt, from the horror of the Munich incident. The entry was extremely productive but Miller, Gray and I did not find out until it was a fait accompli. Miller firmly impressed upon the Unit Chief, who will remain nameless here, that any future requests of this nature should be sent to higher authority. To protect the Unit Chief, Miller assumed full responsibility in his report to me and to Gray. Subsequently, I made a public statement assuming responsibility for the entry.

The [redacted] Office found a bonanza—the names of numerous persons in the United States suspected of being potential terrorists. Instructions were immediately sent out to interview each one to put them on notice that the FBI knew who they were. When [redacted] during the interview, they were fingerprinted and photographed. With one exception, mentioned subsequently, this ended the Palestinian terrorist threat of

* Six changes were made in this chapter at the request of the FBI. Deletions, such as the above, are known as "redactions" in the bureaucratic lexicon.

hijacking, massacres, and bombings in the United States. Convinced that the FBI was all-knowing and ever-present, terrorists refused to accept assignments in the United States. Hopefully, foreign terrorists still feel that way about the FBI.

Gray seemed very pleased when briefed as to the results. He ordered an all-out FBI effort to prevent terrorism in the United States. At a meeting of a group of Special Agents in Charge of several Field Offices, Gray spent considerable time discussing the successful operation at [illegible] and the Munich massacre in the context of the overall threat of Arab terrorism in the United States. When asked if the technique of surreptitious entries would again be used by the FBI, Gray responded in words to the effect, "Yes, in urgent cases such as this, but you had better be damn sure that you get clearance from Bureau Headquarters." Gray now denies making such a statement.

It was crystal clear to me that Gray intended to reinstate the use of surreptitious entries, particularly in cases involving terrorists. There was never any doubt about his extreme interest, for in a note to me on July 18, 1972, concerning the WUO, Gray wrote, "Hunt to exhaustion. No holds barred." Subsequently, in another note he said, "I want no holds barred and I want to hunt Weatherman and similar groups to exhaustion."

To be absolutely sure as to Gray's meaning, Miller specifically asked him if he intended to apply the technique of surreptitious entries to the WUO. According to Miller, Gray replied, "Yes, but be sure they get approval from you and Felt." This was a one-on-one conversation and Gray denies making these comments to Miller.

Speaking for myself, I did not have any further conversations with Gray about techniques to be used in investigating WUO fugitives, but I was convinced from his remarks and by the "no holds barred" orders which Gray had penned to me in his own handwriting that the use of surreptitious entries was to be resumed in domestic terrorist cases and I proceeded on that assumption. I was positive Gray would not have spoken to the SACs as he did without prior clearance from a White House which, since 1969, had been demanding stronger and more effective action against all violence-oriented groups in the United States, or without the approval of the Attorney General.

There was one bombing attempt by Palestinian terrorists. Acting on a tip from [illegible] the FBI alerted the New York City Police of a serious bomb plot. Agents working side by side with the police located three cars with luggage compartments loaded with dynamite and fuel oil. Two had been parked in front of the Israeli Consulate and an Israeli bank, both in midtown New York. The third was parked near the cargo terminal of the Israeli El Al Airline. Police explosive experts, who detonated the bombs in a safe and remote place, reported that if the bombs had been triggered, thousands of persons would have been killed or cruelly maimed by the resulting fireballs.

As a result of what we sincerely believed to be Gray's authorization, Miller and I developed a procedure for handling authority to engage in Black Bag Jobs. When the infrequent requests came in from the Field, they would go to Miller, who would in turn consult me. If we jointly agreed that the operation was feasible and completely justified in the best interests of the United States, Miller would so advise the Field Office and then confirm the transaction in a memorandum to me. On occasion, I learned of the entries after they occurred. In any event, there were only a few such instances when this particular technique was used against the WUO and each is recorded in FBI files.

Since Acting Director Gray had given me complete operational authority, and since he was away from Washington for so much of the time, five authorizations for Black Bag Jobs were given by me without consultation with Gray. I felt then, as I do now, that the actions were wise. We know that it was only during Gray's tenure, at least since 1966 when Hoover discontinued the Black Bag Jobs' use, that there was any top-level control on such matters. Far more important, we were able to give our country a respite from the atrocities of the WUO.

The Weather Underground Organization has not given up and a few isolated incidents have continued. The last serious attempt was in 1977 when the WUO prepared a bomb to be planted in the office of California State Senator John V. Briggs. FBI undercover Agents who had infiltrated the WUO discovered the plot in time and the perpetrators were arrested. Because of cutbacks in Federal domestic security operations, the cases were turned over to the local authorities. The five arrested were all members of the WUO and one was a long-sought fugitive. Four pleaded guilty and are now serving sentences. The fifth was scheduled to go to trial in the spring of 1979.

On June 22, 1973, I retired from the organization which had been my life for almost all my adult years. I left in good conscience, for President Nixon had appointed Clarence M. Kelley to be the new Director. I knew Kelley and felt that his previous FBI service fully qualified him for the position. I had already arranged for a series of lectures before college audiences in order to counteract the mounting criticism of the FBI, and I flatly rejected the importunings of booking agents who argued that I could triple my lecture fees if I attacked rather than defended the Bureau.

I had other retirement "problems" with the Government which were described in the preceding chapter, but in 1975 it seemed for a while that the frenzy to harass and punish those in the Intelligence Community was subsiding. The Justice Department announced that prosecution of Central Intelligence Agency personnel accused of illegal mail openings would be "hypocritical," because of the Government's "failure to provide adequate guidance to its subordinate officials, almost consciously leaving them to take their chances in what was an extremely uncertain legal environment." That case arose from a secret CIA project in which 215,000 letters to and from the Soviet Union were opened, read, and circulated within the Intelligence Community from 1953 to 1973.

The Justice Department also refused to prosecute CIA Director Richard Helms for approving a Black Bag Job in Fairfax, Virginia, because of "National Security" considerations. This surreptitious entry, which was unproductive, involved a suspected leak and was far less urgent than the WUO cases of the FBI.

But the Government's wisdom in the CIA cases created a backlash in some quarters which did not bode well for the FBI. How fortunate were the implicated CIA employees that their cases were the first to be resolved! Facing scathing criticism from civil libertarians who accused the Justice Department of sweeping CIA "excesses" under the carpet, newly appointed Attorney General Bell searched desperately for a way out of the political dilemma. Leaks began to seep from the Justice Department. Playing up to a media which had acquired a taste for blood in the Watergate case, "informed Justice sources" indicated that investigations were in progress concerning alleged violations of the civil rights of supporters and members of the WUO by the FBI. No action was to be taken against the FBI personnel responsible for similar measures used against the suspected Palestinian terrorists, although the Justice Department was well aware of them. The Department argued that the Weather Underground Organization was a movement of "political activists" who, because they were American citizens, must be provided the protection of the Fourth Amendment to the Constitution even though their goals were terrorism and subversion.

The Justice Department's strategy was a novel one, to which it gave the name of "sequential indictments." In plain English, this meant that pressure and intimidation would be used against street Agents in order to force them to testify against the next higher echelon. Moving up the FBI ladder, the Justice Department would be able to strike at the "top dogs," as the leakers put it, who had authorized steps to neutralize the WUO. When this strategy did not work, the Civil Rights Division attorneys resorted to threats and harassments of the Agents, including telephone calls to the wives and telephone calls to the Agents in the middle of the night. In the early stages of this operation, more than 125 present and former FBI Agents were hassled unmercifully. Some were granted immunity from prosecution and others were left dangling for months as to their fate. All were forced to hire lawyers.

It was perfectly obvious that I would be the eventual target of this form of arm-twisting. Though it meant putting my head on the block, subjecting my wife and family to prolonged anguish and uncertainty, I felt honor-bound to act. I had to take the street Agents off the hook in order to prevent the piecemeal laceration of the FBI and the further destruction of its morale. I decided to meet the onslaught head-on by announcing to the press that I had, in fact, authorized "surreptitious entries" which the media had already mislabeled "burglaries."

The New York Times noted that my statement "was the first instance in which a top executive at Bureau Headquarters has taken the responsibility for authorizing any of the burglaries (sic) that are currently the subject of criminal inquiry by the Department of Justice." It noted that I had acted on the strength of assurance by L. Patrick Gray that he would countenance the use of "surreptitious entries" to gather information "in sensitive intelligence investigations," and the *Times* quoted me accurately as saying that at a meeting of Special Agents in Charge, Gray had said that he would "approve these things" but cautioned the SACs to be "damn sure you get Bureau approval."

In a subsequent interview, I noted that the [illegible] entry had been "extremely productive" and had put the Palestinian terrorists "out of circulation." I also defended the WUO entries. "You've got to remember that we were dealing with murderers, terrorists, people who were responsible for mass destruction," I told the reporter. "If you learn in advance of a bomb about to go off, you can't put your fingers in your ears and wait for it to explode. These people claimed responsibility for scores of bombings and we wanted to put them out of circulation. We had an obligation to do so and I think I have observed the spirit and the letter of the Constitution. I'm proud of what I did."

A few days later, I appeared on CBS's "Face the Nation" and said, "You are either going to have an FBI that tries to stop violence before it happens or you are not. Personally, I think this is justified and I'd do it again tomorrow."

Unfortunately, I did not have available then a significant quotation from *A World Split Apart,* written by Alexander Solzhenitsyn, the Russian dissident, who wrote: "When a government earnestly undertakes to route out terrorism, public opinion immediately accuses it of violating the terrorists' civil rights."

All this would hardly impress the liberal politicians who were equally unimpressed by the report of a panel of distinguished Government and industry consultants which said: "The terrorist is the cutting knife against the throat of civilization. Species survival in the end may confirm the necessity of denial of Constitutional protections of society in favor of rude and extreme measures initiated by society as it follows society's basic law—survival."

I was not the only former FBI official to make public disclosure of his involvement in the WUO entries. Edward S. Miller also put himself in jeopardy by making a public statement for reasons similar to mine. Both of us were flooded with letters and telegrams commending us and expressing support. At the Justice Department, the reaction was one of anger and consternation. We had taken the initiative away from them and they could no longer harass the younger Agents. A newspaper reporter told me that one Justice Department official told him, "We'll get that son-of-a-bitch Felt." For attorneys in the Civil Rights Division of the Justice Department, the matter had become not a matter of law enforcement but a personal vendetta. But before the Department turned its guns on me, it found what seemed to be a more vulnerable target.

In April 1977, the Grand Jury in New York City, which had been sifting allegations of FBI illegality, indicted former Special Agent John J. Kearney, who had supervised the investigations to locate the WUO fugitives in the New York area. Kearney testified honestly and openly before the Grand Jury, but this was not enough to satisfy the young lawyers who wanted to implicate FBI officials at the very top. John Kearney is a man of character, well known for his personal courage and conviction. He refused to stretch the truth in what he considered to be an effort to pillory FBI personnel and discredit the Bureau. What first seemed like easy pickings for the Civil Rights Division turned out to be a can of worms.

FBI Agents and former Agents rallied to Kearney's support. More than 300 appeared on the Courthouse steps at Foley Square in New York on April 14, 1977, when he appeared for arraignment. A Special Agents Legal Fund was formed by the Society of Former FBI Agents, and contributions of Agents, former Agents, and supporters have well exceeded $1,500,000 as of this writing. This total included more than $350,000 raised by an Ad Hoc Citizens' Legal Defense Fund organized by former U. S. Senator James L. Buckley, former Ambassador Clare Boothe Luce, and former Secretary of the Treasury William E. Simon.

This generous financial backing enabled Kearney to prepare a strong legal defense and the funds were also used to pay the legal expenses of the many other Agents and former Agents who were caught up in the Justice Department net. Total legal fees of all the hapless victims are now well over $1,250,000 and continue to mount rapidly. Costs to the Justice Department for salaries and incidental expenses in this case have already exceeded $20,000,000 of the taxpayers' money and continue to add up at the rate of $300,000 per month. If the purpose of Attorney General Bell was to bring about a change in FBI policy, he chose a very expensive method to accomplish what could have been done by a simple directive. His problem was the liberal political pressures upon him.

Early in 1978, Bell admitted to the world that the Kearney indictment was a "mistake" and that his mail ran three hundred to one against him. My personal sources told me, however, that the case was far from over because of pressures on Bell from his own Civil Rights Division, as well as outside pressures from the liberal wing of the Carter Administration. My sources proved to be correct.

For a year—a year in which my wife and my family were subjected to the fears and anxieties of what my fate would be—the Kearney case inched ahead. Then, on April 10, 1978, Bell, succumbing to the intensity of public opinion, announced that he was dropping the charges against Kearney. In the same press release, he also announced the indictment of Gray, Miller, and me.

"In the exercise of his prosecutorial discretion," the release read, "the Attorney General has determined that in this case the most severe sanction of criminal prosecution should be brought to bear at the highest levels of authority and responsibility at which the evidence will support prosecution. Mr. Kearney's level of authority and responsibility was substantially below that of the officials who are now to be prosecuted, and was below or equal to that of other officials who will not be prosecuted. To allow the Kearney prosecution to continue under these circumstances would violate the basic tenets of fair and equal justice."

This non sequitur aside, there were three curious aspects to Attorney General Bell's announcement. To begin with, he stated that the investigation which followed the Kearney indictment had allowed the Justice Department to fix responsibility at higher levels. He completely ignored the fact that Miller and I had publicly taken that responsibility *eight months before* the Kearney indictment was returned.

Secondly, and most important of all, if General Bell was honestly seeking the "highest levels of authority and responsibility," he should have indicted top officials in the Justice Department itself at the time the entries were made, since those officials were most certainly aware of them, or others like them.

The third point is that the indictment evaded the question of the legality or illegality of the practice of surreptitious entry by the FBI—a point of law which has never been resolved.

The indictment read:

> From in or about May, 1972, through in or about May, 1973, in the District of Columbia and elsewhere, L. PATRICK GRAY III, W. MARK FELT and EDWARD S. MILLER, the defendants herein, together with others to the Grand Jury known and unknown, did unlawfully, wilfully and knowingly combine, conspire, confederate and agree together and with each other to injure and oppress citizens of the United States who were relatives and acquaintances of the Weatherman fugitives, in the free exercise and enjoyment of certain rights and privileges secured to them by the Constitution and the laws of the United States, including the right secured to them by the Fourth Amendment to the Constitution of the United

> States to be secure in their homes, papers and effects against unreasonable searches and seizures.
>
> It was the purpose of the conspiracy to utilize, and to cause other officials and Agents of the FBI to utilize, the technique of surreptitious entry into the homes and premises of relatives and acquaintances of the Weatherman fugitives, in the hope of discovering something that might in some way assist the FBI in locating the Weatherman fugitives.

Thirty-two "overt acts" were listed in the indictment alleging "conversations" between Miller and Gray, speeches by Gray to FBI officials, approval by Gray of the agenda for an In-Service training course on the Weather Underground Organization, a lecture to FBI Agents on how to conduct surreptitious entries in WUO cases, memoranda on conversations between Miller and me and surreptitious entries conducted by FBI Agents and reported to me by Miller. This was the "conspiracy."

We are charged under a sixty-year-old statute, as revised in Section 241 of the Civil Rights Act of 1969. Until the present case this law was used almost exclusively in the South for the prosecution of Ku Klux Klansmen and local authorities who beat up or otherwise harassed voters at the polls—actions having absolutely nothing to do with National Security.

Attorney General Bell also announced that disciplinary action would be taken against sixty-eight currently employed Agents who had been involved in the WUO cases. At the top of the purge list was J. Wallace LaPrade, Assistant Director in charge of the New York FBI Office. Civil Rights Division lawyers accused LaPrade of less than full cooperation with their investigation because he could not remember everything that they wanted.

Early in April 1978, LaPrade was informally advised that the Attorney General would permit him to retire voluntarily but that if he did not do so he would be dismissed. LaPrade called a press conference in which he disclosed these developments. He said he would not retire under pressure and he challenged the Attorney General to a nationally televised debate on the general subject of current surreptitious entry practices. There was no response, of course, and following this LaPrade was removed from command in New York and ordered to report to Washington, where he was given an office and a secretary but no duties. This is what is known as the "silent treatment," and its purpose is to force out the unwanted employee by ignoring him. LaPrade refused to leave of his own accord and was finally dismissed on July 7, 1978, after being kept in suspense for more than ninety days. He has appealed the action against him and fortunately he is old enough so that he will not lose retirement benefits regardless of the outcome.

On December 5, 1978, Director William H. Webster announced that of the remaining sixty-seven Agents on the carpet, only four would face disciplinary action. He proposed that one be suspended without pay for thirty days and placed on probation and that another be reduced in salary—punishments reminiscent of the old Hoover days. The other two actions which Webster proposed were so sharply severe that even the most hardened were shocked. Webster proposed that both be summarily dismissed from the service. According to Civil Service regulations, each of the four would be given thirty days to respond to the allegations which had been made against him.

One of the Agents to be dismissed was old enough to leave with full retirement benefits, thankful to leave the uncertainties of modern-day FBI life. The other, Horace Beckwith, was only forty-six years of age, and dismissal would strip him of the FBI pension toward which he had worked for twenty years—an incredible hardship, not only on him but also on his family. Hoover may have been a tough boss but he would never have taken such drastic disciplinary action against an Agent who was acting in good faith.

In fairness to Director Webster, let me point out that the charges from the Justice Department against Beckwith were reflective of the bias aginst FBI Agents displayed by the Civil Rights Division throughout this entire affair. When the facts were called to the Director's attention, he reduced Beckwith's punishment to reduction from pay level Grade 14 to Grade 13 and transfer to the office of Beckwith's choice.

That the Attorney General's high-sounding statement of April 10, 1978, at the time of my indictment, was merely for political consumption, became very clear when the Justice Department contacted my lawyer, Brian P. Gettings, and offered to plea bargain. I would be permitted to plead guilty to a reduced charge which would be a misdemeanor instead of a felony. There would be no Government recommendation for probation and I probably would have had to serve time in jail. I flatly refused. Perhaps I should have considered the offer because during these post-Watergate times in the District of Columbia chances for acquittal by a jury are not too bright even though I am convinced my actions were completely justified and certainly not illegal under standards which existed at the time. A guilty plea to a misdemeanor charge would have substantially reduced the potential jail time and it would have avoided putting my family through the strain of this long and drawn-out ordeal. On the other hand, and far more important, was the principle involved. I could not let down the Agents and former Agents who would feel that a plea of guilty would be an admission that they too had been guilty of wrongdoing throughout their years of FBI service. I had no choice but to refuse the offer of the Attorney General.

Over the years there has been constant pressure on the FBI from Presidents and Attorneys General to take all "necessary" or "desirable" measures against anarchists and subversives whose goals are to overthrow the Government by force and violence. On September 14, 1967, one of our Attorneys General most concerned with Governmental incursions upon individual liberties, Ramsey Clark, nonetheless ordered Hoover to take such measures against groups fostering riots and insurrections. He said, "It is most important that you use the maximum available resources, investigative and intelligence, to collect and report all facts bearing upon the question as to whether there has been or is a scheme or conspiracy by any group of whatever size, effectiveness or affiliation to plan, promote or aggravate riot activity." The Director was urged "to take every step possible" in this endeavor, and this was to cover activity "before, during and after any overt acts." When you think of it, concern for the rights of all citizens is not inconsistent with these directions given to Hoover by Attorney General Clark.

All this was brushed aside by Attorney General Bell in his need to play up to the national media which were howling for FBI blood. The consequences for Gray, Miller and me could be very grave. But the United States has the most to lose. Leaving aside for the moment the severe damage to the effectiveness of intelligence gathering and law enforcement at both Federal and State levels, there is a tremendous monetary factor. By its actions, the Justice Department has literally invited hundreds of civil suits which will cost the taxpayers millions of dollars just to defend. If the suits are successful, the cost to taxpayers will be many millions more. The Socialist Workers Party, the Trotskyite Branch of International Communism, is suing the Government for forty million dollars. Members of the Ku Klux Klan, the Black Panthers, and other groups investigated by the FBI have filed suits. Although none of the FBI Agents involved in those cases are being prosecuted, there can be no question that these organizations were the targets of the same kind of conduct General Bell claims, through the indictment, to be illegal.

In the case of the WUO, members and supporters whose apartments were searched for intelligence on the bomber fugitives have filed suit for 100 million dollars.

April 20, 1978, was arraignment day for Gray, Miller and me. It will certainly be a day to remember, partly because of the trauma and unpleasantness, but much more so because of the tremendous show of support on the steps before the U. S. Courthouse in downtown Washington. A group of Agents and former Agents, estimated by the police at 1,200, was assembled in a "silent vigil" to demonstrate support for the defendants. There were no signs or placards, but as each defendant walked across the plaza and up the steps there was loud and sustained applause.

I am not an emotional person but tears welled up in my eyes as I walked with my wife, Audrey, through the crowd. As we paused at the entrance to the building, an Agent and a former Agent read brief statements assuring us of the strong support of both groups. I was asked for a statement but all I could say was, "God bless you all!"

Some of those present came from as far away as Florida. Also represented were FBI Agents from Richmond, Baltimore, New Haven, Boston, as well as Washington, D. C. Three chartered buses filled with Agents of the New York Office left at three o'clock in the morning for the long ride to Washington. It could not have been more impressive.

Proceedings inside the Courthouse were brief. We all entered pleas of "Not Guilty" and the Judge announced that we were to be released on our personal recognizance, which simply means that we promised to appear when ordered. Then there was an unexpected development. The Judge said, "You will now be turned over to the United States Marshal for processing." I knew what this meant. We were to be taken to the Marshal's office for fingerprinting and "mug shots." I had felt this action would not be necessary because all three defendants' fingerprints and photographs were already on file in the FBI. In most cases this indignity is waived when it is not necessary. Many of the Watergate defendants were not fingerprinted at the time of their arraignments. The Justice Department could have recommended that the processing be waived had it been so inclined. There was no doubt in my mind but that it was a deliberate humiliation.

As I waited behind the barred door in the fingerprint and photo room and as I saw my wife standing just outside with tears in her eyes, anger welled up inside me. It would have been very therapeutic for me to have punched someone in the nose, yet I knew very well that the Deputy Marshals were only doing what they had been told. I was frustrated but I had not taken leave of my senses.

Gray was fingerprinted first and as he stepped aside I moved forward for my turn. He was right beside me at the washbasin attempting to wash the black printers' ink from his fingers.

"Pat," I said, "how many years of service have you given your country?"

"Twenty-six years. Twenty years in the Navy and six years with the Government," he answered.

"This is the reward which your country has for you."

Gray did not reply but I knew he shared my feelings of anger and frustration, as did Miller who was waiting his turn to be smeared with printers' ink.

Of course, the indictment, trial, and civil suits against me are personal problems and my wife and I will have to bear the strain as best we can. Thank God for the Special Agents Legal Fund and the Citizens' Legal Defense Fund for the FBI which are paying my legal costs in connection with the criminal charges against me. Costs for defending the civil suits in which I am involved will have to be met in some other way.

I am also deeply grateful for another form of assistance from the Society of Former FBI Agents. Former Agents have volunteered thousands of man hours of service in reviewing documents furnished by the Government through the discovery process, locating witnesses and evidentiary material, interviewing witnesses and many other duties. These services would otherwise have had to be done by private investigators and legal assistants in our lawyers' offices, and the extra costs would have exceeded $100,000. This financial and service support to the "Washington Three" goes beyond all precedent and is indicative of the caliber of personnel you have had working for you in the FBI through the years.

I would like to give recognition by name to all the former Agents who participated but the list would be far too long. Special recognition and thanks is due to J. Allison Conley who coordinated this work.

Imagine, if you can, the impact of these cases upon current personnel of the FBI, the Intelligence Community, other Federal investigative agencies and all law enforcement personnel at the state level. The chilling effect of possible criminal or civil liability next year for something done in good faith today is pervasive and the impact has already been substantial.

The criminal case has moved forward with agonizing slowness. We have encountered still further delays and you will have to read the concluding chapter in the newspapers. The case has gross political overtones. I will never be convinced otherwise, and one of the best indications is the insistence of the Justice Department that the trial be held in the District of Columbia when the Department knows very well that prospects for conviction in other jurisdictions are practically nil.

It has been a period of frustration and trauma which proved to be much harder on wives and families than on the defendants, who by this time were being called the Washington Three. We had expected some delays, and in fact had signed waivers to permit the young lawyers of the Civil Rights Division sufficient time to respond to our requests for documents which we needed to justify and explain to a jury why we had acted as we did. Over a year passed and we still had not received all the documents which the Judge had ordered to be produced for our defense.

"Informed sources" in the Justice Department leaked stories to the media that the defendants were engaged in "graymail" by threatening to expose State Secrets. There was even the inference that the life of an informant might be jeopardized by the release of the documents. Sheer nonsense! No State Secrets were to be exposed; as a matter of fact, we even agreed to stipulate as to the use of a summary of the information at trial which would have eliminated the need for exposure of sensitive documents. The simple truth is that the classified intelligence information which the Justice Department tried so desperately to conceal is positive proof of the use and financing by hostile foreign interests of WUO members for espionage and sabotage missions and as agent provocateurs in the United States.

The duplicity and double standards of the Justice Department in this case defy belief. While resisting our requests for important documents on the one hand, Civil Rights Division lawyers were leaking selective portions of the same material when it served their purposes. For example, John Kearney tried for over a year to obtain the Top Secret FBI report on the Weather Underground Organization. The Washington Three waited another year without success. Yet someone in the Justice Department leaked portions of it to Washington reporter Nicholas Horrock, who then wrote a summary article for *The New York Times*.

Fortunately, I had previously requested the same report under the provisions of the Freedom of Information Act. It took eighteen months of waiting, but I finally received the report in time to help the defense—and, incidentally, to enliven some of the pages of this chapter.

Leak of this report to reporter Horrock was only one of many leaks about this case from the Justice Department over a three-year period. I cannot prove the identity of the leaker. I believe it was either William J. Gardner, Chief of the Criminal Section of the Civil Rights Division, who was by far the most relentless pursuer of the FBI; or J. Stanley Pottinger, former Assistant Attorney General of the Civil Rights Division, who, before his resignation in 1977, had earned for himself the media nickname of "Two-Fisted Leaker."

In early December, 1978, the Government proposed to Chief Judge William B. Bryant, who will try our case, a Protective Order, the scope and breadth of which is probably unparalleled in any other criminal case. Judge Bryant gave the Department lawyers most of what they requested. It sharply limited the defendants' use of the documents which the Judge had previously ordered produced. Under the order, much of the material already furnished had to be returned to the Justice Department for redacting. You have already seen examples of redacting in this chapter, but now we were confronted with hundreds of pages of redacted documents, with thousands of redactions to the point of total unintelligibility.

To be permitted access to further sensitive material, the defendants and their attorneys were ordered to sign a secrecy oath which required, among other things, that there be no disclosure of information at trial unless agreed to by the Justice Department. Witnesses being interviewed prior to trial were also required to sign the secrecy oath. Physical review of the more sensitive material was to be in the Security Information Center (SIC) of the Justice Department—a steel-lined vault on the sixth floor which had been carefully insulated against acoustical intrusion. Gray, Miller and their attorneys, as well as my attorneys, signed the secrecy oath, but under protest and with the added caveat that it restricted the rights of the defendants to a fair and open trial.

I did not sign the oath. To have done so would have

required me to submit this book to the Justice Department for censorship prior to publication, which would have involved endless nitpicking and the possibility of being required to turn over to the Government all profits and royalties therefrom. I regarded this requirement as a gross violation of my First Amendment Rights.

Annoyed by the continued prosecutive delays, Judge Bryant ordered the Government to produce a certification by March 30, 1979, that it had complied with his orders for the production of documents. He also ordered a separate trial for defendant Gray.

On the deadline date, Civil Rights Division lawyer Francis J. Martin, who has been snapping at my heels ever since the days of the Special Watergate Prosecutor, submitted two letters to Judge Bryant—*two letters, not one.* The first letter, which was released to the media, stated that the Government had completed the discovery process, had furnished essentially everything to the defendants, and the trial of Miller and Felt could proceed without further delay. In the second letter, which was submitted under seal and never released, the facts were set out. The Government was withholding documents which contained "State Secrets." Martin requested an opportunity to discuss this privately with the Judge, defense attorneys excluded.

This is where the long, hard hours of work on the part of Brian Gettings; his associate Frank W. Dunham; and his staff of Mark Cummings, a young lawyer in his first year of practice; and Katherine Worthington, a para-legal assistant, really paid off. They were able to establish that Martin was withholding approximately 500 documents. Gettings immediately submitted a motion for dismissal on the grounds of the Government's failure to comply with the Judge's order and supported the motion with a blistering 40-page memorandum of specifics. The Judge has not ruled on the motion as of this writing.

Fearing that the court would awake to the realization that the missing 500 documents would support the defendants' claim of the Weather Underground's "substantial foreign involvement," the circumstances enunciated by the U. S. Supreme Court in the case of *Keith vs. The United States* as probably permitting warrantless searches, the Government prosecutors came forward with what Brian Gettings described as the "flip side" of their case. Martin argued to Judge Bryant that proof of foreign involvement of the WUO was irrelevant. The surreptitious entries, he contended, were illegal, even if the WUO members were foreign agents, because there had been no "specific approval" from the Attorney General. Martin also argued that the technique had never been used in fugitive cases. These arguments were an incestuous mounting of ignorance upon ignorance.

Never, during my entire FBI career, was there a requirement for "specific approval" from the Attorney General. Of course, many Attorneys General and other high Government officials were frequently aware, after the fact, of the results of surreptitious entries. Furthermore, hundreds of important fugitives were located on the basis of leads from such entries. Cases exactly in point involved members of the Communist Party USA who became fugitives and went underground after their conviction under the Smith Act in the early Fifties. A surreptitious entry by Agents of the San Francisco Office provided a clue which led to the successful apprehension of several of the fugitives.

"Specific approval" of the Attorney General *is* required today but only by ruling promulgated by the Department of Justice and not by any statute or even any court decision. Notwithstanding all this, Francis J. Martin wants to apply it retroactively to the Washington Three. It won't wash.

Martin's actions highlight the lack of information, deceit and double dealing by Justice Department attorneys which have been evident in this case from the very beginning. Further indicative of the ramifications was a conversation which I had with a high-placed friend who has many contacts with members of the media.

He told me, "All the reporters I have talked to think you are getting screwed." He paused. "But half of them think you deserve it."

"What do you mean, they think I deserve it?"

My friend hastened to reassure me, "No. No. No. It's

nothing against you personally. In fact most of the reporters like you. It's just that they think the FBI needs to be punished for the alleged abuses of the past. You, Miller and Gray are just symbols."

I hesitated for a moment before asking, "What does the other half think?"

My friend smiled wryly and said, "They feel sorry for you."

I sincerely hope that nothing in this chapter sounds bitter. I certainly don't want that. I have tried to be objective and this version of the chapter eliminates some of the stronger language which appeared in earlier drafts. I am angry and frustrated, yes—but not bitter.

I offer no apologies for what I have done. I admitted responsibility for actions taken against the Weather Underground and I am ready to accept the consequences. I did what I thought was right and my professional obligation. I am willing to stake my honesty and loyalty and dedication to my country against that of anyone. For many years I worked long hours, faced criminals ready to kill and, to the limit of my ability, did what I thought was in the best interests of the United States. So far as the WUO bombers were concerned, I had no criminal intent. My intent was to save lives and property.

Looking back over the years, I know it was worth it. I would do it all again, even with foreknowledge of the parting gift which may be in store for me.

CHAPTER TWENTY-FOUR

> The FBI wouldn't be in this predicament if Clarence Kelley were alive.

The above remark, during Director Kelley's tenure, was an almost everyday observation among Bureau personnel. It reflected the despairing feeling that—buffeted by Congress and the media, manipulated by the politicians, inundated by civil suits for damages, and torn apart by the frivolous use of the Freedom of Information Act—the FBI had no strong and fighting leader to guide and defend it.

Not that Clarence Kelley was uninterested in the welfare and the future of the Bureau. But he had been brought in by a President who wanted a Director acceptable to the career staff but also willing to be subservient to the demands of a White House more interested in political advantage than in the continuation of a semi-independent investigative agency free of Administration pressures.

From the very start, as was quickly apparent to all, Director Kelley was determined not to make waves—to keep his head down and go with the tide. As a consequence, he did little to restore morale, let alone stand up for those working for him.

The changes which Kelley made in the FBI's organizational structure were, with one exception, largely cosmetic. Functions were shifted from one office to another and names of Divisions were changed, but most basic responsibilities were left substantially the same. The one significant exception was Kelley's phasing out of domestic security investigations to placate the media and liberals in Congress. To be sure, if dissidents exploded another bomb in the United States Capitol Building, the FBI would investigate—after the dust had cleared. There was no change in the investigation of foreign espionage operations.

Prior to 1972, the FBI operated under the emergency detention provisions of the Internal Security Act. (Ironically, those provisions had been written into the Act by Senator Hubert Humphrey.) The Act provided for the detention during wartime of persons considered dangerous to the security of the United States. In response to this legislation, the FBI established a Security Index and over the years a list of more than 15,000 individuals was compiled. This was done under the close supervision of the Justice Department. Files were maintained on each person listed, and twice a year a check was made to verify employment and addresses of those considered the most dangerous in the event of war.

The Internal Security Act was repealed in January, 1972, at which time there were some 12,000 names in various categories in the Security Index. The FBI requested instructions from the Justice Department and the Attorney General replied that the FBI's authority to investigate "subversive activities" was "unaffected by the repeal" of the Act. With respect to the continuation of the Security Index, the Attorney General stated:

> The repeal of the aforementioned Act does not alter or limit the FBI's authority and responsibility to record, file and index information secured pursuant to its statutory and Presidential authority. An FBI administrative index compiled and maintained to assist the Bureau in making readily retrievable and available the results of its investigations into subversive activities and related matters is not prohibited by the repeal of the Emergency Detention Act.

Following these instructions, the FBI reconstituted the Security Index as an Administrative Index (ADEX) but with revised and much tighter standards. Even before the repeal of the Emergency Detention Act, Director Hoover had foreseen problems inherent in this program and in 1971 he instructed his newly appointed Assistant Director in charge of the Domestic Intelligence Division, Edward S. Miller, to further tighten the original standards and to reduce substantially the number of individuals in the Security Index. Miller made drastic reductions under Hoover and continued to do so under Gray until the ADEX was reduced to a list of approximately 2,000 individuals who, by the standards set up by the Justice Department, fitted into the category of "dangerous now" to the security of the United States.

Director Kelley, seared by the heat of the Senate Select Committee on Intelligence, headed by Senator Frank Church, and the sensationalizing of the media, moved headlong to completely phase out the Administrative Index, as well as FBI investigations of any subversive activity. The result was summed up by William H. Webster, shortly after he took over as Director of the FBI: "We're practically out of the domestic security field. We have sixty-one individuals and twelve organizations under investigation."

My conception that it is the function of the FBI to prevent violence and other subversive acts rather than to wait until the bomb has exploded before investigating became an abandoned policy under Director Kelley. I was greatly reassured to hear Director Webster say in his confirmation hearings: "If the Bureau receives information that a terrorist organization is considering placing a bomb in a bank or public institution, I think that is a lawful basis for investigation and that the Bureau does not have to wait for the bomb to go off in order to supply the necessary information and authority."

Even when the overt act has been committed, the FBI is criticized when it acts. The FBI was sharply attacked because it arrested two Soviet spies, working out of the United Nations, who were caught red-handed in trying to steal secrets of the United States Navy. The State Department and the Congress complained to the media that the overzealousness of the Bureau put the national security in jeopardy.

The phasing out of domestic intelligence investigations by the FBI has seriously affected all of law enforcement. It has compelled the Secret Service to recommend to the President of the United States that he stay away from certain cities because information from the FBI and local police sources has so dried up that it is impossible to evaluate accurately the possible danger. And it is not only the President who is shortchanged. When a Black Muslim sect took over two public buildings in Washington, spreading murder and terror in the nation's capital, both the FBI and the Metropolitan Police were caught by surprise because they had not been allowed to infiltrate a group openly dedicated to violence.

It is to be hoped that Director William H. Webster will profit from the mistakes of his predecessors. There is every indication that he has. While he need not be as dogmatic and as dictatorial as J. Edgar Hoover, he must be more aggressive than Clarence M. Kelley. The rank and file of FBI employees will respect a leader who will vigorously defend and explain the Bureau's activities. The public will respect and cooperate with a firmly guided FBI.

Director Webster does not have an easy path. Shortly after his confirmation, *Time* Magazine ran an article alleging that the FBI was still being run by Hoover "loyalists" and characterized Webster as a "Charlie McCarthy" of Hoover holdovers. This was a low blow and completely untrue. Actually, all high-ranking FBI officials under Hoover retired either at the time of his death or in 1973. Mid-ranking officials under Hoover retired during Kelley's tenure because of a new law making retirement mandatory for FBI Agents reaching age fifty-five. The FBI is *not* filled with Hoover holdovers. In a speech before Harvard Law School alumni in Washington on December 12, 1978, Webster pointed out that he was the oldest Agent in the FBI and that the average age of all FBI Agents was under thirty-eight.

Webster faces other problems and I do not envy him. In June 1973, when I retired, the Agent complement of the FBI was approximately 8,500. As of January 1, 1979, the number of Agents had been reduced to 7,500. And that is not all: The Office of Management and Budget has projected a flat twenty percent reduction in expenditures for the FBI in fiscal year 1980, which will begin in September 1979. Since most of the FBI budget goes to pay salaries, this will mean an even more drastic cut in personnel at a time when the influx of hostile espionage agents is at an all-time high, when violence and domestic subversion is still a serious problem, when government corruption has become a daily fact of life, and when organized crime thumbs its nose at law enforcement.

And even as FBI personnel is cut back, the Bureau is being strangled by the Freedom of Information and Privacy acts. Under the former, any reporter can go rummaging through the most sensitive of FBI files. Under the latter, any individual must be provided with information from the files about himself, no matter how this may endanger the operations of the FBI or National Security.

The law provides that the Government must respond to these requests within ten days, but the flood of requests has been so great that it often takes the FBI eighteen months to comply. At the inception of the program, the FBI assigned three law-trained Agents and five support personnel to handle requests. This unit rapidly grew to fifty Agents and three hundred and fifty support personnel. At one time, over two hundred Agents were brought in from the Field in an attempt to reduce the ever-growing backlog of requests.

The burden on the taxpayer is far greater than the record shows. *U. S. News & World Report* estimated in June, 1978, that one out of every fifteen FBI Agents was engaged full time in handling these requests. In the first three years of the program, the discoverable costs to the taxpayer for FBI responses to these new laws were more than thirteen million dollars. Current expenditures of the FBI for this program, according to Director Webster, are estimated at nine million dollars per year.

The Freedom of Information and Privacy acts have not only substantially reduced the efficiency of the FBI and other Federal agencies, they have reduced the willingness of these agencies to share information. And the fear of later being exposed as the source of information has seriously inhibited cooperation from informants, absolutely essential to law enforcement agencies, and private citizens. Technically, the disseminating agency deletes the names of sources from file pages which are to be released to the public, but this is frequently inadequate to protect identities. In order to grant one person his "rights" another is deprived of his privacy.

On August 8, 1978, a convicted loan shark and suspected

Mafioso, Gary Bowdach, testified before the Senate Subcommittee on Investigations that he systematically used the Freedom of Information Act to tie up law enforcement officers, to find out what the Government knew about him, and to discover where the information was coming from. From the material supplied to him, he was able to determine the identity of someone who had informed on a criminal colleague. Asked what had happened to the informant, Bowdach replied, "I don't expect him to be living anymore." The lesson will not be lost on those who were once ready to confide to their Government.

Many of the requests for files are thoroughly frivolous. Among some members of the press, it has become a game. Reporters boast at the bar of the National Press Club that they put the FBI through the effort and expense of a search through the files even though they were aware that there was nothing derogatory or significant to be found. One reporter expressed deep chagrin because the FBI had no file on his activities. A schoolteacher had all the members of her class write to the FBI demanding their "dossiers." This, presumably, was in the interest of education and good citizenship.

The purpose of the Freedom of Information Act (FOIA) was to help the media and the public elicit information of cover-up and wrongdoing among Government officials and others. It has had exactly the opposite result. A bank in the South which had suffered a $476,000 loss through embezzlement notified the FBI that because of the Freedom of Information and Privacy acts, it would not provide information without a subpoena. An educational institution in the Northwest refused to furnish information from its records even though the person involved, an applicant for a Government job, had signed a waiver.

FOIA, at the same time that it hamstrings the FBI and other agencies, has additional costs which are hidden from the public. Under the Act, individuals may collect attorney's fees in their efforts to force the Government into debatable areas of disclosure. The children of Julius and Ethel Rosenberg, whose parents were executed for wartime espionage, have been awarded almost two hundred thousand dollars as partial payment for legal work done by their attorneys since they filed an FOIA suit in 1975. What the total bill—paid by the taxpayer—will be, no one knows—just as no one knows what has poured out of the U. S. Treasury to finance other suits against the Government.

The irony, of course, is that while the media clamor for an FBI operating in a goldfish bowl, reporters contend that their investigative notes and the result of their reporting activities must remain sacrosanct—even when they are ordered to deliver them to a judge in a murder case in which the defendant's life is at stake.

All of this is part of the present anti-FBI hysteria and the prevalent attitude in the Congress and among the media that disrupting the work of the FBI is a legitimate First Amendment activity. In time, the pendulum will swing back. But what the Bureau is suffering from today—and it may cause irreparable damage—is a decline in confidence and morale. Once upon a time, an FBI Agent was a respected member of his community. He believed that he was serving his country and did not have to hide his profession from his neighbors.

Career men in the FBI saw that neither Director Kelley, the Attorney General nor the President came to their defense. They were hampered in the performance of their duty by an Administration policy to prosecute Agents for acts undertaken in good faith under rules which were changed without notice. Like a doctor who is afraid to go to the aid of an accident victim because he may be sued for malpractice, all law enforcement representatives may feel that the best way to act is not to act at all.

Now for the good news. I have confidence in Judge Webster. He has displayed leadership qualitites—a fine blend of intelligence, firmness and compassion. I wish him every success. If anyone can, he will restore the image of the FBI and help bring the performance of all law enforcement to the level which citizens have the right to expect.